PRESSURE MAKES DIAMONDS

FROM HOMESCHOOLING TO THE IVY LEAGUE - A PARENTING STORY

CARLINE CREVECOEUR

SHILKA PUBLISHING

For information, or special discount for bulk purchases, please contact carlinecrevecoeur.com.

Library of Congress Cataloging-in-Publication Data

LCCN 2021918252

ISBN: (hardback) 978-1-912680-68-9

ISBN: (paperback) 978-1-912680-64-1

ISBN: (ebook) 978-1-912680-65-8

For Michael Joseph Feffer, my bedrock

There are only two lasting bequests we can hope to give our children. One of these is roots; the other, wings.

— CECILIA LASBURY

From left to right: Mikey, Jackie, Danielle, Joey, Nick (2002)

CONTENTS

PROLOGUE (2012)

You never know how strong you are until being strong is your only option.

— BOB MARLEY

"Leve men'm anlè!" the DJ cried over the loudspeaker.

It was hard to hear him, or anyone really, over the music, but the guests complied, jumping and waving their arms about. The *boom-boom-boom* of the drumbeat shook my bones as I sat, swaying my body and watching the people dance.

I should've been screaming to Boukman Eksperyans' <u>Kè m Pa Sote</u> on the dancefloor along with my husband and children. It's usually the last song my family plays at a Haitian wedding, and everyone knew the words. But instead, I sat in the corner, alone, with a half-eaten plate of jerk chicken and fried plantains keeping me company. I was too tired to dance, so tired. More tired than usual. But why? I began unfurling the events of the last six months, trying to decipher what could justify my worsening fatigue.

In April, Michael and I drove the kids to Chicago for the

National Middle School Quiz Bowl Championships. Then we headed to New York with Mikey for a piano competition in May. In June, we hosted Danielle's high school graduation party back home in State College. Shortly afterward, I accompanied her to D.C. for her Presidential Scholars award ceremony. When we got back, I helped her pack for a summer exchange program in Beijing.

With Danielle off traveling again, I focused my attention on my four other children. I took Mikey to Indiana for the Telluride camp, then the twins to D.C. for their math camp, and Nick back to Pennsylvania for his biotechnology camp. Of course, I then had to retrace my routes and shuttle them home after each program concluded. When Danielle returned from China, we shopped for school supplies, gathered her belongings, and moved her into her freshman dorm. After hugs and kisses, I left to plan out the school year for my remaining children, inquired about the quiz bowl team, and packed for my trip. Then the Benghazi attack happened and—

"Come dance with me!" my brother Rony shouted over the crowd, bopping over to me with his arms outstretched as if asking for a hug.

I pulled back, crossing my arms, and sinking into the plush French baroque chair. I smiled at him, but shook my head, no.

Rony's smile melted. He grabbed an empty chair and set it down next to mine. He looked quite handsome in his tuxedo, and his boyish oval face made him seem younger than a man in his fifties, but his graying widow's peak dispelled any doubts.

"Why aren't you dancing?" he asked.

"Congratulations," I said, leaving his question hanging in the air, "the wedding was beautiful, and the food was delicious." The half-eaten plate of food in front of me didn't seem to convince him. "That's my second plate," I added quickly.

"Why are you sitting alone back here? I haven't seen you dance all evening. Is everything ok?"

"I'm fine," I replied, waving his concern away.

He squinted as he studied my face. "Tic," he said, "are you losing weight?" He gave my right arm a gentle squeeze.

"I don't know... Probably... I think I'm just tired from all the running around I've been doing. It's been exhausting." I said, slumping deeper into the chair. "I don't ever recall being this tired."

"I don't know how you do it, kiddo," he said with half a smile. "You're doing an amazing job with the kids, but," he hesitated for a moment before continuing with a worried expression, "you need to slow down."

"Tell me how with five children," I said, "there's no slowing down for me. I'll slow down when I'm dead."

Rony knitted his eyebrows with an expression I couldn't quite read. Sighing and rising from his chair, he asked, "Are you staying in New York for the weekend?"

"I wish I could," I said, tilting my head up to catch his eyes. "I'd love to stay and spend time with Mom, but I have a busy week coming up. Michael's niece is getting married next Saturday; I need to go shopping. And, well before that, actually this Monday, I'm scheduled for a colonoscopy."

"Why? You've only just turned forty-nine." That look of dread materialized on his face again.

"I know. It's overkill. It's Michael's idea. There was a tinge of blood the other day, and, well, it's probably nothing. Michael said the colonoscopy schedule was light for next week, so he spoke with the GI doctor and convinced him to put me on the list. He said it's better to endure it now and dismiss it for the next ten years. I mean, who wants to celebrate the big five-oh with a colonoscopy?" I added, downplaying any need for concern.

"I had it done a few years ago. It's a breeze." Rony said as he patted my back. "The prep is worse than the procedure," he assured me, his trademark smile returning to his face.

Three days later, I was in Macy's fitting room when my cell phone rang. It was Michael.

"Where are you?" he asked.

"Shopping, trying on a dress for your niece's wedding. Why? Where are *you*?"

"I'm home," Michael said.

"Home? It's only noon. What are you doing at home? Is everything okay?"

"Can you please come home? We need to talk." His voice was a fragile whisper.

"What is it, Michael? Are the kids okay?" I asked quickly.

"It's your pathology results." His tone panicked me.

My mirrored reflection shivered as I stood transfixed in my spot. During my colonoscopy earlier that week, the GI doctor biopsied a small tumor in my large intestine. Still, Michael and I concluded it was benign. I wasn't sick. I felt fine, so I abandoned any negative thoughts—until now.

"What—well—what is it?" I asked, reluctant to finish the question. I heard nothing, but a sigh on the other end. "Is it bad?" I whispered, suddenly afraid of being overheard.

"Yes," he said at last.

I hung up the phone and haphazardly assembled the red dress on its hanger and placed it on the rack. I rushed to my car, buckled my seat belt but couldn't turn the key. I sat petrified, hypnotized in a whirlwind of thoughts. It must be some mistake, a mix-up, a clerical error. I tried to remain calm until I was sure of the findings. But I also knew as soon as Michael received the report, as my husband-physician, he'd seek out the GI doctor, the pathologist, and the lab clerk, anyone involved to discover if there was indeed a mistake. He'd ask all the pertinent questions before burdening me with this news. I gripped the steering wheel tightly as my brain searched for something to hold onto. I didn't want to deal with the information just yet. I thought about where I could drive. Somewhere. Anywhere. Not home. I didn't want to go there. If I didn't *know* I had it, if I didn't see the results for myself, if I escaped to Canada or flew to Florida to visit my sister and left the results behind, maybe, just maybe, I could pretend it never happened. It could be the tree that fell in the forest...

Thirty minutes later, I found myself in front of my house. I don't remember driving there, but after ten years in State College, the drive was instinctual. Michael waited outside, still dressed in his

4

green scrubs, which he hardly ever wore outside the hospital. He stood looming by the front door with crossed arms, appearing taller than his 5'7" frame would suggest. *All right then.* I tensed up in my minivan—*time to face the music.* I took a deep breath to calm myself as I stepped out of the car but was unsuccessful. My legs buckled as I approached him and collapsed in his arms. We stood there, silently entwined in an embrace. Grief and worry were captured in his dark brown eyes. There was no need to talk; there were no mistakes, no clerical errors. The eerie tranquility amplified my fears. I had cancer.

Michael showed me pictures of the mass in my colon, and we discussed our next steps. Michael contacted a general surgeon, and we met with him the following day to discuss the procedure. During the meeting, I asked all the relevant questions as if deliberating on one of my patients. Somehow, I still couldn't register that this was happening to *me. I'm* supposed to be the one with the scalpel, not on the hospital bed. I left the doctor's office fixating on two things he had said: Due to the mass's location, I could wake up with a colostomy bag—forever condemned to carry my waste around with me. And, if the tumor spread outside of the colon, chemo or radiation would be required. How would I share those terrible prospects with my parents, brothers, sisters, and most of all, my children? Despite the grim news, by the time Michael and I reached the sanctuary of our home, I was feeling optimistic. I realized the awful possibilities were just that—possibilities. I may just as likely not require a colostomy bag, and the surgery may cure me. Everything was not doomed, not yet. That's how I considered presenting my illness to my family.

The surgeon pushed for an immediate operation on Monday, following Michael's niece's wedding. So, I decided to postpone telling my in-laws and my kids. My misery needed no one. I didn't want to ruin the blissful occasion, nor did I want pity or feelings of discomfort to suffuse around me at the reception. Michael would tell them afterward.

I told my siblings later that week over a conference call. "Hey guys remember the colonoscopy I had a few days ago well the results came back positive for colon cancer and I'm going for surgery next Monday." I blurted everything out in one breath, trying desperately not to cry. I was trying to be tough for them. After a flurry of questions and answers ricocheted back and forth, there was a terrible silence.

Finally, Edith, my oldest sister, said, "What about Mom and Dad? Are we going to tell them?"

"No, I thought about that. You can tell Dad on a need-to-know basis only. Spare him details and keep it positive. I don't want Mom knowing. After her third stroke..." I trailed off. "Well, she's been through enough."

My siblings agreed. They commiserated with me for an hour or so, trying to remain hopeful. Occasionally, sniffles and cracked voices punctuated our call. Upon hanging up the phone, I screamed and freed the flood of tears dammed during the conversation. My siblings wanted to come for the surgery, but I vetoed that idea. I told them Michael would be in contact throughout the day. I was trying to keep things as normal as could be. I wanted my kids to go to school that day and convinced them their mom was tougher than this cancer. Surprisingly, my teenagers believed me and accepted my illness better than I could have predicted.

After the surgery, I woke up from the anesthesia and immediately probed my side, searching for a colostomy bag; I was relieved to find none. The next day, the surgeon stopped by my room to discuss the results.

"Unfortunately," he said, looking down at his clipboard, "in addition to the primary tumor, we found a second mass in your abdomen." He paused to gauge my reaction. I lowered my head and pulled absentmindedly at a stray thread from the white hospital blanket. "You're now a stage three colon cancer," he continued, "because malignancy was found beyond the colon but localized near it."

"What is my five-year survival rate?" I asked as I rubbed my eye as if removing an irritant.

"We don't have to deal with that now. I'm sure your—"

"Excuse me. What is my five-year survival rate?" I repeated, slower this time.

"About 53%."

"A coin toss," I mumbled.

My friends and family tried to encourage me, telling me I could beat this cancer. I had my kids to live for, they had said. Although I agreed, I saw my situation differently. I had my kids to live for because I hadn't yet completed my job of raising and educating them. I've never abandoned a project, and I wasn't about to start now. Danielle was the only one in college; I had four more to go. Giving up was not an option. That's what I've always preached to my kids. It was time to follow my own advice.

On November 5, 2012, my twins' thirteenth birthday, I had a bloodstream access port inserted in my neck, connecting directly into the right jugular vein for my chemo infusion. I felt miserable about having this procedure done on their birthday, but I was anxious to start my chemo so I could be done with it quickly.

My chemo regimen began a week before Thanksgiving and consisted of a cocktail of three different drugs. The staff monitored the first part at the hospital, and then a visiting nurse attached the more extended infusion at my home to run overnight. It was a twenty-four-week plan, with treatments every other week. Rony wanted me to live in New York with him and his family and go to Sloan Kettering. As thoughtful as the offer was, I couldn't be a burden to him, especially since he had already been taking care of our ailing eighty-two-year-old mom. Danielle suggested I receive treatments at Mass General in Boston. I refused her, too. I didn't want her worrying about me when she should be concentrating on being a college student. In reality, I didn't want to be away from the rest of the family. In the end, I settled on our local hospital. I figured the protocol for my diagnosis would be the same regardless of the locale. But I had overlooked one crucial factor. Only later would I realize different doctors managed the side effects of chemo (of which there are many) differently.

My husband accompanied me to my first chemotherapy appointment. After the nurse began the injection of anti-nausea medications, I sent him away. I didn't need him lingering there for the hour or more it took the pretreatment and the chemo drugs to course through my veins. Five other patients were gathered in the small, bland, sterile-looking room, lying in light blue vinyl recliners, identical to mine. Only white, plastic hospital curtains separated us, enabling us to listen in on conversations on either side of those dividers. I was trying to nap when I heard a woman's voice whisper to the patient next to me.

"Sir, you're behind in your payments. We won't be able to administer your next chemo until you've caught up."

"I understand," he mumbled.

I felt miserable for him. Cancer is bad enough on its own, but worrying about paying for it made it that much more distressing. I felt the weight of our privilege, our premium healthcare coverage, and our comfortable lifestyle as the medication dripped into me.

When the nurse drew back the curtain, I craned my neck backward, trying to steal a casual glance at my forlorn neighbor. He was an elderly gentleman, probably in his late seventies, with thinning grayish hair. Crevices on his face and a shriveled prune of a body highlighted his fragile appearance. Older people shouldn't fall victim to cancer, the treatment alone could kill them. I had heard how debilitated you could feel after a chemo session, and I wasn't sure that frail man would survive it. I surveyed the room as I wheeled my IV pole to the restroom and noticed I was the youngest person there. The sight disturbed me. You're supposed to enjoy your golden years, not suffer through them. But then, when *was* the best age to be afflicted with cancer? I already ruled out the old. I also excluded the young because they're just beginning to enjoy life; their brains are still developing. I bleakly concluded my age was probably the best time to incur this disease. At least I had that going for me.

Traveling along this train of thought to the next stop, I debated the best time for *a mother* to get cancer? Not when her kids are young, because it would be impossible to explain an illness like that to her toddlers, and they still needed to be taken care of. But also, not when her kids are adults because they probably would be just starting their careers and may be raising their own children. Having also to take care of an ailing parent might be exasperating. When they're teenagers—like mine—I concluded, would be the best age; they can take care of themselves with limited supervision. They're so self-absorbed at this stage in their lives that a parent's illness wouldn't impact them as much anyways. Hey, I was two for two. I half-heartedly smiled to myself as I slowly maneuvered my way back to the recliner. The nurse waited with my medication. I sat down, clasped my hands, and held my breath as she hooked me to the chemo drugs, bracing for the tempest.

When you enter a dark and fearful part of your life, it is only natural that you look for a time when there emitted an ethereal light powered by laughter and aspiration, a time when things were controllable, fixable. For me, this would begin with raising my children. Those years gave me the chance to laugh with my kids, play with them, cry with them, and know them. As the toxic treatment squirmed through my veins, I closed my eyes, made myself comfortable, and reminisced about the beginning.

PART I

HATCHING

They know me in a way no one ever has.
  They open me up to things I never knew existed.
  They drive me to insanity and push me to my depths.
  They are the beat of my heart.
  The pulse of my veins and the energy in my soul.
  They are my kids.

— ANONYMOUS

THE FAMILY (1998–1999)

Family, where life begins, and love never ends.

— ANONYMOUS

My reason for wanting a large family was simple: I wanted my children to be each other's playmates, as my siblings were mine. We grew up in Brooklyn in the late sixties, but as a family of Haitian immigrants, we spoke primarily French and Kreyòl at home. My five siblings and I were raised in a typical Haitian household, listening to compas music, and eating fried plantains, fried pork, and, of course, rice and beans. My siblings were my best friends, and with good reason—we were the first Black family to move into a white neighborhood on Nostrand Avenue. The other kids were not allowed to play with us or didn't want to play with us. We never found out which. It didn't matter; we played with each other and kept to ourselves. Sadly, this didn't stop the white kids from teasing us, throwing rocks at us, and calling us names.

My father, like most immigrant parents, was averse to

confrontation and told us to ignore them. He kept us indoors after school, where we hunkered down at the kitchen table to do homework. My grandmother, the family's matriarch, disagreed with my father and told us to defend ourselves. One late October afternoon, we did. We sustained some scratches and bruises, but we gave the neighborhood kids swollen eyes and bloody noses. Upon reflection, I guess they were more shocked that we fought back than afraid. They respected us afterward, and the teasing ended. Some of us even became friends. A few years later, more Hispanic and Black families moved in, and the white families moved out. Although making friends then became a lot easier, my siblings remained my closest companions. If my biracial children received the same "welcome" in central Pennsylvania that we received in Brooklyn, I wanted them to rely on each other.

While wanting a large family was easy, acquiring one was far more complicated. My pregnancies refused to cooperate. Preterm labor aggravated every pregnancy, which resulted in bed rest and medications. My last pregnancy, at thirty-five years of age, was a harrowing experience. I was an obstetrician's worst nightmare.

One night during that pregnancy, I was at the kitchen sink rinsing out a glass. It slipped from my hands and shattered on the beige tile floor, sending pieces of glass sliding like ice cubes across the floor. Startled, my three children spun their heads up. I couldn't speak or move. I grasped the sink with closed eyes as discomfort seared through my lower abdomen.

"Mommy, are you okay?" asked Danielle, my oldest.

I had almost forgotten the kids were there. I didn't want them anywhere near the broken glass, but luckily the shards skated away from them. "Sorry, guys, Mommy's not feeling well. She has a tummy ache," I said as I put my arms across my belly and limped to the family room's brown sofa. "Danielle, my big girl." I grimaced as I caught my breath. "Can you help the boys with their pajamas and... and put them to bed for me, please? You can read them a bedtime story if you want... Dad's on call, and Mommy's not feeling well, so... you're in charge. Can you handle it?"

"Yes, Mommy, I can," she said with no hesitation.

"Thank you, darling." I could not fathom how mature she was for a four-year-old. I wondered, was that an oxymoron? Nonetheless, Danielle was destined to be in charge.

"Come on, boys, let's go," she ordered her younger siblings as she shepherded them to bed. I was apprehensive as I saw my six-month-old, Nicky, crawling up the stairs while Mikey and Danielle trailed behind.

As soon as my kids were out of earshot range, I called my husband to inform him of my imminent miscarriage.

"Do you want to see a doctor? Do you want to come to the hospital?"

I knew there was nothing my doctor would be able to do for an eight-week pregnancy because, as an obstetrician, I had witnessed some of these hopeless situations. After resolving myself to the circumstances, I simply said, "No, the kids are already in bed, and it'll take too long to try to call a babysitter."

"I'm coming home. I'll find someone to cover me."

"No, no, don't. I'll be okay," I lied. "I just need to rest." I hung up the phone and wiped my eyes. The pain in my abdomen and fear in my chest forbade me to climb the stairs to my bedroom. I couldn't even check in on the children. I made myself as comfortable as I could on the sofa. After what seemed like hours, I fell asleep. Dawn found me—surprisingly—well. The pain had subsided, and there was still no sign of blood. After dropping the kids off at preschool and daycare, I went straight to my hospital's ultrasound room. The sonographer showed me two gestational sacs in my uterus. I was having twins. No, that's not possible, twins didn't run in my family, and Michael and I had compromised on four children, not five. Questions began swirling in my head like debris in a tornado. Then I saw the sonographer's widened eyes reflected my own, but our reasons differed: The smaller sac pictured on the screen was irregularly shaped. There was also a ruptured cyst and fluid behind my womb. This observation made it evident that my pregnancy was still in danger. I prescribed myself progesterone and resolved to rest as much as possible, typical advice I would have given to my patients.

My immediate dilemma, however, was telling Michael we were having twins. His initial reaction consisted of outbursts like, "How could this happen? "We agreed on only one more," and my favorite, "I'll be working until I'm 100. No retirement for me." Michael eventually accepted the situation, and, in the ensuing weeks, we were both eager to welcome the twins.

At sixteen weeks, my sonogram revealed the larger twin was a boy and the smaller one a girl. Since my sisters were my best friends, I was delighted Danielle would have a sister also.

Twenty-eight weeks found me in a panic again. Premature contractions pulled my cerclage apart, a stitch the doctor had placed to help keep my cervix closed. It had now reopened and had bulging membranes. I was admitted to the hospital to stop my labor and to put in another cerclage.

My doctor said, "Carline, you know the risks. With this cerclage, there's a fifty percent chance of rupturing the membranes and losing the babies."

"I know," I said, stifling tears. Years later, I realized the fear of losing one's child either in utero or later in life is a cross all mothers carry. It never disappears, not even after they have gone to college or moved away. The umbilical cord is never truly cut.

My doctor deemed the procedure a success and sent me home on strict bedrest, tocolytic drugs, and a series of steroid injections to help with the babies' lung development. My in-laws came that weekend and helped until my parents showed up that Monday. They cooked, cleaned, and drove the kids to preschool for the next month, awaiting the birth of the twins. I don't know how I would have managed without my family.

At thirty-two weeks, my preterm labor resumed, and the first twin, the boy, was a footling breech, necessitating an immediate cesarean section. My twins did well, and thankfully, they had a short stay in the Neonatal Intensive Care Unit. The three of us were discharged together after three days.

Danielle, my oldest, had been my only full-term pregnancy, delivered at thirty-seven weeks. Mikey and Nick were born at thirty-six and thirty-five weeks, respectively. And my twins, arriving at thirty-two weeks, were my earliest premature deliveries. Preemies, I knew, statistically tend to never quite catch up to their full-term counterparts. They are more likely to suffer from developmental delays, struggle in school and sports, and manifest learning disabilities. I feared my children might suffer a similar fate, but as time would tell, they had other plans.

OUR BEGINNING (2000)

The difference between a beginning teacher and an experienced one is that the beginning teacher asks, 'How am I doing?' and the experienced teacher asks, 'How are the children doing?'

— ESME RAJI CODELL

"Wake up, Sweetie, time for school," I said in a high-pitched voice usually reserved for my kids. I cracked open the door to my five-year-old Danielle's pink and white striped bedroom. Quiet as a library. I stepped inside, stood by her bed, and tried again, softer this time. "Come on, Dani, time to get ready for school," I said, prodding her awake.

As she stirred and yawned, I walked over to her window and opened the blinds to gain the sun's assistance. The morning light filtered through the tree branches and streamed into Danielle's room, radiating patchwork sunbeams on her face. She clenched her eyes and recoiled her small body into a fetal position, pulling the covers over herself.

"Can I stay home today, Mommy? Please?" she moaned.

"Why? Are you sick?" I said, coming towards her bed. She peeked out from under her blankets, and I felt her forehead.

"No," she replied, squinting her eyes. "I don't think so." She yawned again.

"Well, then you can't stay home." I nudged her shoulder. "Come on, Sweetie, up. Once you're dressed, you'll feel fine."

I took off the silk scarf I had tied around her cornrows the night before. It reminded me of when my mom used to do the same to my hair late in the evenings, before leaving the house and heading out to her second job. But Danielle's hair was longer and softer than the natural kinky hair I wore back then.

"You look gorgeous," I said, admiring my handiwork, "now get dressed and come down for breakfast. I'm gonna wake up the others."

I placed Jackie and Joey, my six-month-old twins, in their high-chairs and gave them their pacifiers while their oatmeal cooled. The babysitter would take care of the feeding. Nicky and Mikey were already in their booster seats, downing theirs. I had to send some patients home before starting my office hours, so I'd planned to leave the house early. I also needed to drop Nicky at the daycare, Mikey at Penn Mont Academy, and Danielle at St. John's Elementary. If I kept Mikey at the daycare with Nicky or left Danielle at Penn Mont with Mikey, I would have one fewer detour disrupting my chaotic mornings. Because Montessori school only extended to kindergarten, Michael and I decided to make the lateral move to St. John's kindergarten class to allow Danielle to start with the other kindergarteners. This way, she would—wait, Danielle still had not come down for breakfast. "Danielle, get a move on," I called up to her room.

She ambled downstairs, dressed in a maroon plaid jumper and white starched shirt, and took her usual seat at the kitchen table. Crafted of oak and a marbled inlay of dark green Formica, the octagonal table was Michael's creation. He designed it himself in his workshop just a few months after the twins were born. He was very proud of it. We all were. We all agreed that a family that eats together stays together.

I watched as my oldest daughter dawdled in front of her bowl, fiddling with her spoon while cradling her melancholy face in her other hand. "Eat your breakfast, Dani, and elbows off the table," I reminded her as I hurried for the ear thermometer.

Sighing, she straightened up and removed her elbow from the table. "I'm not hungry," she said. I placed the thermometer in her ear. After the beep, a green "98.7" illuminated the screen.

"Eat your breakfast," I said again, more sternly this time, as I put the device away and rushed to retrieve my medical journals.

The doorbell chimed, and I dashed to the door. "Thanks for coming early," I said to the babysitter as she walked in. We had hired her two months earlier to take care of the twins. Although she knew the daily routine, I still recited directives. "I've already sterilized their bottles, their jars for lunch are on the kitchen counter, my beeper and Michael's beeper numbers are on the refrigerator. I'm in the office today," I said, "so use the office number, the second one under my name."

I glanced over toward Danielle and noticed her breakfast remained untouched. "Danielle," I said, "what's wrong? Why all the gloom?"

"I don't want to go to school, Mommy," she said softly.

"Are you going to be a kindergarten dropout?" I joked. Danielle was not amused. She was blue; I was baffled. "Why not?" I asked.

"I'm bored at school, Mom. I would rather stay home with the twins and read my books."

Bored? How can a five-year-old be bored with school? It's kindergarten. "Ahh, Danielle, I can't do this today. You're going to school. Kids, drink your orange juice and get in the car. You too, Dani." After buckling my three older children into their car seats, I handed Danielle a granola bar. "It'll be okay, Sweetie," I said. "You're probably just tired this morning."

"No, Mom," she said, with a certainty that belied her age, "I'm bored."

DANIELLE (DANI): 0–5 (1994–2000)

The Multi-Talented One

Why fit in when you were born to stand out?

— DR. SEUSS

I BEGAN READING to Danielle when she was only days old. By the time she turned one, Danielle had firmly established the habit. It occurred every evening and consisted of at least two books, one of which was always *The Cat in the Hat*. When I resumed working six months after her birth, Michael and I took turns handling Danielle's reading ritual. Sleepy and exhausted after a grueling day at work, I tiptoed up our carpeted staircase. I longed for my bed as a sailor for his sea. The last thing I wanted was to read *The Cat in the Hat* for the thousandth time to my two-year-old.

"Mommy, is that you?" Danielle squeaked.

Darn it. "Yes, Sweetie, it's me," I said, yawning as I peeped into her room. "It's late. Why aren't you sleeping?"

My question drew a blank stare. *What a foolish question, Mom*, her expression suggested. We both knew the answer, so I decided not to wait for a reply. "Okay, Chérie, give me a minute. I'm going to change into my pajamas."

As I undressed, I noted my husband lying contently in our bed watching *Monday Night Football*. I browsed around the room for something to throw at him. "Why couldn't you read to her?"

Lifting his neck around me for a better view of the television, he said, "It's your turn, and you do a better job with the whole voice thing." He glanced up from his reclined position to see my crossed arms and my arched eyebrows. I hated that we both worked full time, but I still had "mommy chores" to do when I came home, even when Michael had a post-call day off. "Okay, I'm sorry," he said,

21

sitting upright, exposing his hairy chest, "I told Danielle to wait until you got home, but I honestly thought she would be asleep by now. If you're too tired—" I thought he was going to say, 'I'll do it,' but instead, he said, "tell her you'll read to her tomorrow."

"Forget it."

She waited eagerly in her bubblegum pink pajamas, propped up against the white headboard, perfectly blending in with her bedroom's décor. Resting on her lap were Dr. Seuss's *The Cat in the Hat* and *Oh, the Places You'll Go!* When she saw me, she shifted her tiny body aside, creating a space for me on the bed. I grabbed the books, settled in next to her, and began reading.

I was getting tired, so halfway through the book, I cut out a paragraph to finish it faster. Danielle already knew the story, and that section wasn't essential, so I figured she wouldn't miss any details. I got away with it. Impressed with how I surgically excised that paragraph, I attempted it further down the page, but Danielle stopped me.

"You missed these words," she said, pointing to my deleted paragraph.

"How do you know?" I asked, sitting up.

"Because I'm reading with you. I think you missed these words also," she said, pointing to my first skipped paragraph.

"What? You can *read?*"

"Yes, I taught myself. I use this book," Danielle said, reaching for *The Cat in the Hat*, "to help me read other books. I try finding similar words."

"What do you do when you come to a word you don't know?"

"I try to figure it out. Sometimes I have trouble," she admitted.

This awakened me. I began teaching her phonics that evening. After an hour, Michael checked in on us. When I exclaimed Danielle could read, he excitedly grabbed a random book off her shelf to see for himself. He picked *Danny and the Dinosaur*. It was perfect because it was not one of her frequently read books. He handed it to Danielle and then sat on the corner of the bed, by my feet. Bolstered by the attention, she read the first page and proceeded to finish the book. Michael and I beamed as if she had just graduated college. Once Danielle understood phonics, her reading seemed limitless.

When Danielle turned three, an educational decision was thrust upon me: Should she remain in the local daycare with her two-year-old baby brother or transfer to our local Montessori preschool, Penn Mont Academy? Danielle was quite familiar with the daycare, and I hated disturbing her routine. However, most of my colleagues enrolled their children at Penn Mont and spoke highly of the school. At the time, I didn't know what a Montessori education entailed, so I toured it.

Unsure of what I was getting into, my doubts were assuaged when the principal, Mrs. Hartye, spoke at the open house. "I won't guarantee your kids will get accepted to the Ivy League, but I will guarantee your child will have a passion for learning. These early developmental years are critical in laying the groundwork for curiosity and learning."

My toddler's acceptance to the Ivy League was the furthest thing from my mind, but I did want a child who was curious and driven. Danielle began attending Penn Mont the following month. Her teacher, Miss Maryann, was a slender white woman with a dark brown bob that framed her angular face. One day as I was picking Danielle up, she told me that Danielle had a passion for numbers, more specifically, the number board. It was a large wooden board with the numbers one to a hundred in bold black ink, printed in a 10 x 10 grid. Miss Maryann found it surprising Danielle did these activities with the five-year-olds. She said most three-year-olds lacked the patience and the acuity to write the numbers from one to a hundred. The following day, we bought a paper-laminated number board. When I placed marbles on the board to represent the numerals, Danielle noticed patterns in every other number, which I described as the concept of numbers being even and odd. It didn't take long for her to "discover" multiplication. When I picked her up one afternoon, she grabbed my hands, grinning, and hurried me to the numbers area. "See, Mom, three plus three plus three is like saying three times three, which equals nine." By the time she was five, Danielle had memorized her multiplication tables.

After her progress at Penn Mont, Danielle began kindergarten at our local Catholic school. She was eager to start at a new school. Exploring new places had always intrigued her. When she was a baby, we would roam the local malls. She'd listen while I pointed out various objects in the storefront windows. Before the age of two, when her airplane tickets were still free, she traveled everywhere with us. During our trips, Danielle didn't cry or scream. Instead, she quietly observed and listened, taking in her surroundings in an attempt to decipher her environment.

Then my child, who had never been bored with anything, told me she was bored with school. I couldn't shake the disgruntled expression on my child's face that morning. I tried to reassure myself that Danielle was tired and needed more sleep; still, I worried. She didn't seem tired. She looked—depressed. So, during a rare break in my office hours, I darted to Danielle's school. I ran tiptoed through the hallways to Danielle's classroom. I peeked through the door, and to my bewilderment, my daughter was correct. I watched in astonishment as the students in her "math" class circled the answer to the exact numbers of apples on the apple tree. They were learning how to count. I was upset, annoyed, and disappointed all at once. No one had informed me of what she was learning, or rather *not* learning, at school.

I decided to be more proactive in my child's education. Thus began my long streak of complaints to principals. In the beginning, the principal sought to accommodate me by giving Danielle extra work. He also noted the following year, when my daughter was in first grade, it would be more challenging because the school combined first and second grades in one classroom. He told me my daughter would be doing some second-grade work while still being with the first graders. I promised Danielle things would improve. I also reminded her of all the new friends she was making. That seemed to appease her for the time being.

The following year found Danielle in first grade and Mikey in kindergarten at St. John's. Though the younger elementary students left their books in their open-front desk, I instructed Danielle to backpack hers home for inspection. They were less than inspiring. Her math book *ended* with an introduction to arithmetic. This situation was not going to work. I decided to meet with the principal. Again.

I told him the assignments were still not stimulating enough for my daughter, and she should be an official second grader. His solution was to give her an exam usually given to first graders at the end of their school year before skipping her. We waited two weeks for the results. Meanwhile, I further reduced my part-time work schedule to three days a week, allowing more time to observe my kids at school. With my extra time, I volunteered one day per week at the school's library. The first thing I noticed was its size. The library was minuscule compared to what I'd imagined, and it lacked diversity in book selections, particularly for my Black children. I spoke with the principal about making a monetary donation for books to assist my daughter and the entire student body.

He replied, "We have more urgent matters to attend to than new books. We have kids who are failing. Your daughter is ahead. You can donate this money, but the school will use it where we see fit."

I donated books instead.

We received the test results. Danielle got a perfect score, and the principal immediately placed her in second grade. Again, I instructed her to bring home her new books when they arrived. In the meantime, I continued to volunteer at the library, where Danielle was always happy to see me when her class visited.

"Any suggestions, Mom?" she asked, perusing the books on the shelves.

"What about this?" I said, pulling down a small, yellow-bound hardcover of *The Wizard of Oz*. "We don't have it at home."

"Wow, Dani, can you read that book?" asked one of her classmates.

"Would you like one also?" I offered.

"No, thank you," said the child, twirling her pigtail with a finger and looking down at her feet, "I'm not up to that level yet."

"Well, you won't know until you try. But," I said, "I'll have one for you when you're ready."

She beamed up at me, nodding her approval, and scurried away. Half an hour later, the principal called me to his office over the loudspeaker. The bellowing of my name was commonplace in a hospital but a school? Was there an emergency? Climbing the stairs two at a time, sprinting down the hall, I arrived tousled and breathless in the principal's office. My eyes darted around for Mikey or Danielle or some other bleeding or unconscious child but found neither. I only saw a middle-aged, bespectacled white man glaring at me from across his desk.

"How dare you?" he began.

"What?" No infraction registered in my mind. "What did I do?" I gasped.

"You allowed a second-grade child to take out a sixth-grade reading level book, and you forced one on another second grader."

I was speechless. It took me a while to comprehend what was happening. This man had summoned me to his office as if I were one of his—*students?* My pulse had come down, but I felt my blood pressure rising. After taking a deep breath, I asked, "And? One of the second graders happens to be my child, and I know she can read that book."

"And what about the other child?" he said as he removed his glasses and used them as a pointer. "Did it ever occur to you that she might have done her best to read that book on your suggestion and failed?"

"Possibly," I said, still standing by the door, trying to control my fury, "but at least she would have tried. Shouldn't we be encouraging our students to push beyond their comfort zone?"

"No... No. That's not what would happen," he said. "Her parents would have been furious with me for pushing their child. You have no idea how things work in a school and the need to accommodate parents." He rested his glasses on his papers and raked his fingers back through his thick black hair. "If you want to continue working in the library," he said, "then you must follow the rules. Students can take books out *only* on their grade level."

"Even *my* daughter?"

"*Especially* your daughter. We don't want to make any exceptions."

"This makes no sense," I said. "Are you telling me even though Danielle is reading at a sixth-grade level, she can only take out books on a second-grade level? Dr. Seuss's books?"

"Correct."

"Well, how is that accommodating my child and me?"

He repositioned his glasses on his face and began shuffling papers on his desk, indicating that this meeting was now over. Then, as an afterthought, he glowered at me and said, "You can take her to the public library."

Instead of saying something I might regret, I left in a flurry, hell-bent on finding another school for my children. I was shocked by the disrespect this man had shown me and equally appalled one of the library staff had seen it fit to tattle on me. Unfortunately, while interviewing other school principals in the vicinity in the ensuing weeks, I received similarly dismal comments about the school's potential or willingness to accommodate my daughter's reading and math abilities. I wondered if their attitudes were due to my gender, ethnicity, or both. Either way, I was stuck.

Danielle's new second-grade books were still full of concepts my daughter had mastered in preschool. I was madder than a wet cat. But the thought of having to confront this principal again, without having a plan B, left me in despair. I predicted it would not end well. I was right. The principal accused me of putting "too much pressure" on my child (an accusation I would frequently hear over the ensuing years). A parent once boasted that, although my kids might be smart, his kids were "good"—as if these traits were mutually exclusive. Who made him the arbiter of evaluating a "good" child? I thought of telling him how my children had done countless volunteer activities in the community but decided against it because I didn't need to justify myself to him. So, instead of engaging this parent in a mindless debate over who raised the better child, I said nothing. I treated the principal similarly when he accused me of putting too much pressure on my children, and I walked out of his office for the last time.

MICHAEL (MIKEY) 0–5 (1995–2000)

The Musical One

> *I see my life in terms of music.*
>
> — ALBERT EINSTEIN

MIKEY IS ONLY thirteen months younger than Danielle, but they were light years apart on the developmental scale. Seeing how Dr. Seuss worked for Danielle, logic dictated it should work for Mikey too. I soon discovered there was nothing logical about raising children; Mikey never took an interest in *The Cat in the Hat*. When I placed my chubby toddler on my lap and read to him, he squirmed and fussed. Mikey was interested in everything except the book. I tested several books until I noticed the busier the pages seemed, the better he focused.[1] Unlike Danielle, who wanted to read along with me, Mikey wanted to know what was happening on each page. When I realized this, I described the pictures instead of reading the words.

When Mikey was three years old, he developed a fascination with cars. He would pick out different makes and models as they motored down the streets, spotting Dodge Durango to Mercedes Benz cars and everything in between. Besides getting him Matchbox cars and t-shirts embossed with cars, I bought him many books about cars, trucks, and trains. We learned about their engines and their maximum speeds. After the car interest wore off, we moved on to dinosaurs, then pro-football teams. Mikey was never interested in reading, though. He wanted to scan pictures, name the objects, and classify them. Like Danielle, who taught herself how to read by memorizing high-frequency words, Mikey's memorization techniques also required a tremendous amount of concentration on diverse subjects. This learning tactic would later prove helpful in fostering Mikey's musical abilities.

"Mikey, you're humming again. I said no humming at the dinner table."

"I'm sorry, Mommy. I hear music in my head."

I never knew where the tunes came from. They were not from *Barney* or any of the children's shows we watched. He composed them himself, and the soft melodies were pleasing to the ear. Soon after his confession of hearing music in his head, I signed Mikey and Danielle up for piano lessons. Their piano teacher admitted he was unsure how Mikey processed the information he was taught, yet somehow it resonated with Mikey much faster than Danielle.

While Mikey was excelling at the piano, I began teaching him how to read using *Bob* books. He had difficulty understanding punctuation. I taught Mikey the punctuation song I had learned from the *Electric Company* with Rita Moreno eons ago. While he liked the catchy tune and danced to the jingle, it didn't help much. Then I used something his mind could comprehend, music. "A period is like a whole rest," I said, "you pause for a while. A comma is like a half rest. You pause for half as long." Success. After realizing how different Mikey's learning techniques were from Danielle's, I knew I would be customizing their learning, something that continued throughout their education.

The following year, my friend's daughter began playing the violin. Danielle told me it was the sweetest sound she had ever heard and begged for violin lessons. I researched the subject and discovered that if a child played a string instrument before the age of seven, they could develop perfect pitch. I consulted various people about violin lessons for my six-year-old. We met with an experienced violin teacher who agreed to teach Danielle and recommended I purchase a violin from a reputable shop in Harrisburg. It was about two and a half hours away, which seemed like quite the trek to buy a beginner violin for a six-year-old. The teacher claimed the shop owner was quite friendly and knowledgeable enough to fit Danielle with a properly sized violin. She also added that since they made and repaired the violins on-site, it could be a valuable teaching moment for my children. Sold. That last part convinced me. The following Saturday morning, I traveled to Harrisburg with Danielle and Mikey in search of a violin for Danielle.

"Are you getting a violin, too, young man?" asked the white-bearded shop owner.

"No, I'm too little," squealed my five-year-old son.

"Nonsense," the man said. He leaned over like a palm tree as he studied my son. "Why, I was about your age when I began playing."

As I stood watching their interaction, the man reached behind a shelf and pulled out a violin so small, I thought it was a toy. He positioned it gently on Mikey's arm, teaching him how to hold it. Mikey's supplicating eyes caught mine, and he said one word: "Please?"

"You're still crazy," my husband said with a smirk after I finished describing what occurred at the shop and my reason for coming home with *two* violins.

"Well, we'll see how crazy I am when he becomes a world-famous violinist," I said, giving my husband a peck on his cheek.

After Penn Mont, Mikey started kindergarten at Danielle's Catholic school. We celebrated his first day by dressing him in his new clothes and telling him he was now a big boy, no more preschool. He sounded thrilled in the initial days as he threw on his white shirt and khaki slacks and scrambled out of the house with Danielle. I was perplexed when he asked me the following week, "Mommy, how much longer do I have to go to kindergarten?"

"Well, for a long time, and then you'll move on to first grade, and—"

A look of horror appeared on his angelic face as the new reality of his life flashed in front of him. "No! I don't want to go to school anymore!" he shouted.

Afterward, getting Mikey ready for school became a struggle. There was a lot of screaming and crying. His tantrums were incomprehensible. I had never seen any separation issues whenever I dropped him off at daycare or Penn Mont. I needed to investigate the cause of this behavior. I began volunteering at the school for Danielle a year before, but now I had to keep an eye on Mikey as well. The principal gave me his non-medical diagnosis of Mikey's issue.

"Your son," he said in his typical arrogant manner, "may be academically ahead of his peers, like his sister, but he is emotionally immature."

I groaned, realizing a mature five-year-old is an oxymoron, but there was no point in stating the obvious.

While volunteering, I formed my diagnosis. Mikey, too, seemed bored. I noticed this as I spied through the square window of his closed classroom door. When the teacher read to the class, Mikey's attention turned elsewhere. First, outside—he observed the black-capped chickadees tweeting by the window, then at the leaves, just beginning to change into their warm yellow and red fall attires. Back inside again, his gaze traveled to the checker-patterned floor tiles and finally landed on the fluorescent tubes on the ceiling. I'm sure he would have glanced at his watch if he wore one. I contrasted that with the times I observed him at Penn Mont. There he roamed around, lay on the floor and did map puzzles, played with the keys and locks, or sometimes, stayed quietly by himself, observing. Regardless of the activity, he seemed carefree. Being confined to a desk and having no say in the curriculum tortured my son. The more I forced Mikey to go to school, the more distressed he became.

I now had to deal with two children who no longer wanted to attend school. Unbelievable.

NICHOLAS (NICKY): 0–5 (1998–2003)

The Creative One

LEGO has essentially taken the concrete block, the building block of the world, and made it into the building block of our imagination.

— AYAH BDEIR

UNLIKE THE PRECISE and continuous memories I retained of Danielle's and Mikey's early years, my little ones: Nicky's, Joey's, and Jackie's—the Munchkins, as Danielle affectionately nicknamed them—are scattered and blurred with time. I also had my attention divided among more children. The few anecdotes I retrieved were from an earlier website: Seven Heaven, my Facebook precursor. I started the site to share pictures of their latest milestones, adventures, and dilemmas with our distant relatives. Nicky's name change was one of those recollections.

"Nicky Feffer! Nicky Feffer! We're missing a Nicky Feffer!" yelled one of the swim officials. They were calling the six-and-under girls to the seating area.

Nicky seemed troubled. "Why are they calling me to swim with the girls, Mommy?"

"There must be a mix-up. I'll fix it," I told my kids as I rose from my squatting position on the grass. After clarifying the blunder, the officials scratched Nicky's name from all his events off the girl's list and placed it on the boy's. I explained that "Nicky" could be a girl's or a boy's name on our way home after the meet. My other kids in the car snickered. Nicky lowered his head.

"What about Nick?" he suggested after a quick moment of reflection. "Can that be a girl's name too?"

"No," I said, "I'm pretty sure Nick is only a boy's name."

"Then I don't want to be called Nicky anymore, Mommy. I'm Nick."

I looked in the rear-view mirror and caught his doleful, puppy eyes on that adorable, puffy-cheeked face and said, "Okay, Nick."

He smiled.

Nick was Danielle's play toy and Mikey's wrestling partner. But to his two younger siblings, born a year after him, Nick was a mixture of contradictions. They related to him better than the two older ones due to the closeness in age. But they also were wary of him because, like many older siblings, he could be a bit of a bully. One day, after knocking his baby sister to the floor, he spotted me eyeing him and said, "Time-out?" Nick used the time-out wicker chair more than all the other kids combined. Whenever he left for the time-out chair, he'd usually grab a book. I had read that if a parent desired their child to be a lifelong reader, not only should they read because kids imitate parents, but they should also place books in the child's vicinity. I displayed books in prominent areas throughout the house. After half an hour, I asked Nick if he was sorry for what he had done and if he was ready to apologize to his baby sister. Without taking his eyes off his book, he put one finger in the air and said, "In a second, Mommy, I'm on the last page." In times like that, I wasn't quite sure time-out was accomplishing its purpose. But if Nick was reading and not bothering the twins, it was a win for us all.

Nick was also an early reader. By then, I was more confident in my teaching abilities using the primers. He also saw his older siblings reading and wanted to mimic them. Unlike Mikey and Danielle, Nick loved all kinds of books. He was also not fond of memorizing high-frequency words; he preferred phonics. Nick enjoyed understanding the concept of how components functioned. When his Star Wars lightsaber broke, he ran sobbing to me while I was setting the table.

"Honey," I said, taking hold of his toy, "I don't know if it will work anymore. Maybe we can buy a new one for your birthday," I added.

"No, Mommy," he cried. "Daddy will fix it. Dad can fix anything."

Sure enough, my three-year-old waited until his dad returned home that evening. He positioned himself by his father's elbow at the kitchen table and, with balled fingers, surveyed how Michael took apart the nuts and bolts of his beloved toy and repaired it. Observing the restoration of his toys accentuated Nick's creative and doer personality. If Mikey threw minor tantrums for being in a rigid classroom, Nick would cause a rebellion. I was not looking forward to the end of his Montessori education.

JOSEPH (JOEY): 0–5 (1999–2004)

The Critical Thinker

> *Anytime you find someone more successful than you are, especially when you're both engaged in the same business—you know they're doing something you aren't.*

> — MALCOLM X

EVERY MORNING, baby Joey marveled at how the three older kids walked out the door with their father while he remained home with Mommy and his sister until the babysitter arrived. *I could do that,* he thought. *It doesn't seem that difficult if Nicky can do it. He doesn't seem much bigger than me.* And so, the next day, he stood up and walked.

That's how I imagined it, at least, when I watched Joey staring at his older siblings with such intensity, I thought he would burst. Joey began walking the day after his first birthday. Like Danielle's reading, his walking stunned me because I never saw him tottering about. I surmised he practiced in his crib and revealed it to us when he had perfected it. Joey's "practice 'til perfect" motto was a formula he refined during the ensuing years. Now that Joey was a walker, he went to daycare with Nick. At barely a year old, he got dressed early and carried his lunchbox out the door, grinning and waving to me and his twin sister, Jackie, who stayed behind.

On our white refrigerator door was a small red and blue magnetic picture frame that read: World's Most Beautiful Baby. It held a picture of Nick at two months old. This frame was given to me by my older sister, Edwidge, Nick's godmother. The kids always inspected the refrigerator door for the colorful magnetic words I created for them each morning. That picture and its title were Nick's pride and joy. He beamed proudly at his younger self every time he walked by it, which annoyed three-year-old Joey.

"But how did they decide that Nicky was the world's most beautiful baby?" he questioned.

"I don't know," I said with a smothered laugh. "I guess they took pictures of all the babies that were born around that time and determined Nicky was the most beautiful."

"But what about me? Did they do that when I was born?" Joey scratched his cheeks.

"I don't know," I said. "Maybe they didn't want to include twins."

"Face it, Joey," Nick boasted, "I'm the world's most beautiful baby."

Joey was not about to face it, nor was he inclined to agree. I caught how he glared at that picture and seemed to know something was amiss.

A week later, Joey said, "Nicky, why don't you take a look at the refrigerator?"

That sounded ominous. Nick sensed it too, so he shot to the kitchen with me in tow. The World's Most Beautiful Baby frame was there, and it still depicted a baby, but it wasn't Nick; it was Joey. My middle son cried upon witnessing this. Although I was heartbroken for Nick, I was impressed with Joey. Not only was he able to figure out the puzzle of the magnetic frame, but he also pilfered one of his baby pictures and replaced Nick's. Brilliant. Devious but brilliant. When Michael scolded Joey and made him put his brother's picture back in the frame, Joey did not seem bothered; he had debunked the mystery. Restoring his title as The World's Most Beautiful Baby made Nick happy again.

One day, when the twins were about five years old, as they lay together on Jackie's bed reading from one of their fairytale books, I heard them whispering. It piqued my curiosity, so I sneaked over to Jackie's room to eavesdrop on their conversion.

"I think it's her, Jackie," I heard Joey say softly.

"That doesn't make any sense, Joey. Why would Mom go to all of these kids' homes to collect their teeth and give them money?"

"No, you don't understand," Joey exclaimed, raising his voice, "Mom is *our* tooth fairy. Maybe the other kids' moms are *their* tooth fairy."

Jackie sounded unconvinced. "I don't think so, Joey, I—"

"Come on, Joey and Jackie, piano time. Let's go." I said, determined to stop the troubling conversation my twins were having. What would be next, Santa Claus? That youngster was getting too bright.

"Why isn't Mom a Feffer, Dad?" Joey asked one evening at the dinner table.

"Ask your mom," replied Michael with a 'Can't wait to see how you wiggle out of this one' grin.

None of the other kids ever asked me that, nor did Michael seem to object. My gold-framed diploma displayed my name as Dr. Crevecoeur, and my patients knew me by that name. Only my septuagenarian dad had a problem with it, and now apparently, so did my four-year-old son.

"Well," I began, as I stalled for time, "I was a Crevecoeur before I married your father, so I didn't see why I had to change it."

"But then you're not part of this family because we're all Feffers."

"Then what does that make me? Am I not still your mother?" I couldn't believe I was engaging in an existential discussion with a child.

Joey didn't quite know how to answer that. So, he deflected it and asked, "Why can't you change your name so we can all be the same?"

"But what will it change? Will you love me more?"

"No, but I want people to know you're my mother; you're part of *our* family. You belong to us now, not the Crevecoeur family."

I laughed. "The Crevecoeurs are still my family. And they're yours, too—your aunts and uncles and grandparents and cousins. But, Joey, if it means that much to you, I'll consider it."

I never did change my name. Joey realized I probably never would. The truth is, sometimes I wish I did take his advice. Later, when my children were in the newspaper or on television for some award, beaming with pride, I wanted people to know those Feffer kids belonged to me.

JACQUELINE (JACKIE): 0–5 (1999–2004)

The Social One

Life isn't meant to be lived perfectly... but merely to be LIVED. Boldly, wildly, beautifully, uncertainly, imperfectly, magically, LIVED.

— MANDY HALE

JACKIE WAS the smallest and the last of the litter, weighing only four pounds and two ounces at birth. During the first few days of her life, she had difficulty maintaining her body temperature. As a result, we raised the house thermostat to ninety degrees Fahrenheit upon carrying her home on a brisk November day. She also repeated her hearing test a month after birth because the hospital's test was equivocal and suggested she might be deaf. By three months, though, her pediatrician acknowledged her to be developmentally on par with her age.

From the start, I encouraged Jackie to hold her own in interactions with her older siblings. One morning, I had to take Jackie's bottle several times out from Joey's mouth, rinse it, and give it back to Jackie. Whenever Joey finished his bottle or lost his pacifier, he would crawl over to Jackie and pull hers right out of her mouth. Jackie would only raise her eyebrows in disbelief while tears filled her little eyes. I was bothered that she never fought to retrieve it. As irate as I was with Joey, I was almost more annoyed with Jackie.

"Come on, Jackie," I encouraged my baby daughter. "If you're going to live with three older brothers in this family, or the world for that matter, you should learn to take back what belongs to you, sweetie. This world can be a ruthless place for a Black woman." I shook my head, contemplating those words. I worried briefly for my baby daughter and the woman she'd one day become if she didn't learn to stand up for herself. But I was not going to let that happen.

Jackie took her first steps earlier than Joey did; however, he walked three months before her. When Joey waved goodbye to us as he left for daycare, I expected Jackie to be sad, cry even. She did neither. Jackie waved goodbye and resumed playing with her colorful plastic blocks. She would stack them up like skyscrapers and knock them down, stack them up again, then knock them down, over and over, clapping her baby hands and giggling as the blocks tumbled onto the carpet. Joey stood at the doorway, observing his twin. He initially had a braggadocious smirk on his face that said, 'I'm leaving you, Jackie. I'm going to daycare with the big kids. Aren't you jealous? Aren't you sad? You'll be the only baby left at home—with Mommy.' But after watching the fun she was having, his smile faded while Jackie's only grew brighter. Her demeanor replied, 'Suit yourself, Joey. I'm in no rush to grow up. While you guys are all at daycare, I'll be playing. I'll have Mommy all to myself.'

My days off during those three months with Jackie were priceless. We played with her blocks, read stories, walked around the mall, and—her favorite—played dress-up. It reminded me of the times I spent with Danielle as a baby, although it was different with Jackie, less inquisitive, more playful. We grew close during our special times, but when the kids returned from their school and daycare, the magic was gone, and she grew jealous of my time with the others. She would sometimes crouch in the corner, dejected, while I worked with Joey and his alphabet. During those moments, I would glance up at her and ponder my desire for a large family. I wished I could clone myself, allowing for enough time with each one of my children. Jackie's face would brighten as soon as her dad came home from work and hoisted her onto his shoulders. He wobbled and bobbed Jackie about as she laughed hysterically. Then, I became the one to gaze at them with dark, envious eyes.

Jackie walked by fifteen months, making her eligible for our local daycare and ending our special moments. As disheartened as I was over this new development, Jackie was ebullient. She relished being with other toddlers. Two years later, she and Joey transferred to Penn Mont together. By then, it was in a newer, more spacious building than the one the three oldest had attended, and it now taught up to sixth grade. The staff usually liked to split up siblings, yet they kept my twins together at my request. Dropping them off and kissing them goodbye for their first day, I told Jackie and Joey how proud I was of them for starting preschool, and I would pick them up later. With their light-up sneakers and empty Scooby-Doo backpacks, my babies were stepping out into the world, and they both seemed terrified.

Then Joey sniffled and placed his arms around his baby sister's shoulders. "It'll be okay, Jackie," he said. "Mommy will come back. She'll never leave us."

LIVE TO WORK (2001)

Children are the reward of life.

— AFRICAN PROVERB

I don't remember why Nick was home, nor where the twins were at the time, but I can still recall the painful cries I heard that day, along with the helplessness that engulfed me.

"Could you come home—please—now!" my babysitter yelled.

"Why? What happened?" I asked.

"There's... there's been an accident," she said with a frail moan.

Then, there it was, a loud, screeching banshee in the background. It took me a second to discern that it came from my son. "Where is Nicky? What is wrong with him?" I shouted into the receiver.

"There's been an accident," she repeated.

"I'm on my way," I said as I slammed the phone down. Our inescapable problem when the children were infants was finding diligent caretakers. Too frequently, they were late or didn't show up at all, forcing us to scramble to make other arrangements. We considered an au pair; however, the expense and the shaken baby case a couple of years before, resulting in the death of an eight-month-old baby in Boston, soured us against it.

I implored one of the other doctors to see the rest of my patients as I prepared to exit. I was having another personal emergency, the second one that month. Fortunately, I was in the office and not in the delivery room or the operating room doing surgery. Because he was an anesthesiologist, Michael's office *was* the operating room. That's one of the reasons family emergencies usually fell on me. I grabbed my things, ran out of the office and into my car. I decided to call Michael on the way home to tell him what the babysitter said.

"But I don't know what happened to him," I confessed. "I only know there was an accident, and he was howling like a wounded puppy."

"God help her if she hurts my child!" Michael raged. "I'm almost done here. I'll see you at home."

I stepped on the gas, zigzagging through traffic and careening around corners, cutting my usual twenty-minute commute by half. The mantra that played continuously in my head was *God, please let Nicky be okay.* It's a miracle I made it home without being in an accident myself.

"Where is my son?" I hollered, racing into the house. I scanned the room and found him whimpering on the couch next to the babysitter. I was horrified at my disfigured baby's face. The right side was as swollen as a grapefruit, with a purplish discoloration around his red-shot eye. I was fuming. "What did you do to my son?"

"I'm sorry," she said, sobbing. "I'm so sorry."

"What happened?"

"Well, I—I was holding him under my left arm, and—and he was giggling as I cleaned your refrigerator—"

"Cleaning my refrigerator?" I screamed, interrupting her. "How many times did I tell you to stop cleaning my house? Stop rearranging my furniture. It's not your job. You're a babysitter!"

41

"I was trying to do both," she said. "Anyway, with Nicky under my left arm," she continued while demonstrating the action, "I turned around, and his face came crashing into the top of the round banister and—he's fine, though. He wept for a while, but I assure you he's fine now—I'm so sorry."

My husband walked in as the blubbering, middle-aged babysitter was apologizing. I too, was crying and caressing my son's face while ensuring there were no broken bones.

"Get out of this house right now!" he yelled. That was the kindest thing he shouted at her. Although Nicky didn't manifest any catastrophic injury, Michael took him to the hospital just in case while I picked up the rest of the kids.

That evening, after our children were in bed, Michael and I rehashed the frightening events of the day. "When I saw Nicky's face today, I went numb. I was scared. Shaking. I've never been this scared in all my life. Children do that, you know. They amplify your emotions to unimaginable levels," Michael said. He paused as he pondered on his pronouncement. "I wish we had family in the area that could help us with the kids, but we don't," he continued. "We only found unreliable and unqualified people taking care of our most precious jewels. We were lucky this time that Nicky wasn't badly hurt, but what about the next time? Carline, we can't go on like this," he said softly. "One of us has to quit our job."

There was silence because we both knew which one of us it would be. Michael escaped to bed. He lay on his left side, facing away from me, covered his head with the blanket, and pretended to go to sleep. I also retired to bed, although I lay awake for most of the night.

"Wake up," I said to him, hours later, as I heard him move about on the bed. It seemed he didn't sleep much either. "By one of us, you meant me. Didn't you?"

He shifted onto his right side and said, "You're the one who wanted more kids. I wanted to stop at two." Lack of sleep probably caused him to make such an asinine statement. He knew it was a mistake as soon as he saw the anguished look on my face. "I'm sorry.

That was mean. I love the kids. I'm just convinced you'll be better at raising them—and you're already working part-time—but if you don't want to, I'll quit my job. One of us has to."

"I know you're just saying that. You don't have any intention of quitting your job," I said, sitting up.

"I will," he said, trying to sound as if he meant it. The slight quiver in his voice gave him away.

Deep down, I too, knew I would be better than Michael at raising the kids. Despite that, the notion of quitting my profession was inconceivable. I couldn't imagine it. I loved my patients. Sure, there were hectic moments, yet most days were uplifting. I chose obstetrics and gynecology because it was gratifying to deliver beautiful babies for loving couples. I felt privileged being a part of that moment. Besides, I invested an enormous amount of time, energy, and money to become a doctor. I remembered how proud my mom was of me. With the pressures she faced raising us and working as a nurse's aide, my mom never found the time to go back to school to fulfill her dream of becoming a nurse, so she lived vicariously through my accomplishments. I couldn't disappoint her; I couldn't quit. But what about my children? Increasingly, I realized I was never where I needed to be at any given time. When I was home with the kids, I worried about my patients and their medical needs. And when I was with my patients, I worried about my kids and their dilemmas: Danielle being bored with her school, Mikey not wanting to go to school at all, and continually hiring new babysitters for Nick and the twins.

Another reason I found quitting so onerous was that I would become dependent on Michael to care for me. I began working at the age of fourteen. I have never depended on anyone. It was not in my DNA. What if we split up? Would I be begging him for alimony? Child support? How long would I stay home taking care of the kids? Would I be able to go back to work? How would I manage the changing surgical procedures and technology? Countless questions competed in my mind for attention.

The winner was money—would we have enough? My family had

lived comfortably in Haiti, and like most immigrants, we had to leave everything behind and start over. I arrived in this country in 1968 at the age of five. My two working parents raised their six children on a modest income. After I rose to an upper-middle-class status, I became acutely aware of what money provided in this country: comprehensive healthcare, quality education, and even peace of mind. I was afraid of losing that. My salary was higher than it had been at any point in my life, and I didn't want to give it up. If I did, could we afford to raise the kids, pay for their college, take care of our parents, and secure our retirement? Maybe not. "I don't think we can live on one income," I finally said.

"I make a decent amount," Michael replied.

"It's not enough with five kids."

"My God, Carline," he said, rising from his recumbent position. "How much money is enough for you?"

Was that a trick question? Was there a correct answer? As much as we can make. Wasn't that the American dream?

"We'll manage," he said with a half-shrug of his shoulders after noticing my impassive expression.

"Manage? What does that mean?"

"Well, for one thing," he said, "we'll start budgeting our expenses and paying closer attention to our spending. I don't suspect we'll be cutting coupons, but we may not be able to travel as often. And, if necessary..." Michael hesitated, swiping his fingers across his forehead. "I'll moonlight—work at other hospitals during my vacation."

I still didn't like the sound of "managing," only I didn't see any alternative. I thought maybe we could decrease the cost of flying for our trips by buying an RV and roam around the country. "Okay," I conceded as I wrapped my arms around me as a chill swept through. "I'll be a stay-at-home mom"—boy, I didn't like the sound of that— "and then in a few years, I'll go back to work."

"Are you sure?" he asked.

"No, I'm not sure, but you're right; we can't keep going on this way."

PART II

WALKING

Education is the passport to the future, for tomorrow belongs to those who prepare for it today.

— MALCOLM X

THE LEAP (2001–2004)

In January 2001, with five kids under the age of six, I officially became a homeschool mom. I didn't entirely quit medicine (for the time being), but I significantly reduced my working hours.

Like most Haitian immigrants, I learned the value of education from an early age. Watching my father get his master's in economics at Brooklyn College's night school after working long days at Merrill Lynch, my five siblings and I applied that diligence to our homework and truly enjoyed our studies. We all attended college, and some continued to graduate school as well. We joke that Edwidge, who is a college professor, still hasn't left school. Even before I considered the idea of homeschooling, I knew I wanted my children to share my dedication and passion for learning. Only I wasn't sure if I was the best teacher to accomplish it. The kids seemed to believe that I was and were thrilled that I would be homeschooling them. Still, I was not as confident. No longer could I blame the school or the teachers for not sufficiently motivating my children. As they say, "the buck stops here." I was about to navigate uncharted seas, which was daunting; nevertheless, I was determined to make it work. Gradually, the fear gave way to exhilaration.

During the Christmas break, I contacted local homeschooling

parents to learn how to proceed. I learned that, as a Pennsylvania homeschool teacher, I had to submit an affidavit to the school district stating my intent to homeschool my children each school year. This form was to be notarized and handed in, along with my yearly objectives, which consisted of the subjects I proposed to teach and the textbooks I planned to use. This process allowed me to design each child's curriculum and set specific goals for the year. Rather than mandating what each of my kids would take, I involved my kids in choosing their courses and set their own goals. We continued this annual goal-setting exercise well into my kids' high school years. We established three main categories: academics, music, and sports, and utilized field trips to provide context for our lessons.

While most homeschooling parents were fearful to modify the objectives, it was permissible if appropriate learning still took place. Therefore, to me, the objectives were guidelines. Once, when learning about King Arthur and the Knights of the Round Table, the kids became so engrossed that I stayed on that subject instead of moving to the next. We learned about castles, and I supplemented the unit with a model castle kit.[1] We discussed the geography of our castle's location and calculated the dimensions of our clay moat. For Halloween, each of the kids dressed up as a medieval character. Of course, all this medieval castle education derailed some of our other goals for that year—but again, they were guidelines.

The school district maintained considerable oversight. They required documentation of current immunizations as well as dental and eye exams. They also provided general outlines for what should be taught at each grade level. What caused most homeschool parents' angst was the dreaded portfolio. At the end of every school year, each homeschooled child had to turn in a portfolio, a large binder chronicling the child's learning for that year. These binders contained samples from each subject, standardized test results, awards, and the state's three mandated sections on health, physical education, and fire safety.

Once finished, the portfolios were reviewed either by a school administrator or by an independent licensed educator.[2] Many homeschoolers opted for the independent educator to eliminate any potential bias from an administrator. At the end of the school year, the portfolio reviewer would meet with each student, quizzing them on each subject to determine what they had learned. Afterward, they sent a summary and the child's portfolio to the school, explaining whether appropriate learning had occurred. The school based its decision on its review of the portfolio along with the educator's recommendation. Rarely would the school disagree with an examiner.

The state also required an attendance log verifying 180 days of instruction. I used two methods to document this: a calendar and memo pads. Each of my kids had a dated notepad in which I detailed the assignments that needed completing for the day. The calendar primarily kept track of sporting practices and games, academic competitions, and other extracurricular activities. I color-coded the events specifically for each child. It allowed me to prepare an overview of the school year and plan selected field trips. Later, I continued with the color-coded calendars to plan summer camps.

I enjoyed constructing the portfolios and documenting their achievements. It also served as a memento of the school year. I made their first few portfolios, and by the time the children were in fourth or fifth grade, they knew how to make their own and took delight in decorating the covers with their artwork or photos.

When I first presented my notarized application to homeschool Dani and Mikey, I intentionally omitted their grade levels because I didn't know where they belonged. After I told her what they were learning with me, the female administrator then assigned them to third and first grades, respectively. She skipped them a whole grade level from where they previously were at their Catholic school. The school district supplied me with schoolbooks but also gave me the option of using my own. Their books were outdated and in poor condition. I initially used them, but by the time I was home-schooling my three little ones, I became adept at using the internet and networking with other parents to obtain the best books for my kids in every subject.[3]

Like oil in a pool of water, homeschoolers did not mingle with regular students in the Altoona School District. As a result, the homeschool parents formed their own club—a loose affiliation of moms who wanted the freedom to teach their children what they wanted. Some families homeschooled for religious or political reasons; I did it for no other reason than to provide intriguing work for my children, something the local schools were unable or unwilling to do. Still, I joined the homeschooling parents group. We met at the Hollidaysburg YMCA (a suburb of Altoona), where our children participated in similar extracurricular activities. We organized field trips, used the same music teachers, and held science, history, and spelling competitions. Additionally, whenever we saw an opportunity to compete against public or parochial school children, we did.

My favorite contest was the Interscholastic Reading Competition organized by Intermediate Unit 8.[4] These reading quiz competitions were held twice each school year, with divisions for elementary, junior, and high school students. Mikey, Danielle, and the other homeschoolers in our group competed in the youngest division. We assembled twelve students and had forty books for them to read, after which we would test them. Thus, we moms also had to read the books our kids were assigned and write questions. As the competition approached, we met at each other's homes once or twice a week to prepare the students in a fun and vibrant atmosphere. We entered our first competition in the spring of 2001 and placed third. For the following three consecutive times, we took first. This exuberant book event spun my two oldest into avid readers.

DANIELLE: 6–10 (2000–2004)

A month into our homeschooling adventure, the school district informed me that every third grader must take the PSSAs, Pennsylvania's Scholastic Standardized Test. Since Danielle had only recently become a third grader, I told them that she should be exempt from the exam. My protests were in vain. I requested sample materials to at least help my daughter prepare. As I perused the booklet, I realized she could already answer most of the problems, except for fractions—we had only recently broached that topic.

"Okay, Danielle," I said after we returned home. "Let's attack those fractions." We parked ourselves at Michael's kitchen table and learned fractions that afternoon.

"Mommy, how do we add and subtract fractions when the denominators are different?"

"Oh, you don't have to worry about that for now," I said, closing the book. "It won't be on the test."

"But why can't I still learn it?"

That was a noble question. I was doing what I had heard teachers complaining about—teaching to the test. Here was a child eager to learn, and I was discouraging it. "Okay," I said, reopening the math book, "let's start changing denominators." I vowed never to stop any of my children from going beyond their assignments from that day forward. I encouraged asking questions and fostering curiosity.

In May, Danielle scored "Advanced" in every subject on the test. While I wasn't surprised, her achievement pressed me to evaluate further her intelligence and what I should be doing to help her achieve her full potential. I reached out to Mensa, the world's largest and oldest IQ society, and inquired about my daughter's criteria for membership. They gave specific instructions for acceptance into Mensa. I then contacted a child psychologist at Pennsylvania State University in State College, about an hour from our home, who was willing to administer the Wechsler Intelligence Scale for Children-Third Edition (WISC-III) to Danielle according to Mensa's requirements.

On July 26, 2001, my six-year-old, with her hair in pigtails and comfortably dressed in a white sleeveless shirt, a dark blue pleated skirt, and white sandals, accompanied the examiner to a nonde-script beige office. The other kids and I settled in the waiting room.

A month later, I received the three-page report. I jumped to the summary page:

Danielle Feffer, a six-year-old female, was evaluated to determine eligibility for the Mensa Society.

Intellectual assessment results indicated that Danielle was in the very superior range of intellectual functioning. This indicates that Danielle is eligible for admission to the Mensa Society.

During the 2003–04 school year, when Danielle was eight years old and doing fifth-grade work, a friend suggested we try the magnet school in the area. I hoped the gifted program would be well suited for her and made an appointment with the director the following day. Although I gave them the results of Danielle's WISC-III test and the coursework she was doing with me, they specified she had to undergo "additional psycho-educational test-ing." They claimed this test assessed her for the gifted support she would require. I was wary of signing my daughter up for any more testing, but I eventually relented. I didn't think I had a choice.

We drove to the designated testing area the following week. Again, I lingered in the waiting room, working with the other kids, while Danielle marched into the office. Half an hour later, the examiner raced towards me. I leaped out of my chair, fearing the worst. He stood before me, rubbing his hands.

"I have never seen an eight-year-old use the Pythagorean theorem correctly," he said. "I didn't believe an eight-year-old could even pronounce the word," he added, seemingly more so to himself. Then he whirled back into his office to resume administering the test to Danielle. I exhaled.

After the assessment, the examiner said that although Danielle was mature for her chronological age and had a superior intellectual ability, he feared Danielle was still a child. "She should spend time being a child," he said. "Brilliant children like Danielle can learn in one year what would take the average child at least two, so we tend to push these gifted kids because they seem to demand it, even crave it. However, it's important to balance it out with playtime."

"Of course," I agreed. "With all of Danielle's younger siblings, they won't allow her to forget to be a child."

"Good," he said as he shook my hand. He added that I would receive his report within a week.

On the way home, I kept mulling over what the examiner had said. Was I giving Danielle enough playtime? She was taking violin, piano, trumpet, ballet, baton, and chess lessons. Anyone would assume it was too much, but they didn't know my Danielle. She enjoyed those things; most of these activities were *her* idea. I had wished that as she discovered new things, she would discontinue others. But not my baby girl; she insisted on doing all of them. As for her schoolwork, that too was fun. Our days usually began with our daily Holey Cards, which we used to drill math problems. We'd then focus our attention on critical thinking and logic by playing chess, doing jigsaw puzzles, or working on our Mind Benders brain teaser books. After that, we would do other schoolwork, which was also engaging. For instance, in our physics classes, with Danielle and Mikey, we experimented with pulleys and gears, electricity, and magnetism; in biology, we bisected flatworms to learn about regeneration.

My teaching was a combination of play and learning. It was spontaneous and dynamic. Instead of the dull, nine-to-three brick-and-mortar classroom, mine was the living, breathing world; my hours were undefined. I wanted to instill in them that learning was everywhere around them, from the stars in the sky to the phytoplankton in the ocean. Danielle loved it. They all did. I would have liked to believe what I was reflecting on if not for that one nagging incident: the chess episode.

Shortly after Danielle taught herself chess by watching her father and I play our nightly matches, I began enrolling her in tournaments. While she competed, I purchased a variety of chess books.[5] It didn't take long for her chess rankings to rise as she won most of her games. However, as my elementary child began playing against older middle school students, the fear of losing, or the pressure to win, took its toll. One episode ended in Danielle having a panic attack, forcing her to resign from her games that day. We stopped with chess for a while and resumed it months later as part of our daily schoolwork. We entered tournaments again with all the five children—with less intensity or pressure.

By the time we arrived home from the magnet school examiner's office, I had replayed the entire chess scene in my mind. Although I felt comfortable with its resolution, I knew I still had to remain vigilant about my children's anxieties.

As promised, we received Danielle's evaluation from the Altoona Area School District in a week. The conclusion:

... Danielle meets PA State Standards to be deemed mentally gifted and in need of gifted support services. Further, given Danielle's level of skill development and educational needs, it is recommended that she receive a full-time Gifted Support Program.

We met with the Gifted Individualized Educational Program team members to discuss and outline Danielle's plan. She was to take all her classes with other gifted kids her age, except for her math classes. She was so advanced she would be given her own math teacher who would work with her exclusively. I was overjoyed. A school had finally acknowledged the intelligence of my daughter.

My euphoria was short lived. Due to school budget cuts, they did not provide a math teacher for Danielle, and she had previously read all the books assigned in her advanced English class. It didn't take long for Danielle to complain she was bored again. She spent that September in school before being pulled out. The one positive note from the magnet school experience was my exposure to some fantastic literature about working with gifted children. One was a magazine article titled "Acceleration of Gifted Students—An Option That Works."[6] The authors wrote:

Our society finds it easy to recognize the need for those gifted in the arts to move at their own pace. Even those gifted in athletics are given this opportunity. We must give intellectual ability the same recognition and respect, or our gifted children will never reach the performance levels of our gifted artists and athletes.

Twenty years later, I still find this to be true.

Another useful reading material was *Resources for Academically Talented Students*, from the Carnegie Mellon Institute for Talented Elementary Students, or C-MITES. This spiral-bound yellow book contained a wealth of information and became my educational bible; I kept it on my bedside table with other informative guidebooks.[7] C-MITES's book included ways to advocate for your gifted child and recommended museums and educational places to visit in Pittsburgh and Philadelphia. More importantly, it provided instruction on how to apply to C-MITES.

Danielle had to take yet another exam. This time it was the EXPLORE test, administered in Pittsburgh at Carnegie Mellon. She excelled once again, obtaining her highest scores in the English and math sections.

In the summer of 2003, I enrolled her in a week-long C-MITES's day-course program in Pittsburgh: The Math Olympiad 2. Since we lived two hours away, commuting was not an option. I decided to stay in a hotel with the children for the duration of Danielle's camp. On Sunday, the morning of our departure, Joey woke up with an ear infection. He was very irritable. The pediatrician prescribed antibiotics, and we got ready to go. Michael discouraged me from proceeding with my plans due to Joey's illness, but I assured him we would be fine. Besides, Danielle still had her course to attend. I packed up the van with my five children and headed west.

Our hotel was no five star, but it was clean and well located. On top of that, it had a valet service, which I loved having when I was without Michael. I disliked traversing parking lots in the evening with all our bags and the children—the extra cost was well worth the convenience and peace of mind.

We planned trips to the Pittsburgh Zoo while Danielle was in class and to the museums and Carnegie Science Center in the afternoon when Danielle returned. Of course, plans never go the way you envision. I awoke to Joey wailing at two in the morning. Hives covered his entire body. My poor baby was having an allergic reaction to the antibiotics and was scratching his bumpy skin. I attempted to soothe him by rocking him gently in my arms, but his cries grew louder. I had to do something, fast. I had children's Tylenol but no Benadryl. I called the front desk. Instead of any children's medications, I was given directions to a twenty-four-hour CVS pharmacy five minutes from the hotel. After quietly hanging up the phone, I surveyed the room. The boys were curled up on the mattress that I had pulled off the convertible sofa, and the girls were sound asleep on the king-sized bed, Jackie perfectly cradled in Danielle's arms.

I had a dilemma: Do I wake them all up and drive to the CVS together, which would take about an hour, or do I only take Joey, which would take about ten minutes? Or do I wait until 9 am when we leave for Danielle's class? Or do I call Michael for advice? I ruled out the last two choices. My husband was too far away, and it would only cause him to worry. And Joey was too uncomfortable now. It couldn't wait. He was still sobbing, but now intermittently as he watched and wondered about my decision. My sleeping angels were too peaceful to wake up. I made up my mind—I would only take Joey. Before I had a chance to consider other alternatives, I called the valet service and asked them to bring my car out. I placed my still-sniffling two-year-old on the couch and put on his jacket. I then left a note on the bedside table for Danielle: *Took Joey to get some medicine. Be back soon. Take care of your siblings. Please be very quiet. Love forever, Mommy.*

I reached for my jacket, zipped on my jeans, picked up Joey, snatched my bag and room key, and exited. There sat my van, waiting for me in front of the hotel, like a co-conspirator. I got in the car, buckled Joey in his car seat, and drove like the wind, trying not to think of all the things that could go wrong with my plan. Maybe Mikey would yell for me to bring him water, or maybe Nick would wake up his siblings with one of his night terrors. All these scenarios culminated in the kids waking up and not finding me. That's when fear would set in, and the crying would start shortly after. They would miss my note during the commotion, and the boys, no, maybe Jackie, would notice that her twin was also missing. Thinking that someone took Joey and me away, the kids would become even more frightened. Finally, Danielle would get the bright idea to call 911, and then a mugshot of my face would be splashed across the front page of all the major newspapers in the country. The caption would read: **Worst Mom Ever Leaves Four Children in Hotel Room Alone.**

I would, of course, argue that I had no choice; I had to get medicine for Joey. He had hives all over his body. And besides, was Danielle *really* a child? Although she was only seven years old, I would explain that she is more mature and responsible than most teenagers. She has a very high IQ; I would say, and—what on earth am I thinking? They will arrest me. I am going to go to jail. They will take my children away. This is crazy. Sweat dripped from my face. Turn back. I should turn back. But before I knew it, I had arrived.

I parked, unbuckled Joey from his car seat, and swiftly carried him inside. Unsurprisingly, Joey and I were the only customers in the store at that time of the morning. I bought some children's Benadryl along with anti-itch cream. I placed Joey on the counter and gave him his oral medication. I then took off his jacket and rubbed the cream all over his body. I thanked the clerk and headed back to the hotel. By the time we arrived at the hotel, Joey had fallen into a comfortable slumber. As I pulled up to the valet parking area, I was relieved at the absence of any siren-blaring police cars. I carried my sleeping baby to the elevator and hurried back to our room. As eager as I was to be back in the room with my children, I was also nervous. Holding Joey in my left arm, I placed the key card in the slot. The green light flashed above the handle. I cracked the door open ever so slowly to find the room exactly as I had left it a few minutes before. My kids were still there, unharmed, and sound asleep. I took Joey's jacket off and placed him alongside his brothers.

I ripped up my note, pulled up the chair by the writing desk, sat down, and cried.

The early morning's events with Joey felt like a dream. Luckily, Joey didn't have any more infections or reactions for the rest of the week. Danielle attended her math camp while I took the kids to the zoo. At the end of the program, Danielle and some of the other high scorers won trophies. The most satisfying moment of that camp experience was when the instructor shared her thoughts with me.

"There is a common way most students solve a given math problem, and then there's another way I demonstrate to the class. What stunned me about your daughter," announced the teacher, pausing momentarily to heighten the suspense, "is Danielle always found a third way." She stopped again, considerably longer this time, allowing me time to process the revelation. "Danielle's originality is remarkable. Don't allow others to structure it," she warned as she shook my hand.

As I thanked her and watched her walk away to mingle with the other parents, I stood relieved and delighted at my daughter's successful week.

MIKEY: 6–10 (2001–2005)

In the 2003–04 school year, I enrolled Danielle and Mikey in the Central Pennsylvania Digital Learning Foundation, an online charter school, in the hopes of cutting down on the glut of paperwork that came with homeschooling. They sent us computers along with a stipend for internet service, books, lab supplies, and a copious amount of art material. My kids' report cards were straight As, and they always made the online honor roll. Although I used the school for its supplies, scheduled standardized exams, and as a stamp of approval to satisfy the school district, I was still their teacher. I taught the classes and checked my kids' work with them before sending their assignments back.

Mikey's math book began with the subjects of time and money. It quickly became problematic when he could not grasp the concept of time. So, we made paper plate clocks using fasteners and construction paper. It was a fun art project, yet it failed to teach him to tell time. I purchased an educational toy clock with large eyes and a smiling mouth on a yellow background. It also didn't help. Finally, I bought Mikey a real child's watch. That too, was ineffective.

"I'm useless," I said, lamenting to my husband. "I'm a failure. How can I call myself a teacher when I can't even teach my son to tell time? What possessed me to homeschool them? I can't do this." Just like that, I wanted to give up, quit, throw in the towel. Michael endured this rant night after night until he grew weary.

"Skip it. Go on to something else. Come back to it later," he said finally.

It hadn't yet dawned on me that I could teach the subjects in any order I chose. Although Michael proposed it out of frustration, it was sound advice. We skipped it and moved on to multiplication. Once Mikey understood the concept, the memorization part came naturally.

Toward the end of the school year, I revisited the subject of time with my son. I was apprehensive, but this time around, it only took an hour before I saw the glimmer in his dark brown eyes and a broad smile on his young face. With his new watch, Mikey proceeded to tell us the time every hour, every minute, every second.

Mikey loved music; it was akin to Danielle's love of math. My only requirement for a music teacher in the early years was simply someone capable of teaching my kids. I viewed music as learning another language: good to know, but not a necessity. I wanted them to enjoy music: learn the classics, read the notes, play at recitals. Things I wished my parents could have afforded. I didn't want strict teachers criticizing their finger curves or bow hold, making practicing their instrument a hated chore. I wanted playful teachers to elicit their creativity and love for making music. When playing the piano became frustrating for Danielle, I accompanied her on the bench, playing the left-handed part until she could. I wasn't perfect.

I was learning the notes and chords along with her while struggling and having fun. With Mikey, it was different. He was serious about his musical ability and wanted to take it further.

When Mikey was six years old, he and Danielle auditioned and were selected for the Altoona All-City Orchestra. Later that same year, they played a trumpet duet rendition of the national anthem at a crowded swim championship meet. After seeing a video of Danielle and Mikey's national anthem performance, the Altoona Curve, a local minor-league baseball team, chose them to repeat it at their stadium. At seven years old, Mikey took first place at a local talent show competition when he played *Wipe Out* on his guitar. By the age of eight, Mikey played the piano, violin, trumpet, and guitar. In February of the following year, he played a piano duet with Danielle at Penn State for Martin Luther King Day. As Mikey's musical talent increased, so too did his dreams.

THE MOVE (2004–)

When the two hospitals in our community merged, my husband found himself suddenly out of work. While searching for a job, Michael received an employment offer from the Centre County Anesthesia group in State College. Since the State College School District had a good reputation, I contemplated enrolling my kids in public school and going back to work. However, remembering what occurred with the magnet school, I tempered any expectations. I contacted several homeschoolers in the district willing to share their experiences with me. As I expected, their reasons for home-schooling were diverse and personal. The statewide homeschool laws applied to State College just as they had in Altoona. However, State College was unique in one vital aspect: The school district had a dual-enrollment policy.

In Altoona, a student was either a full-time enrollee or a home-schooler, and homeschoolers could only join the other kids in non-graded after-school activities. In State College, homeschoolers and traditional students were miscible; they could take classes together. The district categorized students as homeschoolers even if they only learned one subject at home. The parents could send the child to school for courses they felt uncomfortable teaching, with the added benefit of the kids having better chances to make friends. I was delighted. And the best thing about it was I, the parent—not the school or the teachers—decided which classes I found appropriate for my child. The school district preferred to cooperate with home-schoolers rather than cede them to charter schools, which effectively siphoned money away from the district. The homeschool moms told me it was the best of both worlds, yet few took advantage of it.

When I moved to enroll Danielle in a few advanced classes in State College in 2004, it seemed no one in the school—not the teachers, not the counselors, not even the principals—were familiar with their own policies on dual schoolers. Ultimately, the Director of Student Services defended my title as the counselor of my children and helped enforce the dual-enrollment policies. Unfortunately, he retired a year later and left me to fight the battles alone. To further complicate matters, the district was a revolving door of new principals, acting principals, or superintendents. I braced myself for the inevitable arguments that would undoubtedly ensue with each new hire because they often resurrected problems I had previously resolved.

Our first year in State College brought many changes to our homeschooling structure. Danielle, now nine years old, was dual enrolled and took an advanced geometry class at the Park Forest Middle School, just two minutes from our rented property. The twins were four years old and attended the half-day Park Forest Montessori Preschool, two minutes from our home but in the opposite direction from the middle school. Mikey and Nick were homeschooling with me until it was time to pick up the other three. If Mikey finished his studies or got stuck on a problem while I taught his younger brother, he could occupy himself with the piano or the violin while waiting for me. He was disciplined, even at that young age.

Nick, on the other hand, was an enthusiastic, hyper child, flooded with questions. This deluge of energy sometimes interfered with his focusing ability. He'd unconsciously twiddle a small object, usually one of his LEGO pieces, between his thumb and index finger. It irritated me. My efforts to put an end to his fidgeting were futile. Upon realizing it was how Nick processed information, I came to accept it.

Nick's tendency to live in his imagination was a wonder. When our local library held its annual "Write and Illustrate Your Own Book" contest, I encouraged Nick, Jackie, and Joey to submit a book. (Mikey and Danielle were usually busy with science fair projects.) Nick set out to work on his epic fantasy titled *Drachewelt*, which, he had googled, meant dragon world in German. Nick didn't win, but I maintain that he deserved to. His *Drachewelt* calls to mind a kid-friendly version of *Game of Thrones*. The planet, *Drachewelt*, had two landmasses connected by a strip of forested land. Zauber-erland, to the east, was inhabited by dwarfs and ice dragons. Gnomerian, to the west, had elves, gnomes, and fire dragons. Despite their differences, these two societies learned how to live and help each other.

When Mikey and Nick worked independently on book reports, math assignments, or music, it freed me for other tasks. I prepared Danielle's and the twins' work for the day, made plans for our upcoming field trips, did the laundry, folded clothes, and prepped meals for lunch and dinner. My only "me" time in those early years in State College was when I would best the sun by rising around 4 am. I would drag myself out of bed, with eyes partly opened; I'd stagger to the kitchen and brew a wake-me-up cup of coffee. The dark roast aroma began the percolating process in my nostrils. I'd then stroll to my office, sipping its smooth chocolate flavor with a hint of licorice, unhurried, allowing the caffeine to jump-start my brain. I'd remain motionless in my chair, savoring the feeling of comfort and warmth that accompanies a noiseless house. After fifteen minutes, this luxury would end as I put down the empty cup and reached for my red marking pen.

One afternoon, upon returning home with Danielle and the twins, Joey asked what Nick was doing.

"Mommy is teaching me multiplication," he said.

"What's that?" asked Joey.

Usually, I encouraged the kids to share what they'd learned with their dad or siblings that day. It let me know how much they retained, how well they understood the concepts, and how effectively they explained the lesson. That day, it troubled me because my Joey was beginning to develop a competitive nature, chiefly when it came to his older brother, Nick.

"Come, let me show you," Nick exclaimed, yanking his baby brother to the family room and pulling him down onto the carpeted floor. There, he proceeded to teach him how to multiply.

When I arrived at the twins' preschool the next day, I noticed Jackie, surrounded by her usual group of friends in the corner, seemed visibly bothered when it was time to go home. In the adjacent corner, Joey was alone at his desk. The teacher drew me aside and whispered that Joey was concentrating on his multiplication work. He told her he'd mastered addition and subtraction and insisted on learning multiplication. After quizzing him, she reached the same conclusion.

As soon as I opened the front door, Joey ran into the house yelling for his big brother.

"Nick, Nick, I'm doing multiplication at school just like you."

"That's great, Joey. We can do multiplication together," Nick said as he hugged him.

While Mikey played the piano, Jackie worked on her book, Nick and Joey practiced multiplication problems, and Danielle and I reviewed her geometry homework.

"Mom, I understand the work. There's nothing to go over with me," she said in an exasperated tone.

"Well, let's go over it anyway," I said. "Sometimes, there are better and faster ways to write a proof. Even if you solve it correctly, you might waste time on a test. Speaking of tests, we need to prepare for the upcoming one. When is it again?"

"It was yesterday," she said as she handed me a paper.

"But, but—we didn't prepare," I stammered as I reached for the paper. Turning it over, I saw it was her geometry test. It read, "Excellent! 100%."

Danielle noticed my shocked expression and said, "I know."

"Dani, it's obvious you understand your assignments. So, from now on, I'll help you only when you ask, okay? And we'll go over it together."

"Okay, Mom," she replied, "I will."

She never did.

That first year in State College set the framework for what was to come.

SUBJECTS

He who is not courageous enough to take risks will accomplish nothing in life.

— MUHAMMED ALI

Despite my outstanding grades, my undergraduate advisor, a short, red-headed white woman at St. John's University, informed me a career in medicine would be too arduous for me. I should instead consider one in nursing. She eyed me, convinced she knew what a doctor should resemble, and I, presumably, didn't reflect that image. Although I thanked the advisor as I left her office, I was more committed than ever to become a physician. My medical diploma, which hangs on my office wall, serves as a constant reminder of that episode. After two years of homeschooling in State College, arranging and rearranging course curricula for my children, I became more comfortable and bolder about the subjects I wanted to teach them. No one would hinder my children's ambition.

I taught my children the traditional school subjects and added atypical ones due to their requests or circumstances. Some of these included World Religions, Mythology, History of Jazz, and SAT/PSAT/ACT Prep Classes. I also expanded on subjects like Geography, Writing, Poetry, and Art. While educating them, I often counseled them to seek opportunities to compete. "Like it or not," I told them, "competition is an inescapable fact of life. It sets the stage for the challenges that lie ahead." In my experience, those who chastised my competitive mentality are often well-connected or fortunate enough that "everything works out fine in the end" for them. My humble upbringing did not allow such indulgent thinking. I fought for the bare necessities and, in doing so, found strength within myself I never knew existed. Thus, with almost every subject, I found competitions for my children to enter.

GEOGRAPHY

My children needed to become proficient in geography, not only to learn where countries were but also to understand the world. I wanted them to see themselves as global citizens. The kids began their geography lessons at Penn Mont Academy, and I continued them at home with many geographic jigsaw puzzles and map coloring books. Later, I enrolled Nick, Joey, and Jackie in a geography course called Mapping the World through Art, offered by a State College homeschooling co-op called the Solid Foundation Educational Association (SFEA).

As the three youngest became more knowledgeable in geography, I began searching for a contest in our area. Coincidently, the local middle school was to host a regional Geography Bee the following week. The winner would compete with the other regional winners to advance to the Pennsylvania State Geography Bee. After calling the school, they green-lighted my children. Excited, we entered the school a week later and joined the other competitors— about fifteen students—assembling in the designated classroom. The teacher invited them to the front of the room, but a woman barged in before she continued any further.

"According to the National Geography Bee rules, and I quote," the woman said, looking in my direction, "homeschoolers must compete with other homeschoolers." Satisfied with the decree, she pointed to my three children and added, "They can't participate."

The teacher avoided our gaze as she asked us to leave. As we walked out, with our chins to our chests, the veins in my head began throbbing. I had to find a way to mitigate this humiliating disaster. So, as soon as I reached home with my despondent kids, I sent emails to my homeschool group to see if there were any interest in holding a Geography Bee. Finding no takers, I googled "Pennsylvania Homeschool Geography Bee" and found one by Susan Richman. She published a homeschool newsletter and was hosting a Geography Bee that coming weekend at her home in the rural part of western Pennsylvania. It was a harrowing two-hour drive through the state's backwoods, but on that frigid and icy day, I was relentless.

As usual, we were the only African American family in attendance. However, Ms. Richman and the other parents were very welcoming. A jolt of excitement permeated the air as the nine children gathered around the table for the competition. Ms. Richman read questions, and we parents watched as students were eliminated one by one, leaving only my trio. Jackie was the first of the group to be cut. Nick was a strong adversary; despite that, he too succumbed to Joey's intellect. Since Joey became the regional winner, Ms. Richman said he would need to revisit her the following week for the written test to qualify for the state competition. We were elated. Even the weather turned sunny and warm as we made our way home. That week, I hounded Joey with geography questions, quizzing him in the early mornings before school and late in the evenings. He complained to his dad, "Mom has turned my life into a geography class."

We drove back to Ms. Richman's a week later for the written test. I corrected my children's assignments in another room while Joey took the exam. A week passed before Ms. Richman notified us of the news: Joey had qualified for the Pennsylvania Geography Bee to be held at Penn State University.

Joey competed for two successive years at the state-level Geography Bee, doing better the second time. Although I felt he could have been among the finalists the third time around, he no longer wanted to compete. He said he would instead focus on his math.

WRITING

Because excellent writing skills are essential in life, writing played a significant part in our curricula. After every vacation, every field trip, every summer camp, a well-written summary of the excursion had to be prepared and handed to me. It was a lot of work for the kids *and* me. Reviewing their writing gave me a lot of sympathy for English teachers.

In the beginning, these reports were handwritten, as we practiced our print and cursive handwriting.[1] As the kids grew older, they had to be typewritten.[2] For spelling, I made a variety of word lists from books, and it was one of Mikey's favorite subjects. For grammar and punctuation, I had to be more creative. To keep the children focused and engaged, I made the work about them. I personalized each child's Language Arts work, where they had to use capitalization and correct punctuation marks. A typical assignment would be to ask Mikey to share his thoughts about his upcoming birthday. I would then type it, summarizing some of the essential points using words he could read. I would then print it out and ask him to circle and explain the words needing capitalization.

I also sought reading and writing materials the kids would find interesting. Sometimes I used educational children's magazines.[3] These magazines featured innovative projects we later used in our science and history classes. One, found in *Weekly Reader*, was a national competition called Eyewitness to History. Danielle's essay "Front of the Bus" was based on her grandfather's time spent in Jim Crow Tennessee during the late 1950s and described the humiliation he endured when forced to sit in the back of the bus.[4] The interview she conducted with my dad was among the magazine's winners.

Her successful essay, published in April 2003, ignited the kids' participation in local, state, and national writing competitions. Various organizations, including Veterans of Foreign Wars, EngineerGirl, and Reading Rainbow, sponsored these competitions. My favorite was the annual Letters About Literature contest, promoted by the Center for the Book in the Library of Congress. It was a national competition where students choose a book, speech, or poem and write to the author describing its impact on them. During the summer, I would remind my kids to reflect on a book they planned to use for their Letters About Literature contest in the fall. In 2011, after Nick and I read *The Secret Life of Walter Mitty* by James Thurber, he said, "Mom, he sounds a lot like me. I love daydreaming about all the things I wish I could do."

"Well," I said, "you should write to him."

Nick's letter to Mr. Thurber won him an honorable mention at the state level. In 2012, Joey's sixth-grade essay letter, penned to Robert Frost for his poem "The Road Not Taken," earned him first place at the Pennsylvania state level. In his letter, Joey compared the road to a choice many students face: Whether to silently watch as classmates are bullied in school or to be courageous and speak out against it. He concluded by writing...*thank you for writing this radical poem that tells individuals like me that being different is fine and that you do not have to change yourself to please others.* By "different," I assumed he meant being the youngest, typically the smartest, and the only Black student in his classes. I also believed this unique perspective on a classic poem helped him win.

POETRY

The study of poetry enhanced my children's use of imagery and creativity in their writing. It helped them express their emotions in personal yet entertaining ways. April was our scheduled poetry month. Every April, beginning when Danielle and Mikey were in elementary grades, we made a four-foot tree out of green and brown construction paper and taped it on our basement school-room door. It was our "poet-tree." On it, the kids posted the haiku, acrostics, limericks, persuasive, and diamond poems they studied that month.[5] As the children got older, they applied more complex poetic devices such as alliteration, onomatopoeia, and assonance. Danielle's "Seven Ways of Seeing a Pencil" and Nick's poem "Aging" embodied these poetic devices and won them the Wind In The Willows middle school writing awards in 2008 and 2012, respectively. Danielle's five-stanza poem about child soldiers, "Fightin' in Africa," was written as part of a history project I assigned her. I entered it in the 2006 Blair County Arts Festival contest. A week later, she read her winning poem at the festival.

Over the years, the children continued to write poems without the tree construction. We studied and memorized some for our monthly recital nights, at which the kids would perform them for Michael and me. Some verses were from Shakespeare's sonnets, Langston Hughes' "Dreams" and "Mother to Son," Shelley's "Ozymandias," and many more.

WORLD RELIGIONS

The teaching of world religions occurred unintentionally. We were seated at the dinner table when my unassuming nine-year-old Joey posed a troubling question "Mom, how can I kill myself?"

I nearly choked on my piece of honey-glazed ham. It was Easter Sunday, so I had an idea as to why this question arose. I took a sip of water. "Why, Sweetie?"

"I want to see God and talk to Him. I have a few questions for Him," replied Joey.

"You can talk to Him now. Here. He hears you, and He'll answer in His own way."

"No, Mom," he insisted. "I want to sit down with God, look at Him, and talk with Him."

"Well, Darling, you can't. If you ki—if you go and talk to Him, then you'll be leaving us."

"No, Mom," he said, smiling as if he knew something I didn't. "I'll come back in three days, just like Jesus did."

"No, my pumpkin, it doesn't work like that. Once you go, you can't come back. Jesus could because He is the Son of God. You can't. You must wait for God to call you."

"Of course, He'll let me come back when I explain everything to Him. I only want to ask Him a few questions. I don't want to stay there. He has to let me come back. He wouldn't keep me from my family; I'm still a kid. Isn't that—kidnapping?"

I wasn't getting through to him. Michael and the other kids slowly chewed their food as they waited for my answer. My only thought at the time was *he is so bright; what if he did know how to kill himself? Would he still be here, now, talking with me?* I shuddered at the thought. I changed tactic.

"What kind of questions do you have for God? Maybe your dad and I could answer them," I said as my pleading eyes beckoned for Michael's help.

"Well," Joey began, laying down his fork, "I've been wondering about lots of things lately, Mom, like why did He create us? Why are we here?" Like kernels popping in his head, his questions picked up speed. "Why does He let people get sick? Why do we die? Why did Grandpa Feffer have to die? Where do we go when we die?"

The silence was tumultuous. No one spoke as we contemplated our *own* questions for God. Number one on my list would be why He created a world with so much injustice, hatred, and prejudice. How can He allow 1% of people to own half of the world's wealth, leaving most in dire poverty? Where is the fairness in that, and why aren't more people upset? How can there be hundreds of NGOs in Haiti, yet somehow, things never seem to change? In fact, they seem to worsen. Why are there third-world countries, or "shithole" countries, as some have referred to them in the twenty-first century? And why are these countries filled predominantly with Black or Brown people? Why do countries wage wars? Why—

"Oh," Joey said, jolting me back to the present as he remembered something else. "What are gays? And why does God hate them?"

Michael finally spoke up. "Where did you hear that?"

"I'm not sure. I guess, maybe from some kids at the high school."

"Joey," I said, caressing his innocent face. "People try to interpret what they assume God demands, but they're wrong because God created everyone, so how could He hate anyone? And as far as your other questions, God will answer them when He feels you're ready to understand."

Please, please let him be satisfied with that, I prayed. But, when he looked at me as if I had just sprouted an extra head, it confirmed he wasn't. Who could blame him? I was dubious about God myself, and more specifically, about organized religion. Like many people, I believed the church offered direction and a moral compass for the family. It also granted a sense of belonging in a community, primarily the Black and Haitian churches, like the ones my family attended in my youthful days in New York. They were the drum-beating, hand-clapping, hugging-your-fellow-parishioner kind of services. I missed the songs, the people, and my favorite priest, Father Sansaricq. His sermons, in Kreyòl, were engaging and always relevant to the circumstances. Even though I had doubts about God's existence, I didn't feel I had the right to impose those doubts on my children and rob them of the direction and sense of belonging they could gather from a church. I wanted them to come to their own conclusions.

Joey spoke again, "Why can't I speak with God, Mom? Is it because He's not real? He doesn't exist, does He, Mom? Is it just like Santa Claus again?"

My shame silenced me as I reflected on the Santa Claus fiasco.

"We saw him, Mommy," Jackie said.

"No, honey, that was your father dressed as Santa Claus."

"But last year, Daddy was next to me, and we saw him," said Nick.

"That year, we asked our neighbor to help. I was Santa Claus for his kids, and he was for us. You guys were getting too smart and suspicious," said Michael.

"Is that why we saw him walk across the street?" asked Jackie, laughing.

"Yes," I said, laughing along with her.

"You told us that Santa Claus left his reindeer down the block so that the noise wouldn't wake us," said Nick, joining in the laughter.

Everyone was laughing, everyone except Joey. He smoldered silently in his chair, his countenance darkening as his confusion transitioned to anger. "Why did you lie to us?" he suddenly demanded. "You told us not to lie. You said you would wash out our mouths with soap if we ever lied, and yet you and Dad have been lying to us all this time."

"I'm sorry," I said, reaching for his arms, but he pulled away. "We did lie to you, all of you, and I apologize. I'm sorry. We shouldn't have. It was fun when you were younger, but somewhere along the way, it stopped being fun and became simply lying. Please, guys, come here."

Jackie, Joey, and Nick gathered around Michael and me. I reached out for Joey again, and this time, he didn't pull back. "From this moment on, I promise never to lie to you, and I expect you to do the same, okay?"

"Okay, Mommy," they all echoed, even Joey. But he added, "Maybe you and Dad should wash your mouths out with soap."

"Careful, young man," I said.

"Does God exist?" Joey asked again.

"Honestly? I don't know, Sweetie. I don't know if anyone does."

"Then why should I believe in Him?"

"Because of *faith*." It sounded more like a question than an answer.

"Doesn't that go against the scientific method *you* taught us, Mom?" Danielle asked in a snarky tone.

"Dani has a point, Mom," Mikey added. "What happened to the critical thinking you've always talked about?"

"Why do we even go to church then?" asked Jackie.

Et tu, Jackie? It was a mutiny. I was under attack from all sides.

"Uh, for the donuts? Duh," Nick chimed in.

Everyone laughed. It was what this inquisitive milieu needed. Nick could always be counted on to deliver comic relief.

"Seriously, Mom. Why do we go to church? Dad falls asleep half the time during the mass," Danielle said. Everyone chuckled again.

"Hey," Michael objected. "Not fair. I'm awake for the other half."

"Also," she added, "I could use that time to study for my physics class, go over my gov notes, or simply sleep."

Since becoming a teenager, Danielle often questioned my decisions, which annoyed me. Barring that, she did have a point. My daughter was handling quite a course load this year. Despite being only thirteen, she enrolled in several high school classes, three of which were advanced placement.

"Okay," I said, dismissing Danielle's tone. "Let's take a vote. Those who don't want to go to church anymore, raise your hands."

It was unanimous. Mikey, Jackie, and Michael each raised one hand, but Joey and Danielle raised both. They all glanced at each other and grinned.

"I guess it's decided: no more church." The kids applauded. Michael grinned. "But," I added, pointing a finger at them, "Sundays will not be sleep-in days. It will be a day to learn about all religions, the current ones, and the ancient ones. Dani, this can be an elective class for you. You can join us when you're able, particularly on our field trips to mosques, temples, and synagogues, if we're allowed in. Remember to respect other people's religions."

"Are you okay with it, Mommy?" Jackie asked.

"Yeah, it'll be fun learning about all the different religions out there. It'll tell us a lot about the people of that religion and gain insight on how they view the world."

"Isn't it bad, Mom, though, if we don't go to church? Will we be punished?" asked Nick.

"Hey, remember when we discussed the Golden Rule, which hangs on our classroom wall?" I asked my kids. "Well, I believe if we follow that rule in our lives by continuing to do good things like volunteering at the Special Olympics, donating vegetables from our garden to the food bank, and just being kind to people, primarily those with less than us, we'll be fine. And, yeah, I'll miss the donuts, too."

We all laughed again and resumed eating our now-cold dinner.

I bought several books for our Sunday world religions class. Although I used many theological books about God, our course wasn't about questioning the existence of a Christian God; it was about studying the other faiths of the world.[6] We learned about the more prevalent Christian, Jewish, and Muslim religions, and we also explored lesser-known ones, like Voodoo, Rastafarianism, and Sikhism.[7]

Several weeks after we started our world religions class, I was late picking Nick up from soccer practice because I had to get the twins first. When I arrived at the freshly mowed soccer field, it was empty. Looking around with cupped hands across my forehead, I made out a shadowy image of two small boys sitting cross-legged under one of the surrounding trees on the far left side of the field. It was Nick and another boy. The coach had vanished, leaving them unattended. I would've taken my son home right away, but I couldn't abandon the other child. I texted Danielle and Mikey, letting them know I would be late picking them up from their soccer practice. I sat on the cool grass with my kids and the boy as we waited for his mother. She finally arrived twenty minutes later and thanked me.

"You're welcome," I replied. "It was my pleasure."

"Well, that was a very Christian thing to do," she said, hurrying away with her son.

Not kind, not noble, but *Christian*. That struck me. Before we had started studying world religions, I probably wouldn't have thought anything of it—she was just expressing thanks, in *her* way. Now, it sounded—smug.

While pondering the situation, Nick asked, "What did she mean by that, Mom? Do only Christian people know how to be nice to others? What about Muslims? Or Jews?"

"Or Black or White?" asked Jackie.

"Or tall or short?" asked Joey, laughing.

They continued with this line of questions, joking, and substituting nouns and adjectives until we reached Danielle and Mikey's pick-up area. Nick and the twins filled them in on what transpired, and they began adding other terms such as teachers and lawyers, swimmers and dancers. Perched behind the steering wheel, I occasionally glanced at them through the rear-view mirror. I was proud my kids didn't believe in the superiority or inferiority of any group. No one group of people had a monopoly on being kind or smart or even evil. Smiling to myself, I figured I must be doing something right.

MYTHOLOGY

World religions class soon led to a new mythology class. The three younger ones were the main participants of that class. We read the familiar Greek and Norse myths and learned about myths worldwide, from Mesopotamia, India, Africa, and elsewhere.[8] It wasn't long before I acquired a library full of mythology books. To complete our study, I took the family to see a marvelous performance of Ovid's *Metamorphoses* at Juniata College.

I scoured the internet, searching for a mythology contest. This time, I was striving to discover a way to bolster Nick's confidence. He was brilliant, but Joey was a fierce competitor. What had started as natural sibling rivalry was snowballing into an outright battle. I was afraid Joey was crushing his older brother's ego. A couple of years earlier, I heard Nick sobbing in his LEGO room (his closet). Through the half-opened door, I watched as he whimpered while playing with his toys.

"Hey, Sweetie, what's wrong?" I said as I squatted down beside him, giving him a gentle squeeze. "What's up, darling? Why the tears?"

"It's Joey, Mommy." Nick sniffled. "He said he's better than me at everything."

"That's false. There is no better LEGO builder than you." He gave me a feeble, not wholly convincing, smile. I tried again. "Sweetie, don't let him bother you. He wants to be like you. Remember the other day when he wanted to take trumpet lessons because you were? Okay, he was teasing you, but he also did it because he wants to be like you. You're his big brother. You know what, Nick? If there were no Nick, there would be no Joey. You are the one who motivates Joey. You make Joey who he is. He's nothing without you."

"Really, Mommy?"

"Really."

He smiled authentically this time. I chose not to share with Nick the corollary to that statement: He, too, was nothing without Joey. Joey challenged him and kept him motivated as well. They were two sides of the same coin.

"You know what, Mom? I'm glad I have my LEGOs. Whenever I'm sad, they always cheer me up."

"I'm glad you have your LEGOs too, Sweetie," I said as I left him to his toys.

As if the gods were smiling upon me, I found the contest I sought: The National Mythology Exam, held by Excellence Through Classics. The kids enjoyed it and earned medals and certificates. When they were older, we switched over to the much harder Medusa Mythology exam. Nick occasionally beat Joey by a few points, but most of the time, they tied.

THE HISTORY OF JAZZ

I chose to teach the history of jazz as an alternative history class because we had completed all the district's required history courses. The concept arose when a lovely piece played on the radio. I knew the melody but drew a blank on the name. Nick said it was Dave Brubeck's "Take Five" and mentioned he played it in jazz band. All my children had taken piano and violin lessons when they were younger. With those came Bach, Beethoven, Liszt, Haydn, and all the other European masters. We played their music and studied the life and times of these famous composers. I believed it was time for America's classical music.[9] Not only did studying jazz complement Nick's trumpet and Jackie's flute playing, but it also exposed the kids to this African American form of music developed in the communities of New Orleans. It was time to learn about jazz legends such as Louis Armstrong, Duke Ellington, Billie Holiday, and Charlie Parker.

It wasn't an easy subject to teach, as I had initially thought. Each musician that we studied came with their unique musical style and personal failings, all wrapped in the violent history of the time. For their end-of-the-year project, Jackie wrote a piece about Django Reinhardt. Joey's was on Thelonious Monk. Nick analyzed Billie Holiday's "Strange Fruit." He concluded:

> *Holiday released "Strange Fruit" during a very turbulent and discriminatory period, and had she not been so successful and well-guarded, she very well could have been lynched herself for such a song. The piece is interesting because of the lyrics; the speaker never says any words to describe herself or anyone in particular, never using complete sentences with first-, second-, or third-person points of view. It's almost as though the speaker is trying to distance themselves from the murder, to displace themselves from the harsh reality of racism.*

My kids never cease to amaze me.

SAT/ PSAT/ ACT PREP CLASSES

Before the children took any of the standardized tests, we practiced at home. These sessions were often scheduled on weekends when there were no other planned activities. I would mark the date on the large wall calendar that hung in our entryway as a "PRACTICE (Name of Test) DAY," giving the kids at least one week's notice. They all knew what those words meant: Rise early, eat a good breakfast, and be desk-bound for a three-hour timed test. I was preparing them for the types of questions they would face on these exams, as well as the intensity and duration of a grueling three-hour test. I photocopied and collated five sets of exams the night prior and set up tables and chairs in the basement. Afterward, we'd discuss the incorrect answers together.

Danielle took her first SAT exam at the age of twelve. It was a requirement for acceptance to the Johns Hopkins Center for Talented Youth (CTY) subdivision program known as SET, or Study for Exceptional Talent. Our method of using Princeton Review and Barron's SAT prep books and online math and grammar resources paid off, for Danielle gained admittance to SET. It wasn't long before I intertwined SAT preparation with our regular schoolwork. Eventually, we branched into PSAT and ACT prep books.

At fifteen, Danielle found herself away from home and had to study for the PSAT independently. I called to ask her if she needed to enroll in a PSAT prep class over there.

"Of course not, Mom," she assured me. "I do well on these exams. You've been preparing us for them since we were barely able to walk." She was only slightly exaggerating.

"Well," I said. "I'm not there now to schedule PSAT practice days."

"I know, Mom," she said. "But I can do it myself. I brought the PSAT workbooks, and I've already made myself a schedule. I'll do fine."

And she kept to her word. Danielle's score earned her a National Achievement Award and a National Merit Finalist. She set the bar drastically high for her siblings. By the time the Munchkins took their PSAT/SAT/ACT, my involvement had decreased to only scheduling and photocopying. They timed themselves and checked the answers together. Occasionally, I would linger by the doorway and listen as they went over their work.

Joey: "Math section, questions 1–10, did any of you guys get any of them wrong?"

Nick: "I got three and four."

Joey: "Number three was tricky. Did you remember to subtract from the total?"

Nick: "No, that's what messed me up."

Jackie: "I didn't get number seven."

Nick: "Oh, I got that one. They were asking for..."

I listened as they reviewed all the sections. I relished how they collaborated, contributed, and helped each other. There was never any ridiculing or playing around. They approached these tests with confidence, all earning National Merit and/or National Achievement Finalists awards.

ART

Unlike the rest of the subjects I taught, I didn't feel comfortable teaching art. What was the goal? What was the objective? For math, I could explain geometry and identify incorrect answers. For science, I could teach about the planets and their rings and calculate the sun's distance. But with art, were there any right or wrong answers? If I criticized my kids' works, would that inhibit their creativity?

When I first started homeschooling with Danielle and Mikey, I taught them art by following an online curriculum called K12. Their art lessons were intertwined ingeniously with their history class. When the kids studied Native Americans, they also constructed totem poles and made beaded necklaces.[10] When they learned about Mesopotamia, they replicated cave paintings. I also bought a small pottery wheel so they could make pottery at home.[11] When they studied Colonial America, they drew needle-stitch pictures like those you would see in colonial days.[12] Some of the early paintings by Danielle, Mikey, and Nick were fortunate to grace the walls of the Southern Alleghenies Museum of Art. The kids were thrilled to see their artwork displayed in the Student Art Exhibit Gallery.

After purchasing the pottery wheel, I began straying away from K12's script and taught my ad hoc art classes. We utilized plaster of paris kits, stained glass window sets, and other craft supplies. We also used different media such as charcoal, acrylic paint, chalk, and oil pastels. Our art classes were initially every Friday afternoon. However, as we became more involved with outside activities and sports, we relegated art projects to whenever we could cram them in.

My tenure as an art teacher was short-lived. By the time my Munchkins had joined our homeschooling group, I had grown weary of having paint, clay, feathers, and glitter strewn about the house, leaving my home in a perpetual state of chaos. I also didn't feel as committed to art as I did to other subjects. So, I outsourced my art duties. During the year, I put the children in every local art camp I could find. The younger ones took art classes at SFEA, where Mrs. Horner introduced them to different brush strokes, reflections of light, and abstract art. They utilized the works of Monet, Pissarro, Kandinsky, and Mondrian as guides.

At Millbrook Marsh's Nature Art camp, they learned about landscape art; at the Center for Arts and Crafts on Penn State's campus, they made papier-mâché animals and used color pastels and other media to embellish their creations. Once, when I was picking them up from an art camp in Altoona, the instructor commented how he loved teaching art to my kids' age group because "they are blank canvases, their creativity is pure and untouched, anything is possible for them." He added that as children became older, "we structure their creativity." He seemed bitter as he ended his solemn proclamation. That's why every time my kids came home with an art project, the messier it appeared, the happier I was. Their discombobulated artwork showed their creativity, whereas a more structured piece represented conformity and suggested a teacher-assisted project.

Eventually, we pivoted from doing art to learning about art. While Mikey and Danielle were taking AP Art History in school, I taught it to the Munchkins at home, albeit a more child-friendly version.[13] We also took field trips to various art museums throughout the country. My kids' creativity found its way into other subjects such as music composition, poetry writing, and even math problem-solving.

SPORTS

Sports do not build character; they reveal it.

— HEYWOOD HALE BROUN

Sports always intrigued me beyond the obvious benefit to physical fitness. Although their history, like most things, has been marked with racism, I viewed sports as a community among players that can transcend race and creed. All players and teammates are uniting for one ultimate purpose: winning. Thus, *Remember the Titans*, with Denzel Washington, stands as one of my favorite films. The best line in the movie I frequently quote to my kids is:

> *I don't give a damn about how sensitive these kids are, especially the Black kids. You ain't doin' these kids a favor by patronizing them. You're crippling them; You're crippling them for life.*

Remembering my years on the Brooklyn Tech High School track team evokes grueling memories of shin splints, body aches, and defeat. Regardless, it helped me foster the four Cs of invaluable life skills: Confidence, Courage, Camaraderie, and Commitment. These benefits of sports are what I wanted my children to learn.

SWIMMING

Swimming was our primary sport. The kids started in the local YMCA league, then moved to USA and high school swimming. Danielle began the swimming trend by joining the swim team at the age of four. It happened while waiting in the clamorous hallway of our local YMCA in Hollidaysburg.

"What are they doing, Mommy?" Danielle shouted over the noise.

"I don't know," I said, peering through the windows. "I suspect it's a swim team practice."

"A swim team? I know how to swim. Can I join?" she asked.

"Sweetie, being on a team takes hard work," I said, reaching for her hands. "You must practice every day. And once you're part of that team, you can't quit. Your teammates will depend on you."

"Pleeeeeease, Mommy?"

"Okay," I said. "I'll find out while you're in your ballet class."

While she attended her toddler dance class, I asked the swim coach whether my four-year-old could join the team. I did not expect they would permit such a young child on the team, or clearly, there would be a qualifying time standard for her to meet. The coach astounded me.

"As long as she can swim the entire length of the pool, she can be on the team." I later explained this to my husband. "She does enjoy the water."

So, my small water bug joined the Hollidaysburg Tigersharks the next day. However, her enthusiasm didn't last long. A month into it, she said, "I don't want to go swimming anymore, Mommy."

"You can't quit. Mommy already paid for the season. Besides, you're part of a team now. You'll be letting your teammates down. You can stop once the season is over."

"When will that be?"

"In February. Four more months."

"No, I'm not going for four more months."

"Yes, you are."

This arguing continued every day for about a week, but she usually caved, shuffled out the door, arrived at the pool, and swam.

In those early days, Michael confined his comments regarding the kids' activities to questions beginning with who, when, and where: "Who do I pick up? When do I drop them off? Where should I meet them?" However, he began interceding in the disagreement between my daughter and me. Trying to resolve the situation, he'd say, "Why don't we skip swimming for today? Or why don't we take Mondays off from swimming?"

I was uncompromising. My answer was always no. By the end of the week, Michael became infuriated. It led to one of our worst arguments.

"She doesn't want to go!" He shouted. "Why can't you under-stand that?"

"She has to go because she said she would."

"Being on a swim team is not a life-or-death situation. She can stop if she wants to."

"No, she can't. She can't quit. I don't want Danielle believing it's okay to quit when the going gets tough." I said, briefly reflecting on my life and all the roadblocks I had to overcome.

"She's four!"

"And when is she going to learn this lesson? When she's a teenager?"

"Do you hear yourself? This is crazy. She's not going. I'm not going to allow it."

I may have looked poised, but privately, I was terrified. I envi-sioned the scene's caricature: I'm grabbing Danielle's arms while Michael grabs her legs. The two of us pulling on Danielle in oppo-site directions—a tug of war. But the frayed rope, like the child, unravels and leaves her crying hysterically.

Earlier in the week, Danielle had said to me, "I wish you and Dad would divorce so I can go live with Dad." Danielle had said it after I'd written out her daily math problems. She was composed when she spoke, not at all emotional like a rebellious teenager. It was as if she had been contemplating this, which is what frightened me most.

"Well, until then, you're going to do your math work," I replied, trying to sound as calm as she had. But a bomb had just detonated inside of me. My stomach was a black hole, and my brain fixed on nothing else as I drove to work. Divorce? How did she even know what that word meant? I was distraught.

And now here we were again, a week later, and this uneasy feeling lobbied back to my mind as I argued with Michael. I couldn't let a four-year-old child get the better of me. Would Michael divorce me and take Danielle away? I wanted to call a time-out. Surrender. But my stubbornness stood firm, paying no heed. Unflinching.

"You're not going to allow it?" I asked Michael. "Since when do I need your permission to take our daughter to swim practice? And I don't appreciate you calling me crazy."

"I'll call you crazy if you act like it," he said.

Abruptly, after quietly watching the performance taking place in the kitchen, Danielle jumped down from the stool, grabbed her swim bag, and wandered over to her father. "It's okay, Daddy," she said, acting like the only grown-up in the room. "I'm going to swim."

We didn't argue about it again for the rest of the season. At the end-of-the-year swim team banquet, Danielle received her first trophy and a standing ovation for being the youngest on the team. When we got home, beaming with her new award, she hugged me. "I'm glad I didn't quit swimming, Mommy," she said. "I want to do this again next year."

As for Michael, he resumed his non-interfering ways. And "That's My Daughter in the Water" by Loudon Wainwright III became one of his favorite songs.

I realized afterward tantrums were not uncommon in the swimming world. Once at a swim meet, we saw a six-year-old girl tell her father she had decided not to swim after all.

"You're swimming, young lady! We drove all this way, and you're swimming!" scolded the father.

When they called her event, the child climbed on the starting block and remained motionless after the whistle blew, watching her challengers splash the water. When the race was over, she carefully stepped off the block and gave her father a defiant stare. I felt embarrassed for everyone involved and was secretly thankful it wasn't Danielle—because, well, it could have been.

I don't know why Danielle changed her mind and swam after what happened in the kitchen. Her father had sided with her. Maybe she decided she didn't want us divorcing after all. Whatever it was, she paved the way for her siblings to join the swim team. After that, it was never a question of *if* they would swim, only a matter of *when*.

By the time my kids turned five or six, they were all on the team. When Danielle was eight, she was qualifying for district and state championship meets. By ten, she had broken a few records for her age group.

Once, at the local summer championship swim meet at State College, Joey's goal was to break all the eight-and-under swim records, like he had done to the six-and-under twenty-five-yard freestyle and backstroke records two years prior. He had broken records in the freestyle, backstroke, and breaststroke that day, and before he got ready for the butterfly, I saw him and Nick running toward me. Nick was crying; Joey was laughing. This was not good.

"Mommy, please don't let him break my fly record."

"Mommy," Joey said with a grin, "better take a picture of the record board now. Nick's eight-and-under fly record is coming down."

What a dilemma. How could I encourage my kids to always strive to be the best, but not when it comes to breaking a sibling's record? This was a recurring predicament when Joey and Nick were in the same age group. I always had to remember to cheer loudly for both or be accused of favoritism. Joey got on the diving blocks and gave me a thumbs-up while Nick hid his head in my lap, afraid to watch. The result was unbelievable. Joey missed Nick's record by .02 seconds, prompting my disappointment for Joey and relief for Nick.

A year later, I playfully asked Joey if he were afraid someone would break his records, now that he had moved up an age group.

"No, Mommy," he said. "I checked out the eight-and-unders this morning before you came to pick us up, and I watched how they played around instead of practicing. They have no idea how they should be training. The six-and-unders are worse. Most of them can't even make it to the other end of the pool without holding on to the lane lines. I'm only afraid of the ones with older brothers or sisters. Those kids probably know what they're doing and what a swim meet means. It's a good thing there aren't a lot of them." After a pause, he added, "I imagine my records will be safe for a while."

"Wow, I see you thought about this," I said.

"I always do, Mom," he said, smiling at me.

At the 2010 PIAA district championships held at Penn State's McCoy Natatorium, when Danielle was a sophomore in high school, she tied for first in the 100-yard butterfly. The other swimmer happened to be Danielle's former teammate from when we lived in Altoona. To decide the event winner and determine who moved on to the state championships at Bucknell University, the girls were to compete in a swim-off at the meet's conclusion. Because the State College swim team usually dominated the district meets, all the other non-State College spectators and athletes would root against my daughter. I knew Danielle got nervous in head-to-head competitions, so I sneaked onto the pool deck to calm her. To my amazement, she was giddy as she stretched by the cool-down pool laughing with her teammates.

"You're doing fantabulous," I said as soon as she saw me approaching.

Chuckling, she said, "Thanks, Mom. I feel good."

"What about the swim-off? Ready for it?"

She shrugged off my question. "I got this, Mom."

"That's some confidence."

"She assumes I'm the same little girl she knew back in Hollidaysburg's Y. Well, I got news for her."

I tried to expel her presumptuousness by saying, "After that earth-shattering performance, I don't believe she's going to underestimate you, but darling, you shouldn't either. You did tie."

"Mom," she said as she continued to stretch her arms behind her neck. "There's no way I'm letting her beat me in my backyard. No way." When she saw the unsettled look on my face, she added, "Besides, Coach Todd said I have something she doesn't have."

"What?"

"An amazing coach."

I couldn't help but grin. I hurried back to the viewing area to watch the rest of the meet. Although I knew Coach Todd told Danielle this to help her relax, I knew for a fact the Hollidaysburg coach was also quite good. In the end, like most things, I knew the winner would be the one who wanted it most.

The moment of truth came. Both girls appeared on the starting blocks. The whistle blew. The two rivals exploded off their starting blocks. The spectators were at the edge of their seats, screaming with excitement. I was a kangaroo, jumping up and down, struggling to restrain myself. Three lengths of the pool down and one to go, the girls were coming back down for their last twenty-five yards. They were neck and neck, stroke for stroke. There could only be one winner. The other girl was good, but on that day, good wasn't good enough. In the last length of the pool, Danielle powered away from her competitor and touched the wall half a body length ahead. I smiled as I recalled her toddler swim tantrums. Watching my confident, fifteen-year-old teenager as she climbed out of the pool to hugs and congratulations from her coach and teammates, I realized her anxiety was a thing of the past. I placed my hands on my chest, wishing I could say the same.

Swimming also found its way into many of my children's essays. They applied it in a variety of ways. Danielle's article "Swimming" was published in *Celebrating What is Important to Me*, Spring 2008. Joey's 2012 submission for the National Math Moves You competition, titled "How Swimming Revolves Around Mathematics," won him a scholarship. And Jackie's 2012 Letters about Literature essay about her setbacks in a family of talented swimmers, written to Langston Hughes for his poem "Dreams," was among the finalists that year.

SOCCER

Another sport we enjoyed was the "beautiful game" of soccer. Danielle and Mikey started with biddy instructional soccer at the Hollidaysburg YMCA. Nick, Jackie, and Joey never needed that. They learned to play by watching their older siblings and joining when we played family soccer in our backyard. It was one of our favorite pastimes. While other families gathered before their Thanksgiving meal to play football, we played soccer. Since we were an uneven number of players, I was usually the referee. Frankly, no one wanted me on their team; I've missed easy goals on occasion. That was fine with me. I typically left the games early to check on dinner anyway.

My kids progressed from intramural, to club, to middle school and high school soccer. As parents, we enjoyed soccer the most because we had a good idea when it would end, we could easily distinguish which kid was ours, and, most of all, we got to relax in our folding chairs and watch our children play. There were no events to time, no concession stands to run, or tickets to collect, which was often the case with swim and track meets.

Danielle and Mikey sometimes found themselves on the same team, as did Jackie, Joey, and Nick. I usually put them on the co-ed team to help avoid conflicting game schedules and decrease practice pickups and drop-offs. Danielle did well on the mostly all-boys teams. When she was older, one of the referees pulled her aside. "I know how it feels being the only girl on a boys' team," she told Danielle. "But if you continue to push like that, I will call foul on you."

"Got it," Danielle replied.

I'm not sure if she did indeed "get it" because, in the next play, Danielle and Mikey came charging at each other, both trying to play the ball. Danielle stumbled and fell. She hobbled off the field and was taken to the hospital, where the orthopedist diagnosed a fractured ankle. It was treated with a cast and ended her season.

Joey also competed well in soccer. During one of Joey's U5 (ages five and under) soccer games, he kept stealing the ball from his opponent and scoring. Finally, the child threw himself on the ground in a tantrum and shouted, "Mommy! Stop him! Make him stop! He keeps taking the ball from me." The mother ran to him and carried her crying child off the field and, with a fixed gaze, flared her nostrils at me. Joey was embarrassed, but deep down, he was pleased with his soccer skills.

Jackie was not as fierce a competitor as her older siblings. It seemed she enjoyed sports more for the camaraderie than the game, or perhaps she simply lacked the confidence that seemed innate in her siblings. When she was younger, she and her brothers played on the same team. I noticed whenever her brothers missed a game due to occasional conflict with flag football (where my husband was one of the coaches), Jackie was relaxed, interacted better with her teammates, and played well. But whenever her brothers were around, she was disoriented and squirrely, unsure of which way to run. She was tense and would always pass the ball even when she had a clear shot at the goal. Realizing this, I made her switch to the all-girls team. It made a world of difference. Jackie's level of confidence increased, and her team spirit and her skills significantly improved.

By the time Nick and Joey were on the Mount Nittany Middle School soccer team, their speed and agility playing midfield helped them excel on the field. As a result, they were named team co-captains by their coaches and were admired by their peers. Parents often remarked to us how they loved seeing the Feffer boys dart around on the field.

RUNNING

Running was our summer cross-training sport that prepared the kids for fall soccer and winter swimming. I've always enjoyed it and began running with Mikey and Dani when they were five and six, respectively. My friend Ellen and I would take our kids to Mansion Park in Altoona and jog on its eight-lane running track. We ended with stretches, sitting on the newly installed AstroTurf. Eventually, the kids and I stayed closer to home and did our daily one-to-two-mile runs in our neighborhood.

By the time we moved to State College, all the kids had joined in. We lived in a circular development, almost a mile in circumference. We ran at least three times a week. I felt like a mother hen with her chicks closely following behind. Jackie usually brought up the rear, and Nick always volunteered to keep her company. In the summers, we joined Nittany Track and Field, and it was through this local running club Danielle soon qualified for States in the hurdles. Mikey and Joey qualified for the national Amateur Athletic Union Cross Country Championship meet at Disney World, where they both medaled. Jackie, Joey, and Nick ran in intramural meets in middle school and excelled in middle-distance events. As well as they did in track, swimming remained their favorite sport, with soccer being a solid second.

TRIATHLON

Our children enjoyed riding their bikes in our quiet neighborhoods. We visited Rails-to-Trails and always took our bikes with us on vacation.

Youth triathlons were a natural progression for my already talented swimmers and runners. The kids competed in the annual youth triathlon held at Garver Memorial Park, about a half-hour south of Altoona. Like most things, I took it seriously and trained them by practicing and timing their swimming, running, and biking. Since tying their sneakers lost them a considerable amount of time, I bought elastic, curly shoelaces that they only had to pull to fasten. It worked well. My kids took first in their respective gender and age groups for two consecutive years until we left Altoona. We participated in only one youth triathlon after moving to State College because most of the following summers found the children away participating in various summer camps. Mikey returned to competing in triathlons in college and became the president of his triathlon club. I'd like to presume his youth triathlon experiences left him with fond memories of this unique sport.

TAE KWON DO

Tae Kwon Do was one sport my children did not do mainly for fun but necessity. A couple of weeks before we moved to State College, an incident intertwined my feelings of helplessness and anger. Danielle, Mikey, and I traveled to my friend's home one afternoon for lunch and a playdate. Her kids were similar in age to my own, so she and I thought this would be a good idea, and Danielle and Mikey were both enthused. Danielle rushed inside to play with my friend's daughter when we arrived, while Mikey ran outside to play with her son. The boys were about eight years old. Shortly after, I heard Mikey screaming, "Stop it! Stop it!" I bolted outside to see what was happening, and I saw the other kid hitting my son with a stick. Mikey was cowering among the bushes, placing his arm over his face, trying to lessen the blows. The mother grabbed her son and scolded him. Furious and embarrassed, she made her son apologize to Mikey. She also apologized to me. But it was too late; the play-date was over. I was taking my children home.

"Why did he start hitting me?" Mikey cried once we were in the car.

"I don't know, sweetheart. Some kids can be mean," I said and quickly wiped away an escaped tear as I recalled painful memories of my childhood. While driving home, I decided my children should know how to fight and considered enrolling them in a self-defense class. When I mentioned it to my husband later that evening, he was against it. He reminded me of my dad, who wanted my siblings and me to avoid confrontation; likewise, Michael didn't like the idea of Mikey fighting. Neither did I. My siblings and I didn't hunt for conflicts, but sometimes they find you. I learned years ago that you earned respect if you fought back. I was unwilling to allow some kid to beat up on my child without him defending himself. I couldn't find any boxing classes, so I registered the kids for Tae Kwon Do within a week.

Years later, a similar occurrence took place with a different result. My husband was outraged because the other kid was much older and stronger and could have injured my son. But Mikey didn't shy away from the fight, and the bully scrammed away. I was proud of my firstborn son.

As my children got older, their sport's performance began to plateau while other kids' accelerated. Joey once pointed out, "Mom, remember when Dani and Mikey used to be the best swimmers on the team?"

"The high school team is more competitive, true. But, they're not terrible," I said.

"No, they're not," Joey agreed. "But other kids grew taller and better." I did notice the younger kids we used to see at the pool were now older, taller, and leaner. "There's a pattern here, Mom," he continued. "Thanks to you and Dad, our family is vertically challenged."

"Oh, now it's our fault? Don't you know nice things come in small packages?"

"Nope, not for the swim team. Not for basketball either, but—"

"You're not going to quit? You still have a few good years before high school, and you're still a top swimmer. Your breaststroke is fantastic and—"

"No, Mom. I'm not going to quit now, although I'll be focusing more on soccer. I may try out for the high school team."

That was my Joey. He had four more years before high school, and already he was analyzing, calculating, and planning.

My children were never afraid to try new sports or activities. As they got older, I knew they would abandon some to focus more on others. But in fact, the activities my kids continued all depended on Danielle. Being only one person, I had to allocate my time efficiently between my children; thus, it was helpful to put them in the same activities. Since Danielle was the oldest, she set the stage for what her siblings did. Usually, but not always, whatever she did, they wanted to do as well. Although Danielle was an excellent ballet dancer and was excited when she advanced to lessons on pointe shoes, she later quit to concentrate on swimming. My daughter also confessed she felt out of place with her healthy upper body strength from swimming compared to some other dancers. I didn't want her to retire her dance shoes and worked to convince her she had a beautiful Black woman's body and would be fitting in a troupe like the Alvin Ailey dancers.

"But I'm not dancing with them here, am I?" was her tart reply.

So, once Danielle stopped her dance classes, they all did. Although it made my time management more feasible, I regretted that decision because my social butterflies, Nick and Jackie, were talented dancers and had the potential and confidence to excel.

FIELD TRIPS

People don't take trips; trips take people.

— JOHN STEINBECK

Spending money on kids is probably recession-resistant, if not recession-proof. This assertion may not be accurate for all parents, but it is for me. I would pay for music lessons or buy new sneakers for my children in the blink of an eye and waffle for at least an hour before buying myself a new dress. Anything bought for Michael or me had to be a necessity. I have always been frugal or "budget-conscious," as my younger brother, Roland, likes to say. This comes from many years of conditioning and learning to live on a shoe-string budget for most of my life, notably during my college and medical school years.

Managing our finances, I distributed most of Michael's paychecks between our retirement and college funds. I spent money on educational materials, field trips, and vacations, which to me, were all educational. I searched for discounts whenever possible. One Monday morning, as we prepared to leave for a small zoo in Pennsylvania, I discovered admissions were free on the first

Tuesday of every month. I pulled the kids out of the car and announced, "Kids, there's been a change of plans..."

One of our most frequent excursions was the Pittsburgh Zoo. We aimed to go during the off-peak times or light inclement weather when we hoped the park would be less crowded. It wasn't long before we joined a reciprocal zoo and aquarium program. This reciprocity allowed us to visit more than 100 zoos throughout the country for free or reduced price. Each time we visited the zoo, I assigned the kids to choose a particular animal to write about.

On one of our trips, Nick wrote about the lions; they fascinated him by how they can sleep twenty hours per day. "Boy, how cool would that be," Nick had wondered. Danielle seemed bored visiting the zoo for the umpteenth time but perked up when she saw renovations underway to welcome new animals, such as polar bears. The primate area scared Jackie as the gibbons pounded their bodies on the glass. We didn't stay long.

Some museums offered similar reciprocal membership deals. When we became Pittsburgh Museum members, we were allowed unlimited general admission to the Carnegie Museum of Natural History, the Carnegie Museum of Art, the Andy Warhol Museum, and the Carnegie Science Center. With a family of seven, it was usually more economical for us to pay for a family membership. Whenever there were new exhibits, such as the Science Center's "The Bog People," or the Natural History Museum's "Passages," or the Art Museum's "Light!" show, I'd fill up the van, pack some sandwiches, grab a few notepads and pencils, and head out to Pittsburgh.

After we exhausted that city, I did a 180 and headed east to Philadelphia. Of course, we visited the zoo there (a necessity for the elementary kids). We also took tours of the Liberty Bell, Independence Hall, The Franklin Institute Science Museum, and the University of Pennsylvania Museum of Archaeology and Anthropology.

At the Franklin Institute, a twenty-foot marble statue of Benjamin Franklin himself greeted us in the rotunda. The figure sat proudly beneath the building's massive dome. Rays of natural light streamed through the gilded oculus, which glimmered in the sun. The walls, floors, and sixteen Corinthian columns that framed the rotunda were also made of marble as if the whole room were carved from one massive block. Expansive semicircular windows cut into the dome further illuminated the room.

Upon entering the gallery, Joey exclaimed, "Aaah! I see dead people." And we all laughed. Of course, he was right because we were at the Franklin Institute's Body Worlds: The Anatomical Exhibition of Real Human Bodies exhibit, which displayed over 200 cadavers. We were all astonished to see how well the bodies were preserved, dissected, and posed as if they were playing sports or riding a horse. It showed how muscles, skeletal systems, and other functions of the human body worked.

Mikey claimed that the corpses "felt alive." As much as we enjoyed the museum, we left feeling overwhelmed with many unanswered questions, both ethical and scientific.

We synchronized our field trips with our sports competitions. When Danielle made the USA Eastern Zone Swim Meet for her 100-yard butterfly, we took that opportunity to explore Buffalo's zoo and museum. We also drove to Niagara Falls, where we witnessed the majestic cascading blue-green waters splashing into the rocks below. Tiny water droplets floated into the air as a mist, accentuated by a late-afternoon rainbow. We were all mesmerized by the surreal nature and stood in a trance as we watched the waterfall and felt its wetness on our skin.

We experienced some other marvelous field trips, such as the lighthouses at Cape Hatteras, the glass factory at the Corning Museum, the science of sports at SportsWorks in Pittsburgh, the eighteenth-century cities at Colonial Williamsport, the sea creatures at the Baltimore Aquarium, and many, many more. Our favorite field trip, however, was our three-week RV trip out west.

Ever since purchasing an RV, Michael and I have dreamt of driving out west. It finally came to fruition in September 2005 when he was allowed enough time off from work. Danielle was the only one taking a class at the high school, and no one else had any conflicts. I explained the situation to Danielle's Algebra II teacher, and she gave me the books and assignments, so Danielle wouldn't find herself behind when she resumed classes.

In preparation for our trip, the kids and I plotted our route, calculated how long it would take, and decided how long we would stay at each destination. We purchased an RV campground book and made reservations. By the time we were ready to depart, we were experts in managing our provisions and sleeping arrangements. Previously, we had driven the RV to Florida to visit my family. We also took it to New York, Maryland, Connecticut, North Carolina, and Canada. But the trip out west eclipsed all the others, as we planned to trek through fifteen states from Ohio to Wyoming and back, taking different routes each way to squeeze in more sights.

The kids were always excited about RV trips, primarily because it meant Daddy would be coming with us. He was the driver; my job was to prepare meals and keep the crew occupied by playing games, reading stories, or watching videos. Before we got on the road, I handed each child a black and white composition notebook; this was their "out west" journal. I also gave each of them a disposable camera so they could include pictures.

Our first stop was in Chicago, where we visited with Michael's brother Richie and his family and sailed with them on Lake Michigan. The kids had a fun time jumping and swimming in the lake with their cousins. The following day we visited the Shedd Aquarium and the Field Museum. Then we said our goodbyes and continued west. We saw the Mississippi River upon reaching Minnesota, and the kids all exited the RV to take pictures. When we got to the campsite, Michael showed the kids how to make a fire using kindling and firewood in the campground's stone pit. The kids scattered around, looking for dry, dead pieces of wood to add to the smolder. We sang songs, told stories, and played tag and hide-and-seek until the fire was ready to cook our hotdogs, hamburgers, potatoes, and of course, s'mores.

After a couple of days, we left Minnesota for the Badlands of

South Dakota. We visited Crazy Horse Monument and Mount Rushmore, where the kids vociferously debated which of their faces deserved to grace that mountain.

"Seriously, though," Danielle asked, "Whose face should be on that mountain?" After a moment of reflection, she answered her own question with, "Martin Luther King, Jr."

"I think it should be Beethoven," Mikey said as he began to hum Für Elise.

"He's not American," said Danielle.

"Well, you never said that."

Nick and Joey were too engaged in Yu-Gi-Oh cards to participate in the discussion, but I bet they would have chosen a character from their favorite card game to grace Mount Rushmore.

"I think it should be Mommy," said my loveable, kiss-up, Jackie, with an adorable smile.

"Just for that," I said to Jackie, "you get extra ice cream."

"I think it should be you too, Mommy," said Nick, looking up from his game.

"Me too, Mom," Joey agreed.

We left for Wyoming. We took the scenic byway through the Bighorn National Forest, admiring nature in all its glory. Traffic suddenly stopped when a massive herd of bison encircled our RV on their way across the road. One even stopped to poop while crossing in front of us, which the kids found hilarious.

"I hope he wasn't trying to tell us anything," said Michael, grinning.

When we arrived at our campsite, I immediately started preparing dinner while Michael and Mikey went for a bike ride.

"Mommy," Mikey said upon returning, "Dad and I saw two moose, one male, and one female. They were gorgeous."

"I'm glad you and Dad had fun," I said.

"It was the best."

The following day, we visited Old Faithful at Yellowstone National Park, where we observed the geyser erupting over 100 feet high. We watched at a safe distance to avoid burns from the steam hissing skywards out of the vent. We saw the other smaller geyser in the area before the kids rushed off for scavenger hunts with the tour guide, where they earned Junior Park Ranger badges. Before we departed for Nevada, we visited the breathtaking waterfall at the Grand Canyon of Yellowstone.

In Las Vegas, the kids were mesmerized by the glamor of the hotels. We didn't stay long since we had a date with the Hoover Dam. Arriving at the dam, Nick, the twins, and I admired its exterior, while Dani, Mikey, and Michael went inside to see the generators and learn about their construction.

Our trip peaked at one of the world's seven natural wonders, the awe-inspiring Grand Canyon in Arizona. We gazed in awe at the kaleidoscope of red, green, and violet hues in the canyon's rocky layers. "Kids, you see the multilayered rocks over there," I said, pointing to the side of the canyon across from us. "The colors come from the different minerals found in the layer, and their positionings can give us a timeline of Earth's history. We can tell how old each layer is by the fossils found in them, but the canyon itself is six million years old and carved by the Colorado River below."

"Wow," said Jackie, clearly impressed like the rest of us. "It's beautiful also."

We all agreed and took pictures of the canyon and the various animals that inhabited it. Later, the kids rushed off to get another Junior Park Ranger certification by completing their scavenger hunt pamphlets. That evening, we camped at Grand Canyon National Park. We made a campfire and joyfully watched the golden-orange flame as the wood burned. We felt the fire on our faces as the piney bonfire smell infiltrated our clothes and hair.

After dinner, we sat on the ground, enchanted by the beauty of the night sky. We silently gazed at the stars, trying to see the galaxy. Just then, a hawk came into our view as it flew gracefully overhead.

"What kind of bird would you like to be?" I asked no one in particular.

"I'd like to be a peregrine falcon," Nick answered immediately.

"Mom said they're the fastest animal in the world," he added, smiling at me.

"Actually," I corrected. "They're the fastest *bird* in the world. The fastest land animal is still the cheetah."

"Ha," said Joey to Nick. Facing us, he continued, "I'd like to be an owl. They're the smartest bird."

"That's not quite true," said Michael. "Because of their large eyes, which look like glasses, people thought they were smart. And they can rotate their necks something like this." Michael demonstrated by circularly wobbling his neck, eliciting peals of laughter from his young audience. He joined in the laughter, then continued. "The sparrow, parrot, and even the crows are much smarter than the owl."

"Ha," said Nick to Joey.

"Then I'll be a crow," Joey said, unperturbed.

"I think I'll be a bat," said Mikey. "I know they're not birds, but I think it's pretty cool for mammals to fly."

"Well, if Mikey can be a bat, then I would like to be a butterfly. I like their colorful wings. They're pretty," said Jackie.

"Dani?" I said.

"While the rest of you were talking, I was thinking of a bird with a beautiful voice. I've decided on the nightingale because I love to sing."

Ever since I forced Danielle to audition for the musical *Broadway Babies* at the Mishler Theatre in Altoona, her stage fright disappeared, and she was cast in the role.

Danielle began to sing Bette Midler's song, "From a Distance."

Leave it to my genius daughter to pick such an appropriate song for this perfect moment. We played it so often in the car that we all knew the words and joined in the singing. Danielle had my mother's talent for singing. My mom's dramatic soprano voice created a sense of sacredness when she sang in her church choir. Our extended family always asked her to sing at gatherings. I didn't know then that my mother would lose the ability to speak after her third stroke. I would never again hear her speak, sing, or say my name.

I didn't know I was crying until I instinctively wiped away tears from my cheeks. The serenity of the night, the family cohesiveness, the words of the song, and Danielle's rich voice all combined for a once-in-a-lifetime state of nirvana. Did my kids feel it too? Is that the reason Danielle chose the song? I would have loved to stay there, captured in that time forever. No competition. No SATs. No pressure to be... anything. At that moment, I just wanted to *be*. As the song ended and I sat with closed eyes, I was content. I felt at one with nature, blending into my surroundings.

Then, Nick said, "Dad, let's pitch a tent and sleep out here tonight so we can see a black bear."

"Yeah, please, Dad?" the others added.

"Sure," said Michael. "Great idea."

Not wanting an encounter with a black bear, my one with nature feeling ended abruptly as I rose from the dirt floor and moved to sleep in the RV. The following day, with heavy hearts, we waved goodbye to the west, pointed our RV back east, and began the trip home.

Several years later, when we announced to the kids that we had sold the RV, the twins burst into tears. We were all grief-stricken, for we had such fond memories with our beloved RV. However, as the kids got older, we used it less and less. As recently as 2017, the kids begged for a repeat of our road trip out west, and I did my best to make it a reality, but everyone's schedules conflicted.

Sometimes, you can't go back.

PART III

STRIDING

The function of education is to teach one to think intensively and to think critically. Intelligence plus character—that is the goal of true education.

— MARTIN LUTHER KING, JR.

GROWING PAINS (2004–2009)

DANIELLE: 10–14 (2004–2008)

My twelve-year-old still did a few subjects at home with me, but in 2007, Danielle was now spending most of her days at the high school taking advanced courses. What I remember most about that year, which led me to reevaluate my entire homeschooling structure, was an incident in her physics class. While reading Malcolm Gladwell's book *Outliers*, I heard Danielle's cries of excitement as she shouted my name upon entering the foyer.

"I'm in my office," I replied, not sounding as enthusiastic as Danielle. I would usually be delighted to see her come home from her classes; except I was submerged in Gladwell's book today. My kids were mainly winter babies, and his thesis posited that these kids tended to lag behind their same-age spring and earlier-month counterparts in education and even more in sports. The book was forcing me to reconsider my decision to allow my children to skip grades. Perhaps I was hurting them by putting them in the same class with older, more massive kids.

"Mommy," she said again as she made her way into my office. "My physics class is going on a field trip to Hersheypark for their annual Physics Day at the Park." When she noticed my confused expression, she continued, "Well, can I go? The permission slip is right here." She waved the white piece of paper like a surrender flag in front of me.

I was not happy and not *un*happy either; rather, I was apprehensive.

"Sweetie, we always go to the annual homeschool day at Hershey as a family. Why don't you wait to go with us?"

"Why can't I go twice?"

"Because you'll enjoy it better as a family," I said as I attempted to resume my reading.

"Please, Mom," she said. "This is my first school trip. I love going to Hersheypark with the family, but this is the first time I can be with my friends."

I had feared this moment.

"Sweetheart," I said as I lay down *Outliers* to face her. "They're not your friends; they're your lab partners."

"No, Mom, you're wrong; they're my friends. We've become close while doing our lab projects."

Trying not to sound too cavalier about her so-called friends, I defined the term. "A friend is someone who comes to your house or goes to the movies with you. You never did any of those things with them."

"You're wrong, Mom," she repeated, quieter.

I had to be blunt. "Honey, you're twelve; these girls are probably, what, sixteen? Sixteen-year-old girls do not want to hang out with a twelve-year-old. I'm just afraid that when you reach the park, those girls will dump you and leave you all alone in that huge park."

"Mom," Dani said, with tears now welling in her eyes. "I've done everything you've asked of me this year. I've worked hard in all my courses, especially physics. I've gotten accepted into the Exeter summer program. I've practiced my instruments. All I'm asking now is to go on this field trip." She stopped, sniffed, and wiped away a tear. "If it's as bad as you say, then I won't go on another one, but please let me go on this one."

Staring into those teary eyes, I knew I couldn't refuse her. "Okay," I said. "You can go, but we must go over some guidelines." In the next hour, we discussed field trip logistics: the bus location, number, and pickup time. I also bought her a cell phone that week, her first one.

The day of the field trip dawned too soon. I was on edge. I reviewed the guidelines with her again when I dropped her off at the school that morning. "Remember," I said. "If you miss the bus back home, call me right away, and I'll come get you. It should take me about an hour and a half."

"Okay, Mom," Danielle said and rushed to join her classmates.

I couldn't stop agonizing about the trip the entire day. I wanted to be proven wrong. I wanted Danielle to come home and give me an "I told you so" gloat and eagerly recount the fabulous day she had with her friends.

That evening, I arrived at the school parking lot half an hour before the scheduled time. I paced up and down the empty lot, waiting for the bus. When it finally appeared, I scrutinized each kid as they descended, one by one. When I caught a glimpse of my daughter, I waved both arms in the air as if hailing a cab. She gave me a thumbs-up, and I relaxed. As she walked off the bus, I saw Danielle didn't glance back nor said goodbye to anyone. Not a good sign. When she was safely in the car, I said, "Well, how was it?"

She stared out the window and said, "You were right, Mom. Those girls dumped me as soon as we arrived at the park."

"Oh, no," I said. "Why didn't you call me?"

"No, it was okay," she said, turning towards me. "I was disappointed at first; then I saw another girl my age by herself too. I asked her if she wanted to go on rides with me, and she said yes. We went on all the rides and even had lunch together. We left the park around the same time, so it worked out perfectly. She goes to a private school in Philly." Danielle smiled and added, "I had a good time, Mom."

"I'm glad, Sweetie," I said, pleased by how she improvised on my guidelines.

"Mom?"

"Yes?"

"Thanks for letting me go."

"You're welcome, baby."

I've always told my children the maxim: *Blood is thicker than water* since my siblings are my best friends. But water, I realized, is just as valuable for life. I do have a few cherished friends, and my kids yearned for friends beyond the family as well. In my desire to provide for all her educational and familial needs, I failed Danielle on that front. Another lesson I learned that day was that I won't always be there to solve all the adversities my kids will undoubtedly face; all I can do is provide them with the tools they need to solve them on their own. As much as I would have preferred those older girls not to have abandoned my daughter, I was impressed by how she handled it.

The changes I made to my educational structure directly resulted from the Hersheypark episode and Malcolm Gladwell's *Outliers*. Realizing most kids in the area had known each other since grade school and established cliques by middle school, I had to find a way to inject my kids into the mix to help foster deep friendships later. The following school year, when Danielle was in eighth grade, she continued with some high school courses, and I also placed her in fun middle school activities, like jewelry making. Mikey took a few high school classes and tech ed at the middle school. Jackie, Joey, and Nick participated in band and orchestra at the elementary school and intramural track. They also attended programs offered by SFEA.

Most of my children had winter birthdays, and they were already a year or two ahead of their peers academically, so I took Gladwell's advice and held all my kids back by one year. That made some of them the same age or only a year younger than their counterparts. I would still teach them at their academic abilities or place them in advanced classes. It didn't matter what their scholastic grade levels were, but their age could matter in sports as well as having friends at their maturity level. As competitive a swimmer as

Danielle was when swimming against kids in her age group on the YMCA and USA teams, I was unsure how she would fare on the high school swim team, where age groups no longer existed. I understood I had been doing my kids a disservice when I encouraged them to skip a grade level. If they later decided they wanted to graduate early and were mature enough to make that decision, we could always revisit it.

MIKEY: 10–14 (2005–2009)

The Nintendo Wii came out on November 19, 2006, and Mikey wanted one for Christmas. Gone were the days I could buy them chemistry sets, telescopes, or even calculators as gifts. Mikey never demanded much; he was always the quiet one, and hence, never the squeaky wheel that got his way. My husband was against the Wii because the kids already had a PlayStation and a GameCube. He didn't want "spoiled kids who got all the gaming systems that came out on the market."

"Mikey is different," I said, trying to persuade him. "He knows everything about these systems, the processors, the construction. It's not just the games; he also loves the technology. Who knows, it might even inspire him to be a software designer."

"Playing video games produces a gamer, not a software designer," Michael retorted.

Since Danielle's swimming tantrum years earlier, Michael had mostly withheld any disagreements he may have had with me regarding the kids' education or activities. I too, chose my battles carefully. So, I acquiesced. I can still remember how his lips tightened and his head lowered when Mikey didn't find the coveted gift under the Christmas tree. I hugged him while I explained why his dad and I both voted against it.

"It's okay, Mom," he mumbled, biting his lips.

That summer, Mikey heard of a psychology study being conducted at Penn State, in which he could earn up to $300 as a research subject. He begged me to sign the consent forms before he even knew the terms. The objective of this eight-to-twelve-week project was to determine safe ambient conditions for kids doing strenuous exercise. I told Mikey that he could stop if the workouts were too rigorous. I feared that they might be more taxing than Mikey expected; regardless, he was determined to participate.

After the blood tests and physical exams, Mikey had to swallow an enormous tablet (called a T-pill) the night before exercising in the heat-adjusted lab. The device measured the warmth inside his body. After observing the first two trials proceed as expected, I quit waiting for him in the lobby and started dropping him off and picking him up.

"How was it, Mikey?"

"Okay," was usually his reply as he slid into the car.

After dropping Mikey at home, I ran into one of the staff members at the grocery store. "Your son, Mikey, is quite persistent. I thought he was going to stop today. He was on the treadmill, and sweat was running down his body, and he seemed to be in agony, but he finished it."

"Excuse me?" I asked.

"Didn't he tell you? I was sure he would have told you."

"He was in agony?"

"Well, he seemed to be," the staffer said, now surveying the market, unsure how to continue. "We asked him if he wanted to stop, but he said no. Some of the other kids stopped because, well, I guess it was too strenuous for them, but Mikey didn't. So... well, we were all impressed with him."

I rushed home. My mind was speeding faster than my driving, torn between concern and fury. "Mikey! Mikey!" I shouted upon entering our home. "Mikey, come down here right now," I said when I saw him at the top of the stairs. "Mikey, why didn't you tell me what happened in the lab today?"

"Oh, that."

"Yes, that. Why didn't you tell me?" I repeated.

"Because nothing happened."

"Oh? You were in pain. That's nothing?"

"I mean nothing I couldn't solve... It was a bit painful, but I handled it. I'm fine." Mikey said as he shifted his body. "Besides, today was the last day. I finished it. Tomorrow I'll pick up my check," he said with a mirthless smile.

"That's not the point, Mikey. You should have told me. Do you know how foolish I felt in the supermarket while that guy described how you were struggling, assuming I already knew? Don't ever leave me in the dark again. I'm your mom. It's my job to know these things. I'm here to help you, even if it's just to listen. Okay?" As I hugged him, I added, "You don't ever have to go through something like that alone."

"Yes, Mom."

As he made his way back up the stairs to his room, I realized we had an audience—Joey. I'm not sure how long Joey caught the scene that played out below, and when he glanced in my direction, I said, "And that goes for you too, buddy. No secrets from Mom."

He bobbed his head in agreement as he, too, retreated to his room.

The following day, Mikey asked if he could use his $300 check to buy his Nintendo Wii at the mall. I was so proud of him and approved immediately. I admired the grit and determination it took to accomplish his goal. We purchased his game system, but I deposited the check in his savings account for college, with the rest of his birthday, Christmas, and awards money.

That school year, Mikey had another intense academic schedule. He never had the "I can do it myself" attitude, like his older sister. Yet I, regrettably, painted them with the same brush. I assumed if Mikey needed my help, he would request it. He never did ask. Things seemed fine at first. But by November, teaching him at home became problematic. Mikey seemed distant—like a zombie almost— in a stupor. He hardly hummed or played the piano. He was joyless.

One day I finally asked him, "What happened to my fun-loving baby boy who made up these funny riddles and once told me he could dance all day?"

"He grew up and started taking high school classes," he said.

"Well, maybe he should drop one or two of those classes because I want him back."

"I'll be okay," he said, barely audible as he trudged away.

The pressure was too much for him, but my son doesn't allow himself to give up. He believed what I taught them about not dropping or quitting any activity. In this instance, I was wrong. The next day, I spoke to the principal about pulling Mikey out of the advanced chemistry class. Mikey was unhappy at first when he found out what I did. In the ensuing months, however, he hummed softly as the sparkle in his eyes returned. I got my baby back. After that episode, I recommitted myself to staying abreast of Mikey's work. That's one reason I attended a "Meet the Teacher Night" at the high school later that year.

"Mikey is such a pleasure to have in class. He is doing quite well in this AP class. He has a firm grasp of the material, which I now find funny because I didn't think he belonged in my class the first day he walked in," his teacher said.

"Why not?" I asked, failing to see the humor. Although Mikey was still a middle school student, he appeared like a high school student, having facial hair much earlier than most kids his age. So, her statement confused me. Her delayed response and the change in her bubbling personality hinted at the answer. "Why didn't you believe my child belonged in your AP class?" I asked again.

After a moment of observing the floor's banal tile pattern, she finally faced me and said, "I'm not sure."

As we walked away, I articulated with Mikey the microaggressions Black people face in everyday interactions, even in the classroom. That's when he told me about an Asian student in his AP Calculus class who had complained about the pressures of being Asian. "Society expects too much from us," Mikey quoted him saying.

"Next time," I said to Mikey, "tell that kid to try trading places with you, where society expects nothing from Black males, except maybe in music, sports, and jails. Agreeably, both forms of prejudice are harmful, but I think I would rather the positive type. When people assume you should be good at something, you may start to believe it yourself, and it can encourage you to succeed. Whereas when people have few to no expectations of you, it slowly begins to erode your confidence like a weathered shoreline, and eventually, you lose faith in yourself and don't capitalize on your full human potential."[1]

"Really, Mom?" Asked Mikey.

"Yeah," I replied. Stuck in rural Pennsylvania, my kids were too sheltered from the African American experience; They had no idea of the "real world." I had to find a way to remedy that.

NICK: 6–10 (2004–2008)

I wanted Nick and Jackie to have their own musical instruments. In addition to piano lessons which all the children practiced, Danielle, Mikey, and Joey also took violin lessons. It was time to consider the same for Nick and Jackie. It would enable them to play in the elementary school band or orchestra and become part of a group, like their soccer or track teams. Nick loved the idea. After dissuading him from the drums, I tried convincing him to play the trumpet. Nick refused. He wanted the saxophone for the cool factor. Since Danielle's and Mikey's horns were in the closet collecting dust, I did not want to spend money on yet another instrument that would probably have a similar fate.

"No," he said again, this time adding a stomp with his foot like a spoiled child. "You let the other kids pick their instruments; I want to play the saxophone. I don't want the trumpet."

I was getting annoyed. I guessed Nick only wanted to play the saxophone because the other kids never did. He had no genuine objections against playing the trumpet. So, I stood firm.

"Nick, it's either the trumpet or nothing."

"But—but you said—"

"Trumpet or nothing. Choose."

"Trumpet," he mumbled.

After a couple of months of lessons and taking part in the

elementary school band, he enjoyed playing his trumpet. He practiced diligently and made tremendous progress. Eventually, however, the novelty wore off, and getting him to practice became a chore. One day, Joey picked up Nick's trumpet from the stand and blew. It sounded surprisingly clean, with a smooth, velvety tone.

"Wow," I said, walking over to Joey in the family room. "That was good."

Joey just turned to me and grinned. I walked back to my office and resumed my work with Jackie. Then, I heard thumping charging from the bathroom.

"Give me my trumpet, Joey."

"Can I play it again?"

"No. It's mine."

"Fine. I'll get the other trumpet."

"Why? You can't play it. You don't know what you're doing."

"I will if I take lessons."

"You can't take lessons. Trumpet is my thing."

"Who says it's your thing? I can take lessons if I want to."

"No, you can't."

"Yes, I can. I'm going to ask Mom."

"Don't."

"Mom!" Joey shouted while making his way to my office. "Mom, can I take trumpet lessons?"

"No, Mom, no!" Nick screamed, rushing in behind him. "Please don't let him take trumpet lessons. Trumpet is my thing."

"It's not about you, Nick," Joey said. "I like the sound. Well, Mom? Can I? Please?"

They both analyzed my face, trying to decipher the answer. Joey smiled as if he had just gotten another A on a math test. Nick looked terrified, as though he didn't know there was even going to be a test. I knew Joey just wanted to compete with Nick to prove he could be better than Nick at something again. But maybe it would encourage Nick to practice. I stared into Nick's panic-stricken eyes and realized I couldn't do that to him.

"Joey," I said, "you already have the violin. The trumpet is Nick's instrument."

Nick let out a sigh of relief. "Yes."

Joey said, "Okay, Mom," with that 'I was just doing this to be annoying' smirk on his face and walked away.

Nick resumed his trumpet practice, and I noticed it lasted longer and was more focused than his other times. I mentally thanked my youngest son for unknowingly motivating my middle one.

On October 9, 2008, I took Nick to a Wynton Marsalis concert at the Eisenhower Auditorium at Penn State. We left Michael and the other kids at home.

"It will be just the two of us," I told him.

Nick was ecstatic. We both got dressed in fancy attire and made our way to the concert: Nick in a shirt and tie, and me with my pearls and a knee-length black dress. We spoke to other Marsalis fans and fellow trumpet players while waiting to enter. They remarked on how young Nick was and how lucky he was for this opportunity. Nick agreed and squeezed my hand as we made our way into the concert hall. Mr. Marsalis and his Lincoln Center big band made it a magical night. Nick watched the first performance and promptly fell asleep for the remainder of the show. When we arrived home, Nick hugged me and told me he was the luckiest boy for seeing Mr. Marsalis play his trumpet and for having the best mom in the world. The show didn't accomplish what I had initially hoped—to encourage my son to practice more diligently so he could be like Mr. Marsalis. It had achieved much more: a treasured mother-son memory.

JOEY: 6–10 (2005–2009)

As a fourth grader, Joey began his day by taking the school bus to the high school with Dani and Mikey. They would then walk him to his Advanced Algebra II class. Jackie's and Nick's day began at home, working with me, and then I would drive them to the high school. There they'd join Joey for French II.

I was reluctant for my youngest son to start taking classes at the high school with these older students. "Joey," I said to him before the school year started. "I'm pretty good at math, almost majored in it in college, you know. How about if I taught you Algebra II?"

"No, thank you, Mom," he said. "I want to take classes at the high school like Dani and Mikey. I want to see what it's like."

"Pumpkin, you'll be the only fourth grader with these older ninth—or possibly tenth—graders. It might be intimidating to take classes with them. They may tease you or resent having such a young kid in their class." I thought that some teachers might resent it as well.

"That won't happen, Mom," he assured me. "Besides, I'll have Dani and Mikey with me, and you said Jackie and Nick would join me in French II. I'll be okay. It'll be fun. I like working with you in science, history, and those other classes, but I like taking math classes with other kids to challenge myself."

Noting my son's eagerness to start high school classes, I decided to seek out the teachers assigned to my young children. I wanted to introduce myself and explain our dual-schooling situation. I also wanted them to know I would be protecting my children. Danielle and Mikey had not been as young as the Munchkins when they started attending the high school for classes, so I wasn't as worried about them. I needed to safeguard my little ones.

A regretful memory from my childhood was another reason for my precaution. When I was in third grade, slightly younger than my twins, I attended a Catholic school in Brooklyn, where some teachers were nuns. My teacher, a strict, older white woman with hair tightly pulled back in a bun, said if we had any further questions about the homework, we could come up to her for more explanation. A few of us lined up like penguins by her desk. When it was my turn, she pushed me away with one hand.

"Don't breathe on me," she said with a grimace.

I was stunned and embarrassed and almost fell over the small boy behind me. I hurried back to my seat, with tears on my cheeks, and never asked my question. I didn't ask or answer a single question in her class from that day on. I still studied and did my work diligently in all my other courses, but even in those, I remained quiet, invisible, afraid to speak. I never told my parents or anyone else because I feared I had done something wrong, even though I didn't know what it was. I didn't have a cold. I wasn't sick. I wasn't even close enough to breathe on her; other kids, I observed, were much nearer. I didn't understand. That episode haunted me well into my college years. Only later did it finally dawn on me that I had been the only Black child in the class. The only explanation that made sense was the teacher didn't like my skin color. Unfortunately, in every profession, there are racists and bigots. I vowed a similar occurrence would never happen to any of my children if I could help it.

My fears for them evaporated as soon as I met their teachers. I liked them all, especially their French teacher, Madame Showers. I apologized to her for having to deal with my three young children in her class.

"*Ca va être génial,*" (It's going to be great) she said as she held my hands. "It might also help the other kids to participate more."

It turned out she was right. She was a gifted teacher, and my kids enjoyed her class. *Merci beaucoup.*

JACKIE: 6–10 (2005–2009)

She was not my human calculator, nor was she my budding scientist. She was not my genius child, nor was she my computer whiz. Jackie was my social, fun-loving, people person. Likability may have its virtues, but I worried people weren't recognized or promoted only for being nice. The world wants to see accomplishments. She was above average in all her subjects and sports, but I needed to find one in which Jackie excelled to build her confidence. After all: "success begets success." I decided to convert her love of people to the study of people: history.

Although I used the same curriculum[2] for Dani and Mikey, I wanted to add more when teaching Jackie, Joey, and Nick. Since

119

history is chronological, it should begin with the big bang and the development of the earth. To that end, I ordered two twelve-foot laminated posters depicting the Timeline of the Development of Life and the Timeline of Humans.[3] These new materials enthralled the kids as we discussed the plants and animals that existed during each era. They loved the pamphlet that described the pictures, but they hated the exams.

For third graders, it was a lot to memorize. But I taught spiral learning, reteaching a topic every year while adding more details and expanding their knowledge. However, it backfired. The history of life's development left them, particularly Jackie, with a dislike or indifference toward it until they were older. When we moved on to the Timeline of Humans, it was difficult for my children to grasp the idea of time and how short our time on earth has been in reference to the universe's time scale. However, they enjoyed learning about primitive human tools, clothing, fire, flora and fauna, religious rites, and cultural ceremonies. Field trips to the American Museum of Natural History in New York further solidified their knowledge of early human history.

A couple of months later, in the spring of 2006, my sister, Edwidge, told me she would be lecturing in Richmond, Virginia, at a four-day educational conference. I immediately figured out how the kids and I could hear her presentation and have an illuminating experience in Virginia. At the time, I was teaching Jackie, Joey, and Nick American history before 1865, and we were beginning the section on the Civil War. Mikey and Danielle had finished the Civil War and Reconstruction the previous year, so my sister's conference in Virginia provided a perfect opportunity for a field trip.

All the kids eagerly anticipated the trip, but Jackie was the most anxious. She was a visual learner and loved field trips. Seated at a desk, memorizing names and dates was not ideal for her. She needed to experience the exposed world. For Jackie, learning existed beyond the classroom.

"Bye, Daddy," she said, wrapping her tiny arms around her father's neck. "I wish you were coming with us."

"I wish I were, too, but someone has to work so you guys can go on field trips."

"You got that right," I said, flashing my teeth as I put last-minute snacks in the travel bag.

"It's okay, Daddy," Jackie said, still holding on to her dad as he carried her to the car. "I'll tell you all about it."

"I'm sure I'll read about it in the report your mom will make you write. Bye, kids."

"Bye, Dad!" they all shouted back.

While Jackie buckled herself into the back seat between Joey and Nick, Michael came over to the driver's side. He kissed me goodbye and said, "Please be careful with my most precious jewels."

I always loved it when he said that. We always appreciated his presence when he joined our field trips, but his schedule rarely allowed it. "No wild parties while I'm gone," I joked.

"I won't let it get *too* wild," he replied.

"Dad's going to have a party?" Mikey asked.

"He'd better not," I replied.

Michael stood, waving goodbye. "Call me when you arrive at the hotel."

"Will do," I assured him, and we were on our way.

As always, it was a treat visiting with my sister. Although the conference was only four days, we made the best of it. We spent each day sightseeing and caught up with Edwidge in the evenings. Since her presentation would be on the last day of the conference, we planned to attend her lecture and leave for home shortly afterward. We drove around Monument Avenue, commenting on the Confederate statues that lined this historic district. We passed by the Virginia Holocaust Museum and visited Monticello, Tredegar Iron Works, and the American Civil War Museum: White House of the Confederacy.

The museums were relatively empty, so many of the curators and park rangers at the Tredegar Iron Works, part of Richmond National Battlefield Park, spent their time answering our questions and giving us insights such as how a cannon worked. Because I wanted my children not to be afraid to speak up, I gave them some incentives. I decided that the child who asked and answered the most questions during scheduled tours would earn a souvenir at the end of the day. Mikey was usually the winner.

I frequently used DVDs in conjunction with field trips to help teach my children.[4] We had watched some Civil War videos at home before our Virginia trip. We watched on the way to Virginia on the DVD player in the car, which helped curb the "are we there yet" question. We watched *Roots* a day or two after our return home.

While watching Roots with the kids one afternoon, I realized I might have gone too far in wanting visual effects to highlight our readings. When we got to the part where the slave patrollers captured the runaway slave and were about to cut his foot off, Jackie, Joey, and Nick cried, "Stop it, Mom! Stop it!"

I immediately grabbed the DVD remote and clicked it off. Too late. Jackie was shaking and crying hysterically. Despite my hugs and reassurances that everything was going to be okay, it wasn't. Following that episode, Jackie began having nightmares. She had difficulty sleeping and kept crawling into her sister's or brothers' beds. We never finished the *Roots* series.

"*Roots*? For six-year-olds? How could you?" Michael said. "What on earth were you thinking? Obviously, you weren't."

I felt guilty at first, but the steady crescendo in his criticism provoked me to defend myself. I rose from the dining table. "Well," I said. "I was teaching them about slavery, and I'm sorry, but slavery was heinous and evil, and I can't sugarcoat it like the revisionist textbooks are trying to have me do."

"But Carline—"

"Did you know?" I said, finding my seat again beside my husband. "Did you know there's a Holocaust Museum not too far away from those Confederate statues in Virginia?"

"No, why?"

"Well, it made me wonder, do you believe Jewish people would allow statues erected to Nazis, people who brutalized and tortured them? Of course not. No one would. The Jews hunted everyone involved in the Holocaust: the soldiers who claimed they were only following orders, the doctors, the lawyers, the industrialists— anyone they felt committed crimes against humanity. And any time a Nazi's whereabouts are known, they are arrested and prosecuted. How does the United States remember traitors that fought their government to maintain the right to enslave Black people? They erect statues to honor them." I paused. I was getting too emotional. I felt myself choking on tears. I glanced down at my interlaced fingers on the table and back up at Michael. I said softly, almost in a whisper, "Why isn't slavery considered a crime against humanity? Are Black people not considered human?"

After a moment of contemplation, Michael spoke. "Carline, I get it. Just because I'm white doesn't mean I don't understand the cruelty of slavery, the Holocaust, the Trail of Tears, and other atrocities perpetrated in the world. But," he paused, selecting his words carefully. He placed his hands over mine and said softly, "Nick and the twins are too young to comprehend all that. *Roots* was going a bit too far."

"I'm sorry," I said after I had gotten better control of my emotions. "I had forgotten how graphic some parts were in *Roots*."

I finished our slavery unit by taking the kids to see a play at the Eisenhower Auditorium called *Freedom Train*, performed by TheaterWorksUSA. This musical performance portrayed the life of Harriet Tubman and the Underground Railroad in an age-appropriate way. In the ensuing months, Jackie slept better.

CLUBS

If you have no confidence in yourself, you are twice defeated in the race of life.

— MARCUS GARVEY

I utilized academic clubs to foster learning, teamwork, and confidence in my children. We participated in Youth and Government, Forensics, and Future Business Leaders of America, but Quiz Bowl was my favorite.

YOUTH AND GOVERNMENT

At the end of a week-long National Youth Leadership Council program in Washington, D.C., in 2009, Danielle returned home committed to playing a more active role in politics. She joined the Youth and Government club at the high school. Members of the club portrayed legislators or attorneys, and during the year, they would either write bills or briefs. Danielle became a legislator in the club's House of Representatives. She proposed legislation imposing a tax on indoor tanning. My daughter also co-sponsored two other measures: one on the budget and the other on changing how judges were appointed. In April, at the Model Legislative Convention held at the Pennsylvania State Capitol in Harrisburg, Danielle gave sponsorship and summation speeches for all three of her bills, first in committee and then before the entire Model Congress. Ultimately, her Tanning Tax Bill and Budget Bill passed and were signed into Model Pennsylvania Youth and Government law.

When the Affordable Care Act passed the following year, the number of pages it contained became a media punchline; I remembered how indignant Danielle reacted.

"The people who are complaining about the length of that proposal have no idea what it takes to write one," she had said. "You have to make sure your bill addresses any ambiguity. Remember the one I wrote on taxing indoor tanning?" she asked, briefly pausing for my affirmative nod. "Well, someone might have asked something like, 'are we going to tax people for tanning using the sun?' Although that's a transparent attempt to derail my proposal, I had to ensure that my bill clarified such ambiguities. Otherwise, it could have been voted down. That's why I ended up with twenty pages. I'm shocked that Obama's healthcare bill has *only* 1,000 pages." With a shake of the head, she added, "Youth and Government should be mandatory in school, and everyone should have to write a bill."

I listened with admiration.

Years later, Jackie would also develop an interest in political science by joining Model UN. Jackie's team was assigned to represent Somalia, and the topic was sustainable development.

She argued, "If all countries could educate their citizens about the effects of global warming and teach about the technological advances that can be created, slowly but surely, society will be improved. Somalia hopes for a productive debate at this conference and wishes the best of luck to all countries."

After forming alliances with several countries, Somalia won. The judges selected it as the best delegation.

FORENSICS

The Pennsylvania High School Speech League, commonly known as Speech and Debate or Forensics, was founded in 1961. Its mission statement: To promote curiosity and understanding of speech through the means of competition, aligned with my teaching philosophy. Danielle was the first of my children to join the forensics team at State High. She displayed intuitive debating skills in winning her first Lincoln-Douglas debate, in which she had to argue, in the affirmative, the merits of giving felons the right to vote. She eventually left the debate team due to conflicts with the swim season, as neither coach was pleased with her missing practices.

Later, Joey joined the forensics team at the suggestion of one of his track teammates. When he competed, it became apparent that he, too, was a natural. Joey approached forensics with his customarily meticulous, analytical mind. He presented a thoroughly researched argument and was quick to point out the flaws in his opponent's. His favorite event was Public Forum, a debate between two-person teams about fundamental government questions.

When I first volunteered as a judge for Public Forum in 2015, I was surprised by the relevance of the topics discussed, such as a universal basic income, the moral justification of civil disobedience, and the presidential authorization of extreme military power. All the students supported their positions with facts, background knowledge, and enough professionalism to put many actual legislators to shame.

Jackie and Joey competed in Parliamentary Debate together, which was similar to Public Forum, although with three-person teams. After Joey graduated, Jackie began competing in an event called Congress, in which students would present their arguments on several pre-selected bills and answer questions. The judges scored them based on both the delivery and the content of their cases. After my judging duties were over at the 2018 Pennsylvania State Tournament, I watched Jackie's performance. She conveyed impressive poise and confidence. She coolly stated her arguments and rebutted attacks thrown at her, and her team did the same. As I watched, impassioned by these impressive young adults, I thought optimistically of the future. Their generation could change the world.

FUTURE BUSINESS LEADERS OF AMERICA (FBLA)

Jackie found out about FBLA when she began taking business courses at the high school. She wanted to compete in the Business Math event. I was pleased Jackie was forging her path. That first year, Jackie qualified for the state tournament. Joey, always wanting part of the limelight, declared he too wanted to compete in the Business Math category, except with his mathematical prowess, Joey expected to compete at the national level.

"Mom, Joey has quiz bowl; that's his thing," pleaded Jackie. "Don't let him compete in FBLA; that's my thing."

"It's not a thing, Jackie," Joey said. "It's a club, and you're on the high school quiz bowl team too."

"That's not the same thing; you're on the A team. You always score the highest points for the team. Quiz bowl is synonymous with Joey Feffer."

"Maybe I want to branch out a bit, you know, like forensics, track, and now FBLA."

"Mom, don't let him do it."

It was *Groundhog Day*. Like with Nick's trumpet, I told Joey he couldn't participate in FBLA and overshadow his sister. The following year, after investigating FBLA further, I was overwhelmed by the exhaustive category list. This club had events for everyone— more than enough for my children to avoid stepping on each other's toes. In addition to Business Math, the club had events from Accounting to 3D Animation, Public Speaking, Website Design, and more. I should have allowed Joey to compete. The following year, Joey and Nick did. All three competed at States and qualified for Nationals in their events. Due to summer camp conflicts, only Nick attended Nationals, held at the Marriott hotel in Atlanta. He competed in Computer Game & Simulation Programming.

We arrived in Atlanta the day before Nick's preliminary presentation and checked in at the hotel. We made our way through the bustling crowd of ardent FBLA participants to rendezvous with the teacher and some of Nick's friends from State College who had arrived earlier for their events. After dinner, we retreated to our room for the night. I woke up at the crack of dawn to iron Nick's suit and chastised him for the stain I found on his white shirt.

"No one's going to see it, Mom," was his justification.

I sighed. We took the elevator to the location of his event, and when we arrived, I gave Nick a nervous good luck hug.

"I got this," he said, smiling as he entered the competition room.

I wondered if he meant that statement for him or me. After what seemed like hours, Nick came out with a Cheshire cat grin plastered on his face.

"It went perfectly, Mom. Finals, here I come," he exclaimed.

"Let's hope you're right," I said as we walked to the elevator. "When will you know?"

"Later on, this evening. The committee will post it online."

After arriving back in our room, I washed his white shirt in the sink, trying to remove the smudge. In case he did indeed make it to finals, I wanted him neat and presentable. After dinner, Nick and his friends left for the Georgia Aquarium while I lounged by the indoor pool, reading a book from my summer list. Upon his return, he said he had a great time, and I would have loved it, and he described every facet of the aquarium.

By ten o'clock that evening, the results had still not been posted. Several hours later, Nick blurted, "Mom, Mom, wake up," as he jumped out of his bed and ran over to mine.

"What?" I asked, startled, assuming the hotel was on fire or some other danger.

"I made finals, Mom," he said, shoving his phone in my face and pointing to his name.

"Oh, honey, I'm so proud of you, congratulations. What time do you present?" I asked, yawning as I got out of bed.

"In about five hours, at eight o'clock."

Reaching for my phone on the nightstand, I said, "Wait, what time is it?"

"It's three."

"3 am? What are you doing up at this hour?"

"Well, I got up to use the bathroom and then decided to check the results, and—"

"You better go back to bed," I said as I hastened back into mine. "You have to be sharp for your presentation."

We struggled to fall asleep. Finally, I got up at six o'clock to iron Nick's shirt, grabbed a quick breakfast, and forged ahead to the event. Spectators were allowed to watch the finals quietly, so I took a seat in the front row. Nick's demonstration of the 3D animation game he created was engaging, his speech was eloquent, and his answers to the judges' questions were cogent and concise. It was a poised side of Nick I didn't often witness. He ended up placing sixth. We flew home satisfied.

NATIONAL ACADEMIC QUIZ TOURNAMENT (QUIZ BOWL)

Mikey made a name for himself as an exemplary student by the time he reached high school age. One afternoon after his AP Art History class, an upperclassman approached him and urged him to join the State High Quiz Bowl Team. Mikey was ecstatic and felt honored. The team hosted a potluck dinner the next day to welcome new students and parents. I prepared our go-to pasta dish with Michael's homemade pesto sauce and was one of the first parents in attendance.

The coaches described quiz bowl much like a Jeopardy competition where schools could enter any number of teams at the tournaments. Each side could have as many as six students, but only four could compete against another group at a time. Clubs often designated their most gifted students as the A team, followed by their B, C, and D teams. Like a swim team medley relay, everyone in the group had a different specialty: literature, science, math, etc.

Everything I understood about quiz bowl made me realize it was the ultimate competition club; it focused on *all* the academic subjects. Aside from getting good grades, it gave students a reason to study. The prestige of the State High team and their dedicated coaches were added benefits.

After a series of tests on various topics, the coach placed Mikey on the B team. He competed in his first tournament at Harvard with Michael and me in attendance. The rounds, particularly the final ones, were as nail-biting as a shoot-out in a tied soccer match.

Gradually, we all became hooked on quiz bowl. After Mikey, Joey was the most dedicated. He attended high school practices with his brother, where older team members welcomed him. Joey was always eager to share with me a question he answered correctly on a subject we had recently studied together. It was Joey's idea to start a middle school quiz bowl team.

I met with the Mount Nittany Middle School principal to discuss forming a team. It was a pleasant conversation, and he shared stories about his experience competing on his high school team. He said that although he liked the idea, "Funds are not available for the project in this upcoming budget. But we could consider it for the following school year."

"Well, can I run a pilot program this year?" I persisted. "I could select a few students along with my kids, and we'll start from there."

His eyes narrowed. "We still don't have the funds."

"I understand," I replied, clarifying my statement, "but since this would be on a small scale, and most of the team members would be my children, I'll be willing to pay. I'll also keep a record of how much everything costs so I can hand in an accurate budget proposal for next year."

"Okay, it could work."

"Can I call our team the Mount Nittany Middle School Quiz Bowl team?"

"Be my guest. That's what it is."

"Fantastic," I said, with a bit more enthusiasm than the situation called for. I was relieved the days of my kids being treated as home-schooled pariahs were behind us.

I let Jackie, Joey, and Nick select dedicated students who would complement our team, ensuring we covered all the subjects. After my children made the initial contact with their friends, I followed up with their parents. We met at my house, where I detailed the goals and the logistics: team uniforms, entry fees, practice schedule, and whether they'd allow their child to travel to Nationals in Chicago if we qualified. In the end, our team consisted of the three younger Feffers and two other children.

I ordered middle school practice questions from the National Academic Quiz Tournaments, and we held weekly practices, mostly in our home. To Joey's chagrin, I made Nick the captain of our team because he was the oldest. Danielle and Mikey also volunteered to read tournament questions whenever possible, which helped defray our entry fee.

After winning tournaments, the other coaches congratulated us and inquired how I prepared my team, particularly for the current events questions. I hesitated as I rubbed my chin, contemplating an answer because I couldn't recall reviewing those questions with them. Joey, squeezing between me and the entourage of coaches, came to my rescue.

"It's because we listen to NPR," he replied.

He was right, of course. National Public Radio always played in the car, and a large part of our day took place there. We never wasted a moment. Our car was our home away from home, where squares and square roots, spelling words, and French verb conjugation were memorized. It was also where we listened to *All Things Considered* and *World Have Your Say*. That's how they, unintentionally, learned about current events.

We made it to Nationals our first year and drove to Chicago

with our five-member team. The Hyatt Regency's atmosphere bristled with excitement as middle school kids and their coaches arrived, ready for the two-day battle. The competition was fierce, and the Mount Nittany team advanced to the tournament's second day. However, we lost in the double-elimination round and took eleventh out of seventy-two teams. We had set a high goal of placing among the top ten teams and narrowly missed it. Thus, my small group was naturally disappointed. I wasn't, as I reminded them that making it to Nationals was an outstanding achievement for their first year. "And," I added, "we won't stop trying to reach our goal. We're coming back next year as a formidable opponent."

Our troupe was happy again.

Upon our return, I handed the principal a budget for our quiz bowl team, along with an article on the reason middle schools should have a quiz bowl team. It stipulated that teaching kids how to compete is an essential skill and quiz bowl accomplishes that while also allowing them to be part of a team. The principal seemed pleased and indicated he would pass it along to the school board. I was to receive a reply in a couple of months. I then placed a notice about our performance at Nationals in our local newspaper. Not only did I want the team recognized for their valiant efforts, but I also hoped such publicity might inspire other students to join.

Towards the end of the summer, I received a notice that the school board approved funding for my middle school quiz bowl team. A few weeks later, at the beginning of the 2012–2013 school year, I scheduled a meeting with the middle school principal. I was speechless to learn he no longer held that position. The plump new acting principal confirmed that a middle school quiz bowl team was an excellent idea *to consider*. I was perplexed by his statement. "No, you don't understand," I said. "The school board has already approved us. They already allocated funding for the team."

"I don't know anything about it, but I'll investigate it for you."

I thanked him as I disguised my annoyance and exited. This emotion transformed into anger when I received a phone call about the cancellation of the middle school quiz bowl program ten minutes later. No explanation was forthcoming. I was flabbergasted and furious. I wanted to slam on the brakes, reverse direction, and race to the administration building to demand answers, but I had something urgent that needed doing, packing. I was leaving for a trip, and I was not yet packed. The middle school quiz bowl program would have to wait.

BREAKING AWAY

DANIELLE: 14–16 (2008–2010)

My relationship with my eldest soured upon her becoming a teenager. The 2007–2008 school year proved the most challenging. Danielle was argumentative, messy, and uncharacteristically lackadaisical in her schoolwork. Unbeknownst to me, she also had a Facebook account that kept her up until the early hours of the morning. When I discovered it, I confiscated her laptop, which led to further arguments. Later that summer, a week before her scheduled departure, Danielle declared she no longer wanted to attend a Texas math camp. She had all the needed recommendations and taken the required math tests. She refused to say any more. Even though the forfeited deposit displeased me, I became weary of our fights and dropped it.

However, in the fall of 2008, Danielle was one of the nation's top scorers on the American Math Contest 12 (AMC). She received a letter from Advantage Testing Foundation inviting her to participate in the first Math Prize for Girls contest. It read:

We are pleased to announce the launch of an extraordinary math contest for female students. The Advantage Testing Foundation will hold its first-ever Math Prize for Girls contest on Saturday, November 14, 2009, at New York University in New York City. Our goal is to inspire young women with exceptional potential to become the mathematical and scientific leaders of tomorrow.

We will award $43,000 in cash prizes, including a top prize of $20,000.

The Math Prize contest on November 14 will be a challenging, two-hour-long exam comprising approximately twenty problems that test mathematical creativity and insight. We will announce the winners that afternoon at an awards ceremony for the contestants and their parents.

I was thrilled, but Danielle—not so much. She mumbled, "Wonderful, another contest."

"You could win this, Sweetie," I said as I gently placed my arms around her neck.

"I don't want to do this, Mom," she said, turning away.

"Darling, I don't see why not. It's an honor for the committee to have selected you. There's a lot to gain and nothing to lose. This money could help with college expenses, which you kids are supposed to contribute to. No pressure, though; just take the test and do your best."

"Okay," she said, walking away with her head down.

During the following months, she never prepared for the test. The day before the competition, she attempted to back out again. "I don't want to go, Mom," she said. "These girls are going to know a lot more than me. I'm not going to win anything. It's going to be a complete waste of time."

"Well, whose fault is that? Imagine if you went to the math camp, or if you had at least studied, you might have had a chance. It's too late now; you're going."

We went, and she was right.

At the posh auditorium, with the comfy seats where the organizers held the award ceremony, the room was crowded with parents. One other Black parent made eye contact with me; we smiled and mouthed, "Good luck." The judges never called Danielle to the stage because she didn't win anything. Regardless, it was one of the best days we spent together. The speakers were captivating and inspiring. They all made a point to highlight that all the girls present for this test were already outstanding mathematicians. Afterward, Danielle, Jackie, and I ate dinner at a New York restaurant. While we awaited our food, Danielle peered at me with the saddest eyes I've ever seen on my teenage daughter.

"I'm sorry I didn't study for this test, Mom," she said. After an interlude, she swallowed and continued. "I could have won. The problems weren't difficult. I'm also sorry I didn't go to the math camp last summer." She paused again as she collected her thoughts.

I glanced at Jackie. She seemed oblivious to what her sister was trying to articulate. Instead, she stared at the window, absorbing the New York scene.

"I don't know what happened to me, Mom," Danielle finally continued. "I was feeling tired of it all, the contests, the pressure, the —the sameness. I don't know if you understand, and I'm not trying to make excuses. It's... it's just how I've been feeling lately. I'm sorry. I could have won today if I'd prepared."

"Of course, I understand," I replied. "I do know what it means to be tired. You've been studying, practicing, and competing since you could barely walk. You paved the way for your siblings to follow. You've accomplished more in fourteen years than most people do in their lifetime. Danielle, you're allowed to be tired occasionally." I reached for her hands. "I could never be disappointed in you."

"We're good, Mom?"

"No, we're better than good," I said and squeezed her hands.

From that moment onwards, our relationship dramatically improved. Danielle became the model child again. She helped me correct her siblings' essays; she prepared dinner; she even kept her room clean.

One evening, during her sophomore year, Danielle joined me in the kitchen as I prepared dinner. "Mom, I'm contemplating going away to study abroad next year," Danielle announced.

"Oh?" I said, surprised, but not really. We were talking about Danielle, after all.

"I need a change, Mom; I'm tired of school here."

I stayed silent. I searched my oldest daughter's face and found that determined five-year-old baby girl telling me she was bored with kindergarten all over again. My eyes glistened with tears as I diced peppers and onions.

Danielle continued, "I've been taking your classes and going to that high school since the dawn of man, Mom. After this year, there's not a class I haven't taken."

"You can choose to graduate early," I suggested, ignoring the hyperbole.

"No," she said as she put her elbows on the black granite countertop and rested her face in her hands, "I want to come back for my senior year, give speeches, go to prom, and do all that senior's stuff before I graduate. For now, I want to go abroad for a school year."

"You're serious? You want to go to another country and live with strangers for a year?"

"It's actually nine months, just for the school year, but yes."

"What about your friends? The swim team? Your family? Won't you miss us?"

"Well, as far as the swim team, I'm planning on joining one in France, and as far as friends are concerned, we both know I don't have any. Well, not close ones anyway. Not anyone that's going to miss me when I'm gone."

"I don't believe that's true, Dani."

"Yes, it's true, Mom. You've put me in all these advanced classes with older kids, so by the time I get to know them and become friends, they graduate. I never knew anyone in those summer camps or college classes. I was always the odd one out."

It felt like an accusation. Was I being blamed for her perceived lack of friends again? At some point, I knew my kids would complain about the things I could have done better or maybe even about their education. That's what kids do. Except I wasn't

137

expecting the criticism this soon. I had to battle with principals, administrators, teachers, and now my children?

"It's a two-way street, though, Mom," Danielle continued as she straightened herself up on the stool. "Besides our family, I won't miss anyone either. Being the stranger in these classes forced me to learn how to fit in and make friends, although not close ones. It's a good skill to have. Once other students learn about my home-schooling history, they always want to hear what it was like. It's an eye-opening conversation starter." She paused as she recollected those moments. "I believe they have this view of homeschoolers being poor white families living in rural America, driving around in RVs."

Well, we got two out of four, I thought: the RV and rural America.

"Sometimes I tell them my parents locked me in the basement to study and practice violin and I was only allowed out on certain holi-days to play games. It's funny to watch their reactions. They don't know whether or not I'm joking."

"It's not funny," I said, shaking my head. "I know some teachers around here who would most certainly believe it."

"Also," Danielle added, "I don't let them know I'm smart; that's a turn-off on trying to make new friends."

I quickly closed the refrigerator door without retrieving anything and said, "It's bad enough that Black people are made to feel inferior, and now you're purposely pretending that you are? Don't fall into that trap, Dan. Don't dumb yourself down to make friends. Maybe they're not the right friends for you if they can't accept you for who you are."

"Ok, Mom," she said hastily. "Anyway, getting back to the main conversation, I believe I'll relate well with my French friends and host family."

I opened the refrigerator again, but this time, I retrieved a jar of minced garlic. "So, you've decided on France?" I asked.

"I'm considering it. I speak French already, but I want to be fluent so that I can speak with your family."

"That would be nice."

"I was reading about this program called School Year Abroad on College Confidential, and it sounds like what I want."

"Okay," I said, taking a hiatus from my slicing and dicing and gave her my full attention, "get me all the information about this program, the cost, the application process, other parents I can speak with, and we'll see. If everything pans out and you've convinced me, the hard part will be convincing your father."

"Thanks, Mom," she said as she rushed up the stairs.

"Don't thank me yet," I muttered as I resumed cooking and began contemplating how I would broach the news to Michael.

Three weeks later, when I did tell Michael, he brought the reclining sofa to an upright position and muted the Steelers game.

"Sending her to Exeter in New Hampshire or Luzerne in the Adirondacks was not far enough for you? Now you want to send my fifteen-year-old across the Atlantic to live with strangers? For a year? Are you insane?"

Insane, crazy... Michael should come up with better adjectives. I joined him on the sofa. "It's *actually* nine months, but yes, I mean no, I'm not insane, and yes, I want to send her to France," I said.

"Carline, she's fifteen," he said, shaking his head.

"This is Danielle we're talking about. She's always been independent. I couldn't do it at her age, and maybe neither could you. But we're not her. She wants to do this, and I believe she can handle it." I remembered her Hersheypark experience.

"The world is not safe. My God," he said, smacking his forehead for dramatic effect. "Aren't you afraid? Aren't you scared of sending our daughter—our firstborn, to a foreign country halfway across the world for a year—nine months? Who knows what may happen to her?"

"Of course, I am," I said softly, mindful not to start an all-out argument. "What kind of parent would I be if I wasn't? But I can't allow my fears or yours to stop her from doing what she wants. It's her life."

"Oh, it's her life, anything goes? We're her parents. We're

supposed to keep our kids safe. Not send them gallivanting all over the world."

"Michael, we're not sending her to a war zone. It's France. It's not even in Paris; it's in a nice, safe, small suburb. Honey," I said, wringing my hands, "I'm not taking this lightly, either. But I saw how excited she was, how she did all the research and got all the materials I requested. We spoke with administrators and other parents, and, well, I figure it's going to be fine."

"I guess if you and Danielle already decided, there's nothing further for us to discuss then, is there?"

"It's a long process. We don't even know if they'll accept her."

"I'm supposed to hope my child *doesn't* get accepted? Besides, when was the last time Danielle applied for something and *didn't* get it?"

I thought for a moment.

"Exactly," Michael answered himself. He then rose from his chair and said, "I don't want to talk about this anymore. Do what you want, but for the record, I'm against it."

"Come on, Michael, don't leave. Let's talk about this like adults." But he didn't reply. Instead, he exited the family room without a second glance back at me. I peeked at the screen as the Steelers fumbled the ball.

School Year Abroad accepted Danielle into their program, and we all, even Michael, were delighted for her. As she packed for France, I reflected on Danielle's transition from a teenage brat to a thoughtful young adult. I thought of the Letter About Literature essay she wrote to the poet Linda Pastan, "To a Daughter Leaving Home," earlier that year. Her transition had been the catalyst for our perfect year. She realized she would soon be on her own, in a new country, for nine months. It was time to grow up.

In September 2010, two months shy of Danielle's sixteenth birthday, she left Boalsburg's safety and security to live in Rennes, France, with a new family. We Skyped with her whenever we could, and life continued as normally as possible. But, even on sunny days, the mood in our home seemed overcast.

MIKEY: 14–17 (2009–2012)

Mikey's eighth-grade goals took an unexpected detour as an indirect result of the catastrophic 2010 Haiti earthquake. I was heartbroken by that event. That day, I forgot to be a teacher, wife, or mother. I was a Haitian citizen, overcome with grief at the destruction of her country and the devastating loss of lives. Hundreds of Haitian doctors and nurses from the diaspora, including my older brother Evans, immediately flew to Haiti. A few months later, I arrived with my other brother, Rony, to visit hospitals and deliver medical supplies. Upon Evans's return, he had a conference call with our family.

"Guys, we have to do something," he told us.

That's when we decided to start our non-governmental organization—not an NGO that would stay forever, but one having a five-year term limit. We called it C-Change for Haiti. To that end, we applied for a 501(c)(3) and decided to build a website. The professional website companies we contacted were too expensive. Mikey was our savior. Instead of studying for Mathcounts or practicing his music, he created a phenomenal website for C-Change.

Begging for money was something none of my brothers and sisters felt comfortable doing; thus, our own money made up the principal part of C-Change's funding. However, the State College Area School District and East Silver Spring Elementary in Maryland, where my cousin taught, did support our cause. The Altoona Hospital supplied medications and gauze. The University of Florida, where Edwidge taught, contributed computers. She subsequently began an online educational program between her students in Florida and students in Haiti. We could have done many things differently with our NGO; in any case, I was proud of how my brothers and sister came together and accomplished our small consortium. Furthermore, I was tremendously appreciative of Mikey. He didn't reach his academic and musical goals that year; instead, he helped when needed without complaining.

The following summer, Mikey enrolled in the Digital Media

Academy for Mobile Device Programming at Swarthmore College. Upon returning, he set to work on creating his own app. It took Mikey the rest of the summer to research and work out the bugs, and by the start of the school year, he had finished it. *Route Maker*[1] sold in the Apple store at $0.99 per download. The school, as well as our local newspapers and a bike enthusiast magazine, featured Mikey and his app.

The Haiti earthquake aside, the singular event that disturbed me most during Mikey's high school years happened 1,000 miles away from us in Stanford, Florida: the tragic killing of Trayvon Martin. Along with many Black mothers, my heart raged when I heard the news. We all saw our sons in Trayvon's face and grieved for him, his family, and other Black and Brown youths that needlessly lost their lives. I hugged my sons tightly that evening and discussed the reality of being a Black male in this country. Living relatively safe in State College suburb and having a white father, I didn't think my kids understood the Black American experience. They never had a note left on their windshield that read, "Go back to Africa," signed by the KKK, as I did when I first began working in Altoona. They were never called niggers, as my siblings and I were when we were children. They were never pushed aside, literally and figuratively, by a teacher when they were eight years old for daring to ask a question like similar white children.

One evening, I came across a program description for the Telluride Association Sophomore Seminars. The summer program:

Offers bright, motivated high school sophomores challenging six-week college-level courses in critical Black and ethnic studies. We work with university faculty to create exciting courses designed to inspire young people to explore the histories, politics, and cultural experiences of people of African descent and a variety of other topics.

And my favorite part:

Because we believe that students should have the opportunity to pursue their ideas, we cover all the program costs, including tuition, books, room and board, field trips, and facilities fees.

The Telluride programs were held at three universities:

Michigan, Cornell, and Indiana. Although Cornell was just a car ride away from us, the topic at the Indiana campus—*Don't Believe the Hype: Debunking myths and stereotypes and digging into reasons why the Black community in America continues to struggle*—was more what I was searching for. We celebrated when Mikey received his acceptance to his first-choice program at the Indiana campus.

Mikey's six weeks absence was bittersweet. I missed seeing his slender fingers glide over the ivory and ebony piano keys and hearing his composition of euphonious melodies. But he needed to be around Black students. I wanted him to understand why I would fear his departure for college in the next two years; why I was less afraid for my daughter living in France for nine months than I was for my Black sons walking in America's streets.

Six weeks later, Mikey returned as an expert in African American studies and pestered me to read some of the books he had acquired.[2] I told my son about the gloominess I endured while reading those books, yet how educated and enlightened they made me.

He said, "I guess the teacher is becoming the student."

Mikey always knew he wanted to study computer science in college, and MIT, Cornell, and Carnegie Mellon were among his top choices. One sunny spring day, we left our house at 5 am for our seven-hour drive to Boston's MIT campus. We decided to split up the driving. Mikey would go first, mostly on Route 80, in Pennsylvania, and I would drive the rest.

Since Mikey was my quiet child and not one to volunteer information about his innermost thoughts, I recommended a psychological questionnaire game online. I thought it would be a fun activity for us to do together on the monotonous Route 80. It was a sentence completion game with suggestions like *I'm happy when* _____. Mikey was driving, so I asked the questions, and we took turns answering them. Some were silly, and we responded in kind, while others were serious. Then, I read: *Dad would be proud of me if* _____.

"I was more like Nick and Joey," Mikey finished. Suddenly things weren't funny anymore.

I stared at him. "You're kidding, right?"

"No. Not really."

"You don't believe Dad's proud of you?"

"I don't think he is, Mom," he said. His jaw tensed.

"Why would you say such a thing? That's not true."

"Nick's good with girls, and for some reason, it makes Dad happy. And they make stuff together in his workshop, and Joey watches sports with him. I don't do any of that stuff. I'm into computers and writing music, two areas he doesn't understand or care about."

"Mikey, that's not fair to your father."

"Mom, we don't have to talk about it. It is what it is, and I'm okay with it now," he said as his lower lip quivered.

"Sweetie, Nick works with Dad because he likes building things. Sometimes, Nick would rather not make them with him because Dad tends to micro-manage it, and Nick hates that. And sometimes, Nick leaves Dad's workshop in a mess, and Dad hates that. Remember the other day when Nick broke one of Dad's tools? Dad was furious. Now, if that had happened to you or me, we'd probably never go back in that workshop, but not your brother. He was there just the other day. Nick knows Dad loves him and that Dad's bark is worse than his bite, and he's right. You and me, we tend to be too sensitive.

"Believe it or not, you're more like your father than any of the others. I understand your father better because of you."

Michael stayed silent, so I continued.

"You see this excursion we're on? I could see you and your father driving for seven hours in a welcome silence. The rest of us, myself included, value articulating. But not you, and not your father. Yes, Dad may not understand every line of code you write, and he may not understand your music, but Dad is proud of everything you have accomplished. He is proud of *all* his children. That's why Dad works as hard as he does, to make sure you guys are well taken care of. He's quiet like you and may not always express his sentiments, but he loves you very much. We correctly named you Michael after your father."

I paused again. Mikey seemed to have nothing to refute, so I resumed my monologue.

"Joey and Jackie watch hockey with Dad because they want to feel close to him. What have you done to bond with your dad? It's a two-way street, honey. Dad doesn't push himself on you guys the way I do, but I know he would love to spend more time with you too."

Mikey remained quiet. I could tell he was reflecting on my words as his expression dulled.

"Okay, Mom," he finally said.

"Okay," I echoed, "enough of this game. Let's listen to some of your new music."

"Even better."

I planned a family getaway to New York for the weekend of February 25, 2012. After visiting my mom and having an early dinner with Rony and his family, we drove to see Audra McDonald in *Porgy and Bess* on Broadway. Although we enjoyed it, the show was not the primary reason for our visit to New York. The main event, scheduled for the following afternoon at Hunter College's Brecher Hall, was for Mikey. It was for his piano audition. We arrived at a crowded Brecher Hall, filled primarily with Asian students and their distressed parents. When the event organizer called Mikey's name, I walked up to the audition room with him as he hurried in alone. There, I suffered with the rest of the nervous parents, transfixed in that space, incapable of moving or even breathing. It was essential to hear everything, from the lively allegro section to the gentle adagio, every note, every accent, and every dynamic. The only thing interrupting my listening was the loud drumming in my chest. I wished I could stifle it as I strained to hear Mikey's audition from behind the doors. I finally let out a deep breath when he played his final note. He had nailed it. Beautifully. Flawlessly.

A week later, we received the results. Mikey was among the finalists, and he would be playing Rachmaninov's *Prelude in C-sharp Minor, Op. 3 No. 2,* at the Weill Recital Hall in Carnegie Hall on Saturday, May 19. The concert happened to fall on his dad's 52nd birthday. Tears welled up in his father's eyes while Mikey serenaded the audience. Afterward, we gathered in an all-night diner on Queens Boulevard eating chocolate cake.

"Mikey," Michael said as he put his arm around his oldest son. "I'm so proud of you." Mikey glanced in my direction, and his warm brown eyes told me everything my heart felt.

NICK: 10–14 (2008–2012)

A laminated, glossy, 3'x 4' periodic table hung on the back wall of our yellow-painted schoolroom. Adorning the poster was a visual representation of each element and its namesake. It also depicted the corresponding symbols and atomic and mass numbers.[3]

I began teaching the kids chemistry when they were around eight to ten years old. When I taught Mikey and Dani chemistry, we drew pictures of the atom to depict isotopes and electron configurations. We also drew the periodic table on pillowcases and t-shirts to help us learn the elements. For Jackie, Joey, and Nick, though, Michael had constructed a tabletop version of Bohr's planetary model, carved from wood. We used a small transparent plastic bowl as the nucleus with marbles representing subatomic particles. Each ring or energy level around the nucleus had the correct number of holes to situate the required electrons. The kids added neutrons, protons, and electrons to the nucleus as we discussed the *s, p,* and *d* orbitals and the spin orientation of the electrons. For such a complex topic, the kids grasped it quickly. Each year, I added more information to their basic chemistry knowledge.

"What about fire, Mom?" Nick said during our discussion on the states of matter. "Fire is not a liquid, gas, or solid. What state of matter is fire?"

I had been a chemistry major at Brooklyn Technical High School and St. John's University, but I don't recall ever contemplating such a question at such a young age. My education was one-sided. The teacher taught, and I learned. My kids' learning was nothing like that. Theirs was interactive. They felt safe and secure in their home, in their pajamas, to ask any questions without fear of ridicule.

In retrospect, I should have anticipated that question from Nick. He was a juvenile pyromaniac. More than once, I had smelled smoke coming from his room. One incident occurred when he was in middle school. I had bought him a glass plasma lamp that generated static electricity. Nick quickly discovered that if you put a wire or paper clip on it, the static became more powerful, and if you did it just so, you could produce an actual arc of electricity. Equipped with this newfound knowledge, he then wrapped an elongated paper clip around the lamp's base to take all the charge out of it and then brought another untwisted clip to the wrapped one. The arc crackled and jumped between the paper clips, and he tried using it to light a candle. It's hard to fathom how Nick didn't electrocute himself or burn down the house in those days.

When the kids were older, we built a fire pit in our backyard. Reminiscent of our camping days, making a fire with Dad and roasting hot dogs or making s'mores soon became one of Nick's favorite activities. For my fire-loving kid, we always began the year with the required fire safety precautions.

Although Nick understood and appreciated chemistry, he preferred biology. Over the next couple of years, the kids dissected everything from the occasional frog we found dead in our vegetable garden to crayfish, worms, cow eyes, owl pellets, and starfish.[4] I taught them about each organism in the mornings before dissecting them in the afternoon.

We occasionally brought our biology lessons to the dinner table, where Michael would take a chicken wing and point out the humerus, radius, and ulna. He would then demonstrate the movement of the analogous parts on the kids' arms. He differentiated the tendons from the ligaments. On our school room sidewalls, I hung colorful laminated posters of the muscular, digestive, and respiratory systems. On the adjacent walls hung smaller posters depicting intracellular structures distinguishing between bacterial, plant, and animal cells. In addition, on the corner desk, in front of the school-room, stood a 3D model of the human heart and a four-foot model human skeleton. My favorite, the one I purchased for one dollar at a local yard sale, was the Invisible Woman's vintage model: a trans-parent model showing all her internal organs, including a pregnant uterus with a fetus.

Nick spent his seventh and eighth-grade years as a fully enrolled student at Mount Nittany Middle School and shuttled to and from the high school for some of his other courses. He continued to excel in academics, music, and sports. Nick received many awards at the eighth-grade award ceremony, including the TechEd award and the John Bolash Triple-A award for Academics, Activities, and Attitude. He made many friends and discovered lots of things in middle school. To my displeasure, the female sex was one of them. Nick had begun his transition to the dreaded teenage years.

JOEY: 10–13 (2009–2012)

While searching the internet for unique and affordable summer programs, I came across a flyer by the American Association for the Advancement of Science inviting high school students to "Represent Your Communities in Mathematical Competitions in Africa and Latin America." That got my attention. I continued reading:

> The program starts with a training camp in Washington, D.C., on August 1–10, 2012. We will be training about twenty students, of whom four will be chosen to attend the Pan-African Mathematical Olympiad in Tunisia in September and another four for the Ibero-American Mathematical Olympiad in Bolivia.

The criteria were:

Applicants must still be in high school, under 18 years of age... should have demonstrated an interest in mathematics through advanced coursework or other activities. Experience in mathematical competitions, including Olympiad-style, free-response questions, is highly desirable.

And:

The program is fully funded by the Alfred P. Sloan Foundation. All tuition, travel, materials, and fees will be covered for all participants.

I couldn't wait to share the news with Joey. It occurred to me that although Joey was taking high school courses, he was not *technically* a high school student. He was only twelve years old. I wondered how strict they would be about age. There was no use in rousing Joey's hope if his age would disqualify him. I called and discussed the situation with one of the advisors.

"Although Joey is in sixth grade, he loves math and has taken AP Statistics and AP Calculus. He also qualified for the American Invitational Mathematics Examination (AIME) and was first in Pennsylvania on the AMC8 this year," I boasted.

"Oh, wonderful," the soothing voice on the other end said.

He remained silent after that as if waiting to hear more, so I continued to flood the line with Joey's accolades. "Joey also made it to the invitational round in the Linguistics Olympiad contest. He told me he liked the math puzzles on these tests." More silence. I was beginning to question if the advisor was still there. "By the way," I continued. "Joey is quite mature for his age. If the judges selected him to go to Tunisia for the week-long competition, he'd be fine. He has no separation issues. He spent three weeks at Cornell last summer attending Awesome Math." I was about finished with Joey's most relevant math accomplishments and starting to panic. Should I go to his physics awards? Chess maybe?

Before I could decide, the calm voice spoke, "He sounds like an amazing young man, quite the type of student we want in our program. Please have him apply."

Since the man sounded impressed with Joey, I proceeded to tell him about Jackie. "He has a twin sister," I blurted. "She's quite amazing in her own right. She's taking Advanced Algebra II and—"

"Yes, they can both apply," he replied quickly, abandoning that soft tone, and effectively cutting me off before I delved into Jackie's achievements. "We will await their applications."

I thanked the man, hung up the phone, and left the house. I thought about adding Nick to this math training camp, but he had already accepted an offer to attend the Center for Talented Youth biotechnology summer course in Bethlehem, Pennsylvania. I rushed to pick up the kids from their class to tell them the exciting news. The twins were thrilled, albeit for different reasons. Jackie envisioned a resort with an occasional math class, while Joey envisioned training and participating in a national math competition. Competing in USAMO—the United States of America Mathematical Olympiad—was a dream of his and being selected to compete in Tunisia would be a step toward that goal. Nick seemed relieved he was already committed to a science camp. He liked math but was never enthusiastic about going to a math camp.

Within a week of sending off their applications, they accepted Jackie and Joey into the program. When the day arrived for me to take them to D.C., I watched as they gathered last-minute items. Joey fetched extra batteries for his calculator while Jackie ran for another pair of sunglasses.

The next day, Jackie and Joey called within minutes of each other.

"I can't believe it, Mom," Jackie said. "All we do here is math. We're not even allowed to go to the pool."

"That's awful," I said, grinning.

"I can't believe it, Mom," said Joey. "All we do here is math. I'm learning a lot. The other kids are smart, but I think that I have a good chance of making the top four, Mom."

"That's wonderful," I said.

Was it? Despite my assurances to the advisor on the phone weeks earlier, I wasn't sure if I could send my twelve-year-old off to

Tunisia, halfway around the world, on his own. Danielle had only recently returned from France. I was not ready to allow an even younger child to travel abroad alone again. But, if he did qualify, I knew I couldn't deny him the opportunity. Two weeks later, Joey made the U.S. team and received the invitation to compete in Tunisia in the fall. Given that Joey was several years younger than his teammates, I was permitted to accompany the group, provided I covered my expenses.

Our trip to Tunisia took place in the fall of 2012, shortly after the wave of initial revolutions and protests of the Arab Spring began to fade. Upon arriving in Tunisia, tension still hung in the air. Nonetheless, it was one of the best trips of my life. While Joey stayed at the host university with the U.S. team and fellow competitors, I booked myself into a nearby hotel. My suite was not in the central part of the luxury hotel but across from it. I liked it better; it felt cozy. I quickly unpacked and went for a walk along the sunny promenade. The scenery reminded me of the *Bellagio Promenade* painting by Howard Behrens, with colorful flowers and an expansive view of the crystal blue Mediterranean.

The hospitable Tunisians spoke English, French, and Arabic. I mainly spoke French with them. The best part of the trip was meeting the many exceptionally talented and beautiful students from South Africa, Tanzania, Burkina Faso, Ivory Coast, Egypt, Gambia, Nigeria, and Tunisia. I was particularly impressed with the female competitors and hearing about the hardships they had to endure just to participate in the event. The only thing that could have made the trip more enjoyable would be if the rest of the family could have joined us. And if Joey and I didn't argue.

After breakfast on my first morning in Tunisia, I caught the train to the university to spend time with my son. He was housed and fed in a dorm-like setting with the other participants. I accompanied them on various field trips, including the Carthage Museum, the Medina, and the Central Square. Joey spent most of the time getting to know the other students. At first, I was glad because that was the program's primary purpose—getting kids from different parts of the world to mingle and share their passion for math. Although later, I noticed that whenever Joey saw me coming, his chin raised, his lips tightened, and his brows furrowed. I didn't know how to proceed. I considered that maybe I made him uncomfortable since I was the only parent on the trip. Eventually, I stopped approaching him and spent most of my time with the director and the other students. I overheard one of the students tell Joey what a wonderful mom he had. He didn't respond.

The nine-hour test, given over two days, had four-and-a-half hours for three questions per day. On the first day, I arrived early and read comfortably in a nondescript beige lobby while Joey took the exam. When he walked out of the examination room, he waved when he saw me, leading me to believe Joey was happy to see me or did well in the first part. Either way, I was glad to speak with him briefly before he disappeared with his friends.

The director invited me to join him and his colleagues for dinner at a fashionable Tunisian restaurant that evening. As much as I loved the Ottoman architecture and the place's sublime scenery, along with my spiced couscous and thick lamb chops, it was the dinner guests who made the event memorable. One woman described her unique career traveling to parts of the third world, documenting indigenous people's births and deaths.

"Can you imagine," she said, "that there are people alive today with no written documentation of their existence in the world?"

The impact of that reality disturbed me. "How awful," I said. "How would you begin sorting the family's genealogy with no records of their existence?"

"We're making tremendous progress," she said.

"Well, if you're ever in dire straits for an assistant, I would love to apply for the job," I said, only half-joking.

The next day, after the kids finished the second part of the exam, I restlessly awaited Joey's arrival. When he saw me this time, he did not wave. Instead, he gave me one of his angry expressions. He briefly acknowledged my presence and hurried to his room. I felt humiliated. The other students came over and conversed with me. I hugged them and promised we would exchange email addresses and additional information before departing. After they left, I continued my surveillance for Joey for over three hours. Some of his friends told him I was still there, waiting in the lobby; all the same, it didn't seem to deter him. I hoped Joey would eventually come and talk to me, but he never did. I finally stormed back to my hotel.

The award ceremony was to be held that evening at a downtown location unfamiliar to me, so I decided to leave early for my destination. As I dressed, I felt the unsettling sting of humiliation from Joey's behavior. Why should I tolerate that kind of treatment from a twelve-year-old? What message would I be sending him? The longer I thought about it, the more embittered I became. So, I undressed, put on my pajamas, and switched off the lights.

I had several dreams contributing to a restless night. *Joey won a gold medal, and he was ecstatic. While going up to receive his prize, he gazed out into the crowd and couldn't find me. His joy melted into one of confusion, then sadness. In the end, Joey crouched in a corner, crying, as the other medalists took pictures.* I woke up in a cold sweat around midnight. Removing my pajama top, I patted myself dry and drifted back to sleep around 1 am.

I dreamt again. *Everyone medaled, except Joey. He sunk in his seat, stone-faced, holding back tears. He turned around in search of me. He needed me; I wasn't there.* I woke up at 3 am and realized I'd made a mistake. I should have gone to the ceremony. I failed to remember one of the most basic premises I had learned about raising children: They say and do dumb things they later regret; as a parent, I should never stoop to their level. When kids push their parents away, parents should hold them closer. I was ashamed I had allowed my emotional wound to fester, poisoning my relationship with my youngest son. I should have gone. I also missed the opportunity to say goodbye to the other students. With a headache and tensed muscles, I don't know how I finally dozed off again.

We were to leave later that day. I wanted to check out of the hotel early and go to the bazaar for last-minute souvenirs for my family before meeting with the others at the airport. I took out my ancient laptop and powered it on. As it took its time to rev up, I gazed out of my window at the stunningly clear blue Mediterranean Sea and said my farewell. Returning to my computer, I planned on sending Michael a quick email about our expected departure and arrival times when, instead, I saw he had sent me several urgent messages last night:

Are you OK? How's Joey? This Benghazi thing is scaring us.

Three minutes later:

Where are you? How are you? How's Joey? Please let us know.

The third:

We just heard that a school burned down in Tunisia over the video. I don't believe it's Joey's school, but we're still very anxious. Please respond.

What Benghazi thing? I thought Benghazi was in Libya. What video? What school? I was frantic with worry. I turned on the television and caught up on the news.

I sent Michael a quick email telling him I was okay and heading out to meet Joey. Forget the bazaar. I checked out of the hotel and took a cab to Joey's dorm. What I missed about yesterday's event on the news, the cab driver filled me in. He specified that people were angry over an anti-Islamic video and were protesting and torched a nearby school. When I arrived at Joey's dorm, concern triumphed over anger as I ran to him and hugged him. His tight grasp around my waist told me how much he missed me too. We remained silent as I helped him pack, and we boarded the bus to the airport. Once on the road, we took pictures of the team, sent them to the families, letting them know the kids were safe and began our long journey home.

On the plane home and during the layover in France, Joey didn't tell me what happened at the awards ceremony, and I didn't ask.

Finally, when we were alone in the car driving home, he asked, "Where were you yesterday, Mom?"

"Yesterday?" I asked, feigning forgetfulness. "Oh, yesterday, I was at my hotel."

"Why didn't you come to the award ceremony?" he said.

"I didn't believe you wanted me there," I said.

"Why would you say that?"

"Oh, I don't know. Maybe because you didn't acknowledge me the entire time."

"We had to mingle with the other kids."

I stopped at a red light and turned to him. "Don't insult me, Joey. We both know you were ignoring me."

"I'm sorry it seemed that way."

It's worth noting here that Joey's apologies, or non-apologies, are legendary in our home. We can now joke about it and make up examples of Joey's non-apologies. But at the time, they were very upsetting. Joey was loath to admit his mistakes, and thus apologizing presented itself as a bitter pill to swallow. In the rare moments he'd make amends, he gave non-apologies like, "I'm sorry you were annoyed," or "I'm sorry you didn't understand my joke," in effect, putting the problem on the other person, and never him. Regardless, this time I accepted Joey's non-apology.

"Well, how long are you going to keep me in suspense? I'm dying to find out what happened at the award ceremony."

"Oh, my God, Mom, it was scary," he said. "They called all the winners to the stage and handed them their medals. There were none from our team, the U.S. team. We stared at each other, terrified. 'There must be some mistake,' we whispered to each other. Afterward, our coach pulled us aside and told us we would be getting plaques sent to us instead of medals. He then gave us our scores and correlated them to the medal category we would have received. The captain of our team qualified for a gold medal. We all knew he would. That other guy from Stuyvesant got a silver. I thought we were pretty close in our math abilities, and we would probably win the same medal. But the second day's exam destroyed me. It wasn't hard. I approached the problem wrong and made it much harder than necessary. After that test, I wasn't sure what would happen. I didn't want to come all this way and leave empty-handed. And," he acknowledged, "I didn't. I got a bronze medal."

"Oh, that's fantastic, sweetheart."

"I was ecstatic after that. I searched for you, hoping you were just late or something... anyway, the kids were asking for you, Mom. They liked you. They gave me their email information to give you."

"Oh, thank you."

I drove home as my medal-winner explained the problems on the test and how he solved them. I was so happy for him.

JACKIE: 9–13 (2008–2012)

When I found out that Senator Barack Obama would be speaking at the Old Main lawn on Penn State's University Park campus in a few days, I decided our civics class that year would be on the 2008 presidential campaign. Since I was a Democrat and Michael, a Republican, the kids would see opposing views and form their own opinions. I proposed we listen to the candidates and then choose for whom we would volunteer. They all chose Barack Obama. I did, too, especially after reading *Dreams from My Father*.

On March 8, 2008, I packed the kids in the minivan and headed over to the campus to hear Senator Obama's speech. Unfortunately, 20,000 other people had the same idea, and we were not able to enter. We barely caught a glimpse of him as he was whisked into the yard like a tropical gale. We returned home, bitterly disappointed. The following week, I found out Senator Obama would hold a town hall meeting at Lycoming College in Williamsport, Pennsylvania, in April. Since it would be in the afternoon, and my older kids would be in a class, I decided to take my three little ones.

This time, we arrived two hours early and were among the first to launch into the auditorium when the doors opened. At the end of the senator's speech, he roamed briefly around the room shaking hands. Mr. Obama greeted Joey with a "What's up, little man?" as they shook hands. That made Joey's day. He became more determined than ever to volunteer with the Obama campaign.

The next day, I marched over to the Centre County Democratic headquarters, situated across Schlow Public Library, and signed us up to volunteer. In the ensuing weeks, we learned more about

Obama's positions, made campaign buttons, and helped make phone calls to registered voters. Although they gave us a basic script to read, we occasionally improvised when asked other questions. I remember watching with amusement when Jackie tried elucidating Obama's healthcare policy to a would-be voter.

Overall, it was an incredible learning experience. It wasn't long before my kids were a favorite among the staff. The week of the election, we did some canvassing in various neighborhoods and talked to voters. When we arrived back at the office, we found three small brown paper bags filled with assorted candies atop our desks. Written on each bag was the name of one of my kids: Jackie, Joey, and Nick. On November 4, 2008, I took them along with me when I voted, and we stayed up watching the election results. It was a historic night.

Two years later, Jackie came home from her middle school class, saying, "I've decided to run for Student Council."

"Super," I said. "What do you have to do? Posters? Speeches?"

"No, Mom, nothing like that. All we do is submit a paragraph describing how we would improve the school for our fellow students. Our names go on the back of the paper to keep them anonymous. The teacher will post them up in front of the classroom, and then the students will vote for their favorite paragraph."

"That's a pretty good idea," I said. "This way, it's not a popularity contest, only a vote on real issues that can help the school."

"And also, since it's anonymous, no one will know if you lose."

Hmm, I didn't like where Jackie was going with that lack of confidence.

The day before the scheduled voting, Jackie came storming into my office. "You were wrong, Mom," she said, dropping her backpack onto the floor and crossing her arms.

"What did I do now?" I asked.

"Voting on real issues in middle school is not realistic." After noticing my confusion, she continued, "Someone's paragraph said they'd end homework on Fridays. They can't do that, Mom. They know it. And I'm afraid some of the other students may believe it and vote for them."

"Oh, honey, I don't think so," I said.

"I do, Mom," she said, throwing herself down on the leather armchair across from me. "It's like what you said about Michele Bachmann, remember? She said if she's elected, she'll lower gas prices below $2.00 a gallon. She can't do that, and she knows it, and you said that uninformed voters might believe her."

"Yes, I know I said that," I said, pleased at how she successfully used my words against me. "Sixth graders will see right through the no-homework-Friday ruse. They won't fall for that. They're smarter than you give them credit for. Anyway, worry about your paragraph. Keep it simple, reasonable, and honest. That's how you'll win."

"I hope you're right, Mom."

I was. Jackie won. And we celebrated. Having been bitten by the political bug, she ran for Student Senate Class President in ninth grade and lost by a narrow margin. She was devastated.

"Well, you win some and lose some," I said. But Jackie was inconsolable, feeling the hurt and shame that accompanied failure. This defeat seemed to extinguish her political aspirations until she joined the forensics team.

SUMMER FUN

There are only two lasting bequests we can hope to give our children. One of these is roots; the other, wings.

— CECILIA LASBURY

Unlike most parents, summers were when my children were *not* around me. Summers were *mommy's* time. It was my time for gardening, reading, planning for the next school year, visiting family, or relaxing on the patio.

For my kids, it was camp time. Some were the old-fashioned, squatting-around-a-campfire type I always wished I could have attended when I was young, but most were the modern, specialized educational camps. These programs required them to be away from me, to leave the safety and security of their home to explore the world, learn things from different teachers, meet new kids, and come back and share their experiences.

The downside was that I was the one that drove them to their camps. Even after moving to State College in 2004, the kids still attended some camps and activities in the Altoona vicinity.[1] One mid-morning, after dropping the children off at camp, I succumbed to highway hypnosis and dozed off for a fraction of a second. I awoke just in time to avoid ramming into a tractor-trailer. I slammed on the brakes, sending my white minivan into a tailspin. I swerved and flipped, striking the metal median divider, just barely avoiding crashing onto the oncoming Interstate 99 traffic. Papers flew all over the highway like large white butterflies. The car was totaled, and I was ambulanced to Altoona Hospital. I miraculously managed to leave the hospital with only minor bruises and pain. I was thankful no one died on my account. But most of all, I was grateful none of my children were in the car that day. After that episode, I decided to reduce any long-distance drives, pullover, or spend the night at a hotel if I ever felt too tired to continue.

Sometimes I'd coordinate a mini vacation with a camp. Harvard Technique Swim Camp offered one such opportunity. It was the first camp that admitted all my kids, even my then-six-year-old twins. It was a week-long camp in which they swam from 9 am to 3 pm every day, so we had no option but to lodge in a Boston hotel. After we dropped off the kids at Blodgett Pool, Michael and I found ourselves strolling around Harvard Square. Despite the cacophony of honking cars, groaning buses, and wailing ambulances, we laughed, ate ice cream sundaes, and held hands like honeymooners as the sounds around us became white noise. It was one of the rare occasions we were without our children, and we made the most of it. Spending mindless time chatting with my husband provided a welcome change. When the kids rejoined us in the afternoon, we'd head out to the MIT Museum or the Harvard Museum of Natural History or the movies in Kendall Square before grabbing food. We each fell in love with Boston, although for different reasons.

One summer, I learned about a wilderness camp in Vermont, and I immediately registered Nick and Mikey for it. Although Mikey was not like my hyper-energy, tree-climbing, outdoor-loving middle child, I wanted him to accompany his brother because Nick was too young to be so far away from home by himself. They also seemed to be getting closer due to their experience in the Science Olympiad club together, and I wanted to continue fostering that relationship. Mikey thought the camp was okay, but Nick loved it and conveyed this love of the wilderness in his 2010 Letter About Literature to the children's book author Jean Craighead George for *My Side of the Mountain.*

By the time the kids began high school, our camp selections had become more deliberate and sophisticated. I created a spreadsheet to organize potential summer programs by grade level. Some programs were available for all high school students. Whereas others, like the Telluride Association Sophomore Seminars (TASS) and the Telluride Association Summer Program (TASP), were only for sophomores and juniors, respectively.

Next, I noted location, duration, dates, and cost. These headings were essential and helped us make tentative plans for the summer months. For location, I sought camps in the northeast because driving would cost less than flying. Also, since we had relatives there, my children would stay with family for programs that didn't provide housing. Camps in Florida met the requirements since my sister and parents lived there. I recorded each activity's duration and dates, marking the start and end dates on the calendar to avoid conflicts.

Finally, my attention turned to the most crucial issue—the cost. Sending five kids to summer camps took a toll on our budget, and I began saving months in advance. The price of summer programs skyrocketed astonishingly over the years, even for toddlers and elementary schoolers. The more prestigious programs tended to be free and more competitive, a few with acceptance rates lower than some top colleges. We took the application process seriously, started early, and applied to as many as possible. We also took advantage of early application and family discounts.

Each November, we listed which programs we were applying to for the coming summer, and the kids began writing their first essay drafts. In January, after the teachers and counselors were less overwhelmed by writing college recommendations for their graduating seniors, my children would ask them to write theirs for camps. The applications were usually due in late January and early February. By March or April, we received our responses. The summer camp application process provided the organizational groundwork and discipline integral to the college application process years later.

In addition to the TASS and the TASP, some of my other favorite educational programs were the Johns Hopkins Center for Talented Youth; Research Science Institute; West Point Summer Leadership Experience; Minority Introduction to Engineering and Science at MIT; MIT Online Science, Technology, and Engineering Community; the National Youth Science Foundation; and ACE Quiz Bowl camp. Some of the adventurous and picturesque programs were Summer School Year Abroad in Spain, where Nick spent five weeks, and Jackie's scuba diving camp in Saint Martin with Broadreach. CTY's *Imagine* magazine, May/June 2016 issue, published Jackie's essay about her memorable experience.

My sister once told me her kids' summers involved swimming and relaxing on the Florida beaches. She commented that the school year was stressful enough, and she wanted their summer to be a time to unwind. How could two sisters be so different? If my kids were at the beach, they would learn about marine biology, the disappearing coral reefs, the ebb and flow of tides, or how to scuba dive. They would have to learn... something.

When we were younger, my older sisters, Edwidge by two years and Edith by six, always had more friends than I did. I looked up to them, but they sometimes regarded me as their pesky, tag-along little sister. When it became apparent that they didn't want me around, books became my best friends. All sorts of books. Pre-computer era, I had to take the bus to the Jamaica library in Queens, where I would sit for hours reading books like *Seizing Our Bodies: The Politics of Women's Health*, edited by Claudia Dreifus, which spurred my interest in gynecology, or *The Autobiography of Malcolm X* by Alex Haley and Malcolm X. I loved learning new things. I believed it should be something people wanted to do, not something you required an escape from. Learning should come as naturally as breathing.

Even so, our conversation did strike a nerve. I wondered if my sister was right. Did my kids need a break from all the AP classes and essay contests? Was I stressing them out the way I tend to, at times, stress myself? I picked up the kids' summer calendar that I had just finished color coding with their summer activities. Five bright colors were drawn across the pages, each illustrating one of the five children. I felt dizzy viewing it, and rightly so because I would be the one taking them to and from each place. Danielle joined me in the kitchen, interrupting my thoughts.

"What are you doing, Mom?"

"Just making the final touches to the summer schedule. Are you hungry?"

"No," she replied. "Just want something to munch on before life-guarding at Elks."

"I forgot you were working today. Hey, are you happy with your camp choices this summer?"

"Like always," she said, flashing her white teeth. "But I have to admit, I'm more excited about France."

She looked guilty as she closed the refrigerator door empty-handed. Her eyes landed on the fruit bowl on the kitchen counter. She grabbed an apple and joined me at the table.

"Me too," I said. "I've been reflecting on your upcoming adventure." I still couldn't believe Danielle was going to spend her junior year of high school abroad. "But we have to weather the summer."

"Good one, Mom," she said and took a bite of the apple.

"With your job and all, I've kept it light for you. This way, you'll be able to spend more of the summer at home. With us."

"Us, Mom? Don't you mean you?" she said.

"No, I mean us, smart aleck. Given you're leaving so soon, I kept it light for everyone. See?" I held up the papers. "There aren't as many colors crisscrossing the calendar this year."

"If you say so," she said.

"No, I mean it. I'm in charge of the summer swim league this year; I can't be traipsing all over the country taking you guys to summer camps."

"Aha. It's about you then, not me."

"Okay," I said, "it's about both of us." I motioned to the calendar again. "See this part, right here? Your siblings' names, highlighted in orange? It corresponds to the swim team. This green over here is you. You're the only one going out of state this summer." I paused as I debated how to articulate what had been weighing on my mind like an anvil. "Listen—in wanting to expose all of you kids to opportunities I never had, I might have... well, I might have overdone it a bit."

"No," she said with a surprised tone.

"Seriously, Dani, some people would analyze your school workload and summer and work schedules and assume I'm putting too much pressure on you guys. Remember when I used to take your math books to the summer swim meets, and we would do problems lying on the grass between the events? Parents looked at me strangely. Was that a bit much? Could I be overdoing things? Be honest. Would you rather have more time to relax during the summers, going to the beach, smelling the salt-filled air, and just having fun?"

She calculated this for a moment. "All these summer clichés sound nice, and at first, I would say yes, I want that," she said. "It would probably be nice for a few days, but after that, I'd get bored. I have to do things. I love learning. And Mom, it's not like we don't go water skiing with Dad or visit relatives. We do fun things, but we also like to have a productive summer. So, I would just ignore those people who might be judging you. They don't know us. You're the only one who can determine how much pressure to put on us, and I'm convinced you put the right amount."

Danielle rose, stood behind my chair, bent down, and kissed my cheek. Then she put her strong arms around my shoulders and softly said, "Keep doing *exactly* what you're doing, Mom. You know what they say, coal under pressure makes diamonds."

As much pressure as I might have put on my kids, I recognized I put twice that amount on myself to be the perfect mom, teacher, and wife. I appreciated what Danielle said and took solace in her words. I also acknowledged that parenting didn't come with an algorithm or a training manual. I was doing my best; that was all I could do. It was a relief that my fifteen-year-old daughter thought so as well. I only hoped that when she revisits this conversation in ten years, she still agrees with her younger self: that I set her up for success in life and didn't ruin her childhood in the process.

I rose from my chair and hugged her, probably longer than necessary, as if she was a lifeline I couldn't let go of. I stood there, swaddled in her strong arms. Danielle was more precious to me than any diamond. I wanted to beg her to stay and not go to France. But if I did, I would be undermining all I aimed to do with the summer programs and raising an independent child; she needed to spread her wings and explore the world. For now, I was willing to suffer in silence.

BRINGING HOME THE BACON
(2009–2012)

The 2009–2010 school year was the first time I noticed the writing on the wall: my kids no longer needed me. I was still their taxi driver, picking them up from their classes, taking them to their various music lessons, or taking them to the middle school for Mathcounts or Science Olympiad practices. I still taught them some subjects, including the state's mandated ones at home, and we took field trips, but even those were decreasing. Being replaced hurts. But I remained optimistic when I realized that maybe, just maybe, the time to go back to work had come.

I kept up with medical journals and the Continuing Medical Education program to retain my Obstetrics and Gynecology Board Certification. I also researched with Michael some of the innovative Ob/Gyn surgeries he observed in the operating room. Still, I needed to do procedures to remain proficient. Later that year, I began volunteering a couple of days a week at our local free clinic, Centre Volunteers in Medicine. The following summer, I volunteered to manage our community summer swim league. I loved the sense of control it gave me. It was not the same as being in charge of an operating room, though it did stir nostalgia. I was ready to close the "stay-at-home-mom" chapter of my life.

With Danielle attending school in France for the 2010–2011 school year and the entire family missing her, I decided not to make any more radical changes to our schedule. I still had some free time, so I began working out at the State College YMCA, taking occasional step aerobics and Zumba classes. I even enrolled in an online MBA course because I valued managing our finances and taxes, and I wanted to leave my options open for the future.

When Danielle was back on U.S. soil, I decided it was time to fill them in on my idea. "Hey guys," I said one morning while the kids were grabbing cereal and oatmeal boxes from the cupboard. "Since you're doing quite well managing your schoolwork, I've been considering going back to work this year. Well, at least applying. I've been revamping my resume and pursuing potential job opportunities." After they all stopped what they were doing and locked their five pairs of shocked eyes on me, I added, "Come on, guys, you all knew this day would come." I proceeded to tell them about my plans.

"Oh good, we'll have more money to pay for college," Danielle said, laughing. Aware that it fell flat, she added, "Just kidding, Mom. It's a splendid idea for you to go back to work."

My decision didn't affect Danielle one way or another. She was entering her senior year and was focused on college applications, her research work at the university, and her part-time job teaching toddlers how to swim.

"Yeah, Mom, I agree with Dani," said Mikey. "I'd like that for you."

Mikey, too, wouldn't be much affected by the change. I was eager to hear from the Munchkins. "You say that now," I said. "But no longer will dinner be waiting for you when you return home. And, I might be gone the entire weekend when I'm on call."

"Do you have any prospects, Mom?" Danielle asked.

"Well, I recently saw an Ob/Gyn position in St. Mary's and another one in Altoona."

"That sounds wonderful, Mom," Jackie said, with a smile, glancing at Nick. They were trying hard to contain their excite-

ment. Those two were my social butterflies. The more they social-
ized with their middle school friends, the more they were ready to
be done with homeschooling, Jackie especially. The isolation that
came with home education and the struggle she had keeping up
with her siblings was like adding bricks in her backpack—they
weighed her down. Given a choice, I expected she would prefer
spending more time with her middle school friends, embroiled in
middle school drama. I worried about peer pressure, bullying, and
other downsides that come with school social scenes. Balancing the
desire for them to have more friends with the desire to keep them
safe would be difficult.

"I don't like the idea, Mom," said Joey, resting the gallon of milk
on the counter. "I like coming home to hot dinners, telling you
about my day, and doing work together."

I recoiled a bit when Joey said that, but no one seemed to notice.
Those words affected me because my younger self wished I could
have told them to my mom. My siblings and I always had hot
dinners because my grandmother lived with us and helped raise us.
But I wanted my mom's dinners. I wanted to spend time cooking
with her and telling her about my day. She was mostly home on
weekends. And between market day, laundry day, cleaning the
house day, church day, and raising six kids, the weekends were a
blur, and the closeness I sought with my mom never materialized
until I was married and had children of my own. Things were
different for my kids. I was home during their formative years. And
if I did go back to work, I'd make sure to plan time for them.

"Oh, stop being selfish, Joey," Jackie said as she chewed on her
Frosted Flakes, probably fretting her twin would ruin everything.

"Well, I'm sorry if I like having my mom home," Joey said.
"Besides, Mom, Mathcounts and Science Olympiad are the only
things I do at the middle school. There's nothing left there for me.
All of my classes are with you and at the high school."

He was right, of course. He was far beyond a middle school
curriculum.

"Mom," Mikey said. "What if Joey and I remained dual enrolled when you go back to work? We could keep taking some classes at home, and we can go over them together, with you, on the weekends. As for Joey's violin lessons, I can take him. I should be driving by then."

"I like that, Mikey," said Joey.

"Are... are you all okay with my returning to work?" I asked.

"Yes, Mom, it's *almost* unanimous," Danielle said, glaring at Joey. "It's your time now; you should go for it."

"You're just worried about your college money," muttered Joey.

"Well, you should be too, Joey," said Danielle. "College is expensive. By the way, Mom, I left my college application essays on your desk. Give me your opinion."

That 2011–2012 school year, I implemented my plan to return to work. Danielle enrolled fully at the high school for her graduating year; Jackie and Nick followed suit at the middle school; Mikey and Joey remained dual enrolled. I continued taking the kids to their music lessons and sports practices, ensuring they were on top of their various school assignments, summer camp applications, and competitive essays. I continued working with Joey and Mikey on evenings and weekends. I continued volunteering at CVIM and working on my online MBA course. With Joey's persistence, I also started a pilot Mount Nittany Middle School Quiz Bowl team. Above all, I started applying for jobs in my field. I soon found out that Joey wasn't the only one who had a problem with my returning to work.

I was in a buoyant mood after returning from my job interview in Altoona. "I like the practice," I told my husband that evening while getting ready for bed. "And the two other male doctors were nice enough," I said as I stripped out of my navy blue business suit, trying to remember the last time I wore one. "They want to take me to dinner tomorrow to meet the rest of the team. They want to meet you also."

"I can't make it. I'm on call tomorrow," he said, from the bedroom closet.

"Can't you try to change it?"

"Who'll be home with the kids?" he asked, entering the bedroom in his white underwear and t-shirt.

"They're old enough to take care of themselves for one evening. Are you angry about something?"

"What happens when you're on call, and I'm on call, and the kids have a soccer game or a swim meet, and we have to pick them up and—"

"What are you trying to say, Michael?" I asked.

"I don't believe this is the right time for you to go back to work," he said as he pulled down the comforter and sat on the bed. "The children still need you."

"Are you kidding me? You're telling me this now?" Sensing my blood pressure rising, I too, sat on the bed. "I've been sending out resumes, going to interviews. We talked about this, and we both agreed this was the perfect time."

"No, you talked, and I listened, but I never agreed."

"Then you should have spoken up."

"Okay, maybe I wasn't thrilled with the idea of you going back to work," Michael said, walking over to my side of the bed. "But I was hoping it would at least be here, not far away. I don't want our lives to be hectic again, like before you quit your job. I guess I got comfortable with you being home, taking care of the kids. You did such a wonderful job and had everything under control. I got spoiled."

I remained silent as I reflected on his words. Realizing he might have found a chink in my armor, Michael sat next to me and continued. "But I still believe we would both be affected. Imagine trying to change our call schedules, so we're not both working for one of their concert performances, or trying to request the same vacations, or simply rushing to pick up the kids. Then try throwing in illnesses and doctor's appointments. And what about the multitude of competitions you've entered them in? Are you ready to end that? Even the Middle School Quiz Bowl team you recently started?" Michael pulled out all the stops. He had seen my vulnerability, and I stood wounded. "I want you to go back to work, but around here, not an hour away."

"I would like that too, but there's nothing available around here. I've been searching."

"We'll do it together. I'll help you. I promise," Michael said as he put his arms around me.

"Okay," I said, almost in a whisper.

I kept the dinner engagement and confessed I was having second thoughts about the job offer. The doctor told me to give him a call when I was ready to consider it again. A month later, they hired someone else.

PART IV

FALLING

No one is actually dead until the ripples they cause in the world die away.

— TERRY PRATCHET

THE DARKNESS (2012–2013)

Only when it is dark enough can you see the stars.

— MARTIN LUTHER KING, JR

"Wake up, Darling," my husband said softly, nudging me. "Time to go home. How are you feeling?"

"Ok," I replied, still groggy. I knew the more extended chemo treatment was to come later at home, and this was only the first of twelve appointments. Still, I was glad to be going home. I couldn't believe I had slept for three hours in the recliner.

During my weeks off from chemo, I took care of everything before my week of malaise and vomiting arrived. I prepared meals for the kids, cleaned the house, did the laundry, read my AP Human Geography textbook to develop lesson plans for Joey and Mikey, and read Nick's and Jackie's school essays. I did these things to reclaim my mother-teacher role and convince myself I would not let this cancer take over my life. Despite that, with each passing week, the disease was winning. My activities slowly decreased as I grew weaker and more nauseated until I could barely go over the children's lessons.

I developed peripheral neuropathy, painful sensations of multiple pins and needles attacking my hands and feet, alternating with periods of numbness. This pain only got worse as the temperature dropped. Mikey had gotten his driver's license by then and performed all the mom-taxi duties I no longer could. Eventually, he and Joey took over their AP Human Geography course and studied on their own. I knew they were on autopilot at this point in their lives, and they would excel in the exam with or without my help. But I still wanted to matter. At times it felt as if I was watching a dress rehearsal of a play titled: *Life After Mom*. Everyone seemed to be continuing with their performance, even as the directors wrote my character off the show. Some days, I'd cry into the abyss, "I want to matter."

While I slept or played chess on my phone, trying to resurrect any dying brain cells, Joey would burrow himself by me, doing his British Literature homework. We had begun the course together, but he ended up finishing that alone, too. When I was too sick to correct his work, he checked it himself against the teacher's edition. He was motivated to finish the 1,000-plus page tome because British literature questions came up quite frequently in quiz bowl. Occasionally, I'd open my eyes and catch him staring at me.

"What?" I asked.

"Nothing."

I didn't believe him. He was holding back on me. We used to be close when he was younger, but now he seemed—distant.

"I'm not going to die," I told him, assuming that was on his mind.

"You better not," he replied with a curious expression. His eyes seemed hollow, while his lips labored to curve into a smile, yet didn't quite make it.

"Come over here and give me a hug."

He obediently walked around to my side of the bed and squeezed me.

"I promise," I whispered. "I'm not leaving you."

"Okay," he said, with that curious expression again.

Despite all my chemo complications, side effects, and changing doctors and hospitals twice due to our differences in opinion regarding my care, I always believed I would live. As my condition deteriorated, my brothers and sisters visited. They and a few friends and neighbors took turns cooking and taking care of us. Danielle came home to help take care of me instead of taking optional programs at Harvard during the winter break. I was against the idea, but she did it anyway.

Once again, Danielle was the responsible child. However, she was no longer a child. Or was she ever? I told the examiner years ago I would allow Danielle to be a child, now I don't believe that was ever possible. That's not who she is. Sure, she played around like the rest of them, but her oldest sibling status, and the responsibility that came with it, never permitted her that childhood luxury.

Danielle accompanied me to my chemo appointments. They were at a different hospital than before and provided actual private rooms. She reviewed her course schedules when I slept and read to me when I was awake. My daughter prepared lunch at home on days I could tolerate food, and we listened to audiobooks in my bedroom while drinking my daily ginger tea. Some smells or colors associated with my cancer experience still elicit negative emotions in me. But the sharp, peppery, pungent aroma of ginger tea stirs mixed feelings. It reminds me of my sickly days, yet it also furnishes an odd sort of comfort because Danielle prepared it just for me.

Danielle even took her Munchkins to a quiz bowl tournament when she was home and volunteered as a reader for the competition. Jackie, Joey, and Nick comprised our quiz bowl team that year, and Mikey was their coach. Shortly after my return from Tunisia, I had received my cancer diagnosis and thus never had a chance to schedule a meeting with the principal. I never did find out the reason for the canceling of the team's funding. Even though our group was short a player, we won quite a few tournaments and made it to Nationals in Chicago again. Since Nationals landed on a chemo week, Rony and Edith came from New York to take care of me while my husband and the kids headed out to Chicago. They didn't do quite as well as they had done the previous year, and I heard their cries over the phone when they called to tell me the news.

"We wanted to win the trophy for you, Mommy," Jackie said through sniffles.

"Guys, I want to let you in on a secret. Winning is terrific, I'm not gonna lie, but you had an incredible year without me. You were a player short, you came from behind to win some difficult tournaments, and you all worked very hard as a team to make it to Nationals. You took seventeenth out of ninety-six teams, a lot more than last time. I'm so proud of you. You are all the trophies I need."

"Thanks, Mom," Jackie, Joey, and Nick replied in unison. I hung up the phone, envisioning their wet, droopy faces, but I knew in the end, they would be fine.

By the tenth chemo infusion, my neuropathy had intensified. Walking, or doing just about anything, became pure pain as the sensation of pins and needles pricked continuously at my fingers and toes. It also caused me to lose my sense of balance, and I became unsteady on my feet. Eventually, my oncologist decided to decrease my dosage to 80% and allowed me to skip weeks. Toward the end, around the eleventh chemo treatment, I had no energy to move from my bed, even during my off weeks. I lost a considerable amount of weight, and my hair thinned out. Despite all that, I anxiously anticipated my subsequent chemo treatment, for it was my last. It was scheduled the week before Mother's Day.

Edwidge flew in from Florida to witness and celebrate my last chemo with me. The day began like any other infusion day, on a Thursday morning. She dropped me off at the Lance and Ellen Shaner Cancer Pavilion's entrance and parked the car. We took the elevator to the second floor. I combed for two empty seats in the waiting room while my sister checked me in. Edwidge kept telling me how proud she was of me and how strong and courageous I was while we waited. She held my hands, and I felt like a child again, remembering a happier time in Brooklyn when we walked to school. Afterward, my sisters and I would lie on our bed in our room, sharing secrets about our family, friends, school, and our crushes on the Jackson Five.

They called my name and regretfully woke me from my reverie. We followed the nurse to the room. I glanced at the IV pole with the saline bag and tubing hanging from it, and I could already sense that horrible metallic taste in my mouth. I took a seat in my recliner, and the nurse proceeded to sterilize my port access area and connect me to my pre-chemo anti-nausea medication. After seeing to my comfort, Edwidge took out her laptop and curled up on a chair beside me. Twenty minutes later, the nurse arrived with my first chemo bag. After verifying my name and date of birth and confirming the medication, she attached it to my IV. My sister gave me an 'Okay, this is it' expression and squeezed my hands.

Within minutes of the medication squirming through my veins, I slumped back in my chair. My eyelids and face swelled. I gulped for air as I struggled to speak with a lead-laden tongue. Edwidge glanced up from her computer.

"Help! Help! My sister needs help!"

Two or three nurses came charging into my room. They stopped the medication and took my vitals. My breathing improved, but my face remained swollen for quite a while. No one could make sense of what had happened. Although it was assumed to be an allergic reaction, we were baffled as to why it occurred during my final treatment. After about an hour, the nurse restarted the infusion at a slower rate. We all held our breath. My doctor remained in the room. With no recurrence of the earlier reaction, he left to see his other patients. The rest of the morning proceeded without further incident, and Edwidge took me home to receive the rest of the chemo from the visiting nurse.

Those post-chemo days were among the worst ones. Nevertheless, I forced myself to feel better for my sister, my kids, and my husband. They all yearned to close this painful chapter and resume an ordinary life.

It was Mother's Day.

A few weeks later, I sat in the waiting room, palpating the infusion port in my neck while my mind accessed the dark corner where I kept the "bad events" file and revisited the day of its insertion. It was on the twin's birthday. I remembered how miserable I felt about that. But I also recalled how I smiled, a couple of months later, when I found a message on Jackie's cell phone that said:

Twins, I know it's your birthday, but please be good to Mom. And Joey, apologize. I just talked to her, and I'm sorry if Nick wasn't able to buy an M-rated video game and that you guys didn't get breakfast in bed, but you have to understand that your mother has cancer. Period. You don't even understand how angry I was when I heard that you were so insensitive. Then I thought about how I was when I was 13. I was a brat when I was 12. That was when Mom and I fought basically every day. At 13, I was a little better, but I can admit that I was still pretty selfish. I can understand how you guys feel. The difference, though, between me at 13 and you guys now is that at the time, my mom didn't have cancer. Turning 13 is a big deal. I know. I remember how excited I was, and I know that it's your birthday, and today should be about you. But you guys have to accept that she might not be able to go out to dinner today, she's not going to have a ton of time to dedicate to you, she's going to be sick and exhausted for months. I want you both to enjoy your day since you only become a teenager once, but don't make Mom's life any harder than it already is.

Love,

Your big sis who wishes more than anything that she could be home today.

I was proud that my Danielle was still shepherding her younger siblings, even though she was 400 miles away.

"The doctor will see you now," the nurse said.

I grabbed my jacket and handbag. After getting my vital signs and recording my height and weight, I proceeded to an examining room where I sat and waited again.

Finally, upon entering the room, my oncologist said, "So, how are you feeling?"

"Great," I replied, a little too exuberant. "When does this port thing come out? It's spring, time to put away the turtlenecks and put on sleeveless, low neckline shirts. I don't like this thing protruding here."

"I—I don't believe it would be prudent to pull your port out this soon," he stammered.

"Why? My chemo is over. I survived it."

"Well, not quite," he said. "The cancer may come back. It's too early to tell. I have patients, especially my older ones, who have had their ports for years, even during remissions. They come in every four to six weeks to flush it, maintaining its patency."

"No." I stood up. "I'm not getting the cancer back. I'm done."

"Maybe, but you still have to come in for monthly lab work," he said. "And the port will make it easier to draw blood since you have tiny veins."

I admitted this was true. The phlebotomist always had to try multiple times to draw blood from my arm. "I guess," I said. "Only for a year."

THE FAMILY II (2013–2014)

June 1, 2013, was a picture-perfect day equipped with a shining sun, blooming flowers, and chirping birds. It symbolized my mood. Despite the ongoing painful neuropathy and other residual side effects, I was happy. I had defeated cancer. Like P. Diddy, I was coming home, and I never felt so strong. I was ready to put the nightmare behind me and take part in my children's lives once again. Unfortunately, my dream of going back to practicing medicine ended prematurely. In good faith, I could not perform surgery with alternating numbness and stinging pains in my hands and feet. And I worried about how "chemo brain," a sense of fogginess and forgetfulness that afflicts some cancer survivors, could affect my practice too. But I was eager to resume educating my kids. I was proud of my kids' studiousness and discipline during my illness, but it was time to pick up where I'd left off.

The 2013–2014 academic year was Mikey's graduating year, so he was a fully enrolled student at State High. I longed for my three younger ones to return to our dual-enrollment status.

"What are our educational goals for this school year?" I asked Jackie, Joey, and Nick over lunch at Applebee's.

They went quiet as they glanced at each other in a way that said,

'Is she for real? Is Mom doing this?' It made me nervous. I'd put the cancer behind me, but were my kids beyond me? I feared my teenagers had discovered how to navigate life without me. Danielle had settled in at Harvard. Between Mikey's driver's license and his successful *Route Maker* app the year prior, he navigated his way in the world. But not my three little ones. They still needed me.

Or maybe vice versa.

After the waitress took our orders, the kids still had not answered my question. I finally said, "What? You don't want to be homeschooled anymore?"

Nick finally spoke. "No, it's not that."

"Well, what is it then?"

"Well, Mom—it's kinda hard for us conceptualizing you educating us when you're still carrying a diagnosis of stage three colon cancer."

Was there resentment in that statement? I wasn't sure, but I didn't like it. "I have no idea what that means," I said. "What does my past illness have to do with any—"

"But, Mom," Jackie interrupted. "What Nick is trying to say is what if it comes back, and you're sick again? The doctor said you're in remission. We don't want you to get stressed with our workload."

"My illness is not coming back, Jackie. Besides, your workload is not what caused the cancer. And on the off chance it does return, we'll proceed as we did before and be better prepared the second time. Now, I've already started with outlines for AP Biology for you and Nick and AP Chemistry for Joey and Nick. If you don't have any other questions or fears, let's go over your course schedules and your goals for the upcoming school year."

"Okay, Mom, let's go over our course schedule," said Joey.

"They're right here."

I moved back to allow our waitress to set our drinks on the table before reaching into my oversized gray shoulder bag. I then pulled out three lists and handed one to each of them.

"Do you see anything there that requires changing, either adding or dropping a course?"

"No, it seems fine," said Joey, after a glance at the paper. "Nick and I are still taking AP Chemistry with you?"

"I don't know. It's up to you. Do you still want to with your other classes?"

"Yeah, it'll probably be fine."

"Nick, what about you?" I asked. "Your schedule looks intense. You'll be a real high school student this school year. An official ninth grader. How does it feel?"

"No different. We're all used to being at the high school by now, Mom," he said, drumming his fingers on the table.

"I know that, but now you can't afford even an A- or you won't be in the running for the Principal's Award, like Mikey."

"Mikey didn't get it this year," said Joey.

"Mikey tried correcting it, but because of his workload, he hasn't met with the principal. But I will. I've already scheduled a meeting with him."

"Of course you did," said Joey, smiling. "We expected nothing less from you, Mom."

As I drank my water, I felt proud my kids knew I would always have their backs. I was pleased they watched me stand up for them over the years. I demonstrated how they should defend themselves in the future without me. My generation was not permitted to question authority figures and was thus inclined to accept the status quo. But significant movements like the Arab Spring and Black Lives Matter were taking place worldwide, and changes were coming. Their generation would be different.

"Oh, speaking of complaining," I said, putting down my drink. "Do you want me to try to petition for a middle school quiz bowl team?"

"No," they said in unison.

"Why not?" I asked.

"Well, because Nick is now a ninth grader and can't be on the team," said Jackie. "And Joey and I want—okay, mostly Joey wants—to concentrate on the Mathcounts team."

"Since when can't my kids concentrate on more than one thing?" I said.

"No, Mom, you don't understand," Joey said. "I can't let what happened to me at Mathcounts last year happen again. I felt humiliated. To take sixth at States, missing the cutoff for Nationals by two places. And seeing you guys and the rest of the team out there in the audience feeling sorry for me. Auugh, it was bad."

Right around that time, our waitress brought our salad. "It'll just be another minute for the sandwiches," she said.

"They weren't feeling sorry for you," I said, resuming the conversation.

"Yes, they were," he said. "Riding back home on the bus was extremely painful. Everyone, including the teacher, kept telling me how spectacular I did, and how close I came to making Nationals, and—my favorite—'there's always next year.' Things I, frankly, didn't want to hear. I knew they meant well, but I kept wishing they would leave me alone before I started bawling."

"A tad melodramatic, you think?"

"No, Mom," he said. "Not at all. It was horrible."

"Well, that's why I wanted to take you home that day instead of letting you take the bus with the other kids."

"I know, Mom. I wanted to go home with you too, but it would have made things worse. I had to 'face the music,' as you like to say."

"That took lots of courage, Sweetie. I guess that's why you're going to try again."

"I have to, Mom. What is it you always said? 'Life is a competition, and those who are afraid of competing will finish last?' Something like that. I will compete again, but this time I am going to Nationals."

I beamed. What was this kid made of? He got my quote wrong, but he exemplified my competitive ideals more than any of my other kids.

"Joey, we all have some amount of pressure in our daily lives, from babies to grandparents," I said. "And some pressure is good. It lets you know you're still alive. But you can also have too much, and that's bad. The trick is knowing the perfect amount. It's a delicate balancing act." I imitated a scale with my hands. "You have to apply the correct amount. That's how you're going to make it to Nationals. Also, Joey, you can't be too cocky; these things have ways of backfiring."

"No, Mom," he said. "I'm not cocky; I'm realistic. I'm going to Nationals because I already scoped out my competition."

"Why am I not surprised. Well, I guess going to AwesomeMath at Cornell this summer will also help."

"No, that's not for Mathcounts stuff. That's for AMC and AIME. Since you don't want me to go to Exeter for the training I'll need, I'm finding ways to do it on my own."

"Well, I didn't rule out Exeter completely, just partially. I'm going to the university's math department to search for math professors who would be willing to tutor you. Then we'll see if we need to consider Exeter."

"Right, Mom," he said. That didn't sound convincing. I guess he remembered how I torpedoed Danielle's dream of attending Exeter years ago.

"Well," I continued, "what about the middle school quiz bowl team? It seems you have everything planned well enough to handle it."

"I probably do," he said, "but I still have to study. Besides, I'm already on the high school team and might make the A-team this year."

"Okay."

"Mom, did I tell you this high school kid, Will, is trying to recruit me for the cross-country team?" said Nick.

"Cross-country?"

"Yeah, he said I have a perfect runner's body."

"That's flattering, but did you tell him you're a sprinter, not a long-distance runner?"

"No, I'm not sure I'm a sprinter any more. I used to be the fastest sprinter in seventh grade, but I was down to third by eighth grade. The distance coach told me the 800 meters or even the mile is probably more my speed these days. But definitely *not* long-distance," he said with a chuckle.

"What did you tell him?" I asked.

"I told him I'm planning on trying out for the soccer team, but he tried talking me out of it, saying I'll have more success running."

"Who knows, you might," said Jackie. "What did you decide?"

"I haven't. He wants me to go on a few morning runs with the team. I guess I'll do that. I have nothing to lose, just my pride when this guy realizes I'm not as good as he seems to believe. I'll be sore, but it'll put me in shape for either cross-country or soccer."

"Good for you, Sweetie. Go for the challenge. By the way, are you ready for your chemistry camp?"

"Actually, Mom," Nick said. "I never understood why I have to go to a chemistry camp, and Joey doesn't. And yet you plan to teach us both AP Chemistry in the fall."

"First of all, you chose chemistry, Joey chose math, and Jackie chose a writing camp for the summer. Second, we chose those camps when I was still sick. I didn't even know if I would be working with you this fall. And your schedule this school year, along with sports, will be difficult. Maybe having a head start in chemistry will help."

"It'll help until Joey catches up to me. Isn't that what you mean?" Nick said.

Joey, noticing the conversation now involved him, decided it would be an ideal time to excuse himself to the restroom before the waitress returned with our meals which, by the way, was taking longer than a minute.

"Nick, where's this coming from? What's wrong?"

After a contemptuous sigh, he picked up his school schedule and said, "See, Mom, Joey is in quite a few of my classes this year."

"And?"

"Well, it's just that I'm going to do my best, but somehow, as always, Joey is going to do better. And then some dumb kid will ask me, 'How come your younger brother's smarter than you?' and I'll pretend I didn't hear that insult and pick up my books and walk away. Just like I've been doing every year."

"I put you in some classes with Joey to help each other."

"No, Mom, don't you mean so Joey can help *me?*"

"Nick, if you're going to be on a high school sports team, you might miss classes for away meets. And Joey might miss classes for other reasons. I thought it would be nice to rely on each other instead of asking other students for their notes. Mikey didn't seem to mind when Joey was in his AP Stats class. I would have liked having my sister or brother in my classes in high school."

"No. No, you wouldn't, Mom. Not an annoying younger brother who always tries to outshine you."

"Come on, Nick, Joey's not purposely trying to humiliate you. He takes his work seriously."

"No, he takes these classes like a competition; everything is a competition for Joey." Noting my bemused face, he added, "Oh, I forgot, that's your motto after all, about life being a competition. I guess that's why Joey's your favorite."

"I'm going to ignore that last part," I said, "but I will say this: Out there Nick, out in the world, there'll be fiercer competitors than your brother. I'll advise you to use this opportunity with Joey to push yourself. Yes, sometimes you'll lose, but sometimes you'll win. The point is just put yourself out there and give it your best. Don't let anyone, including Joey, intimidate you. But, if it bothers you that much to be in his classes, I can change them, or you can do them at home with me."

"No, Mom. For the most part, it doesn't bother me. I like it sometimes when we do projects together; we work well together. But other times... when those kids—" He stopped in mid-sentence as he saw Joey approaching.

"Well, you'll have to learn to ignore those kids," I said. While Joey retook his seat, the waitress finally returned with our sandwiches and fries. Picking up a fry, I turned to face Jackie. "Your turn. What are your thoughts on the upcoming school year?"

"Well, I agree with the others about the middle school quiz bowl team. I don't want you jumping through hoops trying to implement this at the middle school when we only have a year left. Would you continue with the team after we're gone?"

"That's a good question," I said. "Maybe. I enjoy quiz bowl. And it would be nice to help other kids develop a passion for learning. Maybe it's time for me to give back to the community."

"Okay, well, I don't believe it'll be the same without our terrific captain," she said as she smiled at Nick. He nodded as he chewed his food. Being Joey's twin, she could relate to Nick's complaints about his younger brother. Beyond that, the two years they had spent together at the middle school forged a camaraderie. I didn't know for how long, though. The dynamics between those three constantly fluctuated. "And I want to start practicing with the high school quiz bowl team with Joey," she continued, "and I also want to do well on the Mathcounts team, too. And," Jackie glanced down at the paper while throwing a fry in her mouth, "my schedule's fine."

With Jackie, it's what she doesn't say that's important. She didn't say anything about trying to make the National Mathcounts team, like Joey. Competing on the team was enough for her. She also didn't say anything about the track team. She had been one of the fastest 800-meter runners the previous year. Then, toward the end of the year, each competition brought more anxiety. Defending her elite position came with some physical pains. I hadn't quite figured out if they were real or psychosomatic.

"What about the journalism class?" I asked. "Are you excited about it?"

"I guess," she replied.

The journalism class was my idea. Again, I was trying to find something different for Jackie, something to propel her out from the shadows of her older siblings. My other kids were heavily STEM-oriented. They did all the AP science and math classes. Jackie liked math but didn't love it like Joey. She liked science but didn't love it like Nick. She liked computers, but not like Mikey. Danielle loved everything, but her baby sister didn't seem to love anything.

"What about business, Jackie?"

I had suggested this idea a few months ago. It came to me when Danielle got an internship at Morgan Stanley for the summer. It confused me because she was a pre-med student. She justified it by saying, "I want to be well-rounded. And the pay is excellent too."

"What about it?" Jackie said.

"Well, there are other courses at the high school to consider. You don't seem to like anything else, why not give business courses a try? They have an impressive curriculum at the high school, and you can take some classes at the university if you want later."

"Okay," she said blandly. Then again, arguing was never her style in those days. She had a getting-along-with-everyone personality. With the decision made, we penciled in Advanced Accounting I on her schedule.

We had cold meals by the time we finished, something we have gotten used to over the years, but at least our goals for the summer and the upcoming school year were all sorted out. As we drove home, Jackie noticed an omission in the course schedule.

"Mom, you left out history," she said. "We have no history class for the coming school year."

When the kids were younger, I had emphasized math and reading, but as they got older, I started focusing more on history. Because, unlike the other subjects, history can be subjective, the winners write it. "You need as much critical thinking reading a historical account as you would with a math problem," I had told them. "You should always ask yourself, 'Whose views am I getting?'" When we studied U.S. history and world history, we did units on Haitian history as well. We learned how 800 Haitian soldiers fought in the Battle of Savannah, Georgia, alongside the French and Americans for America's independence against the British. We learned how Haiti's revolution for independence spurred the Louisiana purchase. And we learned how Haiti had to pay ninety million francs to lift a crippling embargo imposed by France, Britain, Spain, and the United States, sending the first Black republic into a devastating economic decline. When we studied World War II, we learned about the Haitian pilots recruited in 1943 and trained as the Tuskegee Airmen. These were some of the histories not taught in "regular" history classes. Like all our classes, our history classes were unique.

"Do any of you have any suggestions?" I asked them as I envisioned something original to teach them. As we drove home, a beautiful jazz piece began playing on the radio. "I love this piece," I said, humming along.

"It's Brubeck's 'Take Five,'" Nick said. "I played it in jazz band."

I TURNED fifty in October of that year, and I watched my house transform into a floral boutique filled with cards, flowers, and all sorts of gift baskets from family and friends. From my kids, I received a silver necklace containing an elegant pearl pendant. They also made me an oversized card. The cover read: "Happy 50th Birthday, Mom!" with a blown-up picture of me. The inside title said: "50 Reasons Why We Love Mom." They listed the fifty reasons, with accompanying photos. The #1 reason my kids said they loved me captured the mood of that memorable October day and clarified what the multitude of gifts represented. It said: "She is still here with us," and a family photograph accompanied it.

ALL THE KIDS had an exciting school year. Jackie and Joey excelled on the Mathcounts team. The team, taking third at States, made it the school's best finish in history. Several of Jackie's articles graced the school's newspaper, and she seemed to enjoy her accounting class. In swimming, Jackie began having shoulder problems; we wrapped it with ice. She took time off and started concentrating on running. Shortly afterward, however, she developed painful shin splints, which largely stymied her athletic career.

Joey made it to Nationals in the Mathcounts competition as he had predicted. And once again, I was to accompany him to a math competition, this time at Disney World in Florida, which meant I got a chance to visit with my dad and sister. Joey also advanced to the second round of testing in the Physics, Biology, and the North American Computational Linguistics Olympiads.

Nick also had a breakout year. He received the Technology Education and Computer Graphics Award at the high school's end-of-the-year award ceremony. He swam on the high school team alongside Mikey and qualified for district championships in the fifty-yard freestyle. But what made the year most memorable was when he discovered his passion for running. As a freshman, Nick made the varsity cross-country team and helped his team take fourth at States. He was often in our local paper for his running prowess.

"I didn't know you had it in you, Nick," I said. "You were always a fast midfielder in soccer, but cross-country? I never saw that coming."

"Neither did I, Mom. I guess Will had more confidence in me than I had in myself and, well, I didn't want to let him down."

"That's all it took? Someone to have confidence in you? I always have confidence in you."

"Yeah, but it doesn't count. You're my mom."

"Wow, that stings, Nick."

"You know what I mean, Mom," he said.

"Yeah, I know what you mean."

That was the same reason Mikey excelled at quiz bowl, and Joey joined the forensics team: an upperclassman recruited them and made them feel they had something to contribute. If parents want their high school child to join a club or a sport, they should seek a team member's help to recruit them.

At the cross-country banquet that year, I volunteered for the treasurer position for the next season. I figured I might as well be involved. As Joey had correctly predicted years before, my kids moved away from swimming and focused more on track and soccer.

Mikey also had a tremendously successful senior year. Then again, this is Mikey we are talking about. He always had successful years, and he did so in his typical, quiet, unostentatious way. In 2013, along with about a dozen international students, he became a Google Trailblazer member. His recruitment required him to work for several weeks on a computer science project with fellow Trailblazers worldwide. Along with a parent (me), a high school Trailblazer student traveled to Google headquarters in Mountain View, California, to present their projects.

Mikey received the State AP Scholar Award, the Principal's Award, and the Stokes National Educational Scholarship. Best of all, he was accepted to his dream school: the Massachusetts Institute of Technology.

For Mikey's graduation, we planned a party in our backyard. After sprucing up the house, I quickly stopped by the hospital to check my latest lab results. When my chemotherapy finished, I had entered an intensive surveillance program consisting of monthly blood work, quarterly PET scans, and yearly colonoscopy. Besides the dreaded neuropathy in my fingers and toes and my persistently low white blood cell count, I felt fine. My hair was filling in, and I was gaining weight. That's why I was unprepared when I noticed a slight increase in my CEA levels—my colon cancer tumor marker—three months before Mikey's graduation party. My PET scan lit up a three-millimeter lymph node in my right lung's lower lobe six months prior. My oncologist dismissed both new developments.

"I'm not worried," I lied. "I just want to understand the increase. What caused it?"

"It's only by 0.1; anything can cause that, the time of day of your blood drawing, lab fluctuation, anything," said Michael.

"I know you're right, but it's been stable, and now this."

"I agree with your oncologist," Michael said. "0.1 is an ant-sized increase. It's still below the normal values."

"I guess," I said.

But my concern was justified. The following month saw another slight increase in my CEA numbers and further growth of the suspicious lymph node. I didn't wait for my oncologist to take my complaints seriously. I consulted a pulmonologist who recommended a transbronchial aspiration, an outpatient procedure whereby the tiny mass in my lungs could be aspirated and analyzed. The doctor scheduled it a week before Mikey's graduation party.

The process was uneventful, and by the next day, I was running around like a hamster touching up the final details for the party. A couple of days later, the pathology result returned "inconclusive"; I would have to repeat the test. We met with a thoracic surgeon who recommended excision of the node via a thoracoscopy. Meaning he would try to extract this lymph node using a scope. If this approach proved unsuccessful, he would proceed to a thoracotomy, opening my chest cavity. This operation would occur the Monday after Mikey's graduation party.

History was repeating itself.

I was at a party again, delighting in the company of family and friends, pretending everything was fine, while I silenced my fears of a possible cancer recurrence. Whenever someone at the party asked, "So, you're okay? Right?" or, "You look fabulous. So glad the cancer is all behind you." I would only smile and nod, unwilling to utter mistruths. I was terrified. I didn't know if I could go on lying and pretending everything was fine, chiefly to my sisters. But I had to keep reminding myself that this day belonged to Mikey. He worked hard for this moment. I needed to keep it together for him, and I did.

THE SHADOW (2014–2015)

The quality, not the longevity, of one's life, is what is important.

— DR. MARTIN LUTHER KING

On Sunday morning, the day after Mikey's party, I confessed the actual state of my health to close family members gathered around the kitchen table for breakfast. I told them about the surgery scheduled for the following morning. I watched how their joyful, celebratory faces became undone and replaced by anguish as their eyes welled up with tears. I was doing it again.

"It's going to be fine," I said. "I didn't wake up with a colostomy bag, and I won't wake up with a chest tube. The doctor has an impressive bio. He's going to use a scope. Remove the lymph node, send it to pathology, and the result will be negative. Come on, guys, it's not the time for sad faces. I want positive thoughts around me. Okay?"

"Okay," they muttered.

A harbinger of my ensuing nightmare came when I awoke in the recovery room with a tube through my rib cage. My chest cavity had been cut open, my lung deflated and re-inflated with a machine. The pain of having it clamped and unclamped, along with my chest incision, was unbearable. Many months later, it was still difficult to lie on that right side. The doctor expounded how the thoracotomy was necessary and how he removed the node, along with an adjacent one, and sent them to pathology. He also informed me I would always have nerve damage in the area because he had cut into the intercostal nerves around my rib cage. More neuropathy? Would this nightmare ever end? No, I found out later. The answer was no.

The pathology report came back negative; the lymph nodes contained no cancer. Michael and I were thankful, until my next monthly lab showed yet another increase in my CEA.

"Wherever the cancer is, it's not in your lungs," the doctor assured us. "Maybe there's a recurrence in your colon."

Between trying to find out if and where this supposed cancer was hiding, I had to deal with my children's summer programs and the upcoming school year. They were aware the disease might be back and, if it were, whatever subjects I'd start with them, they would probably be required to finish on their own. With that in mind, Jackie, Nick, and I agreed to do AP Human Geography at home because I already had all the notes and exams. Since Joey had completed all the math courses available at the high school, he decided to work independently on a differential equations course using MIT OpenCourseWare and consult a State High teacher for discussion.

For the summer, Danielle lived in New York doing another internship. Mikey attended the National Youth Science Program in West Virginia for the next three weeks. Jackie spent part of her summer at a Leadership, Education, and Development program, the Computer Science Summer Institute at Virginia, and a business leadership camp in Florida. Joey wanted to stay home and take an online course in matrices at Penn State. To my annoyance, he also spent much of the summer on the couch watching the 2014 FIFA World Cup.

Nick was to leave for Spain for a five-week summer immersion with School Year Abroad three weeks after my surgery. The program required all students to fly out of Boston, and I geared up to go with Michael to see my son off.

"You can't come. You're still recuperating," said Michael, as he watched how I grimaced while packing my overnight bag.

"I can recuperate in the car, as long as you try avoiding the bumps," I said.

"Are you kidding me? We're driving to Boston. Of course there'll be bumps."

"Maybe I can take enough pillows to help cushion the pain."

"Carline—"

Michael stood right behind me.

"I have to see Nick off," I said. "Who knows if I'll..." I left that statement unfinished, in a state of uncertainty, similar to how I've come to view my life.

"Okay," Michael said.

"Besides, it's our anniversary weekend," I said. "Why don't we stay in Boston and celebrate it over a nice dinner? We can pretend, even briefly... this... that it's not happening again." My breath rasped in my throat, swallowing tears.

Michael walked over and hugged me. It said everything he couldn't. And it was just what I needed at that precise moment.

We took Nick to Boston the following day, where he rendezvoused with his fellow School Year Abroad classmates and staff. We hugged and kissed him as he prepared to go through security. Despite the bumpy roads, surgical pains, and the precariousness of my health, I delighted in a lovely anniversary weekend accented by cooperating weather and an exquisite dinner with the love of my life for the past twenty years.

Once I tucked the kids away at their respective camps, I went in search of this obscure cancer. I made an appointment for a colonoscopy for the coming month. In the meantime, I contacted oncologists at Johns Hopkins, Sloan Kettering, and the Mayo Clinic about my dilemma. I sent them a summary of my case history, along with relevant lab and imaging data. Hopkins replied first, so I continued conversing with them. The oncologist suggested that, along with the colonoscopy, I should secure a bone marrow biopsy since I still had a low blood cell count. Both the colonoscopy and the biopsy reported negative results.

Hopkins then scheduled me for a repeat transbronchial aspiration. Two days after the procedure, Michael and I drove down to Baltimore for the results:

1. *Lymph node, FNA [the "FNA" stood for "fine needle aspiration"]*
   Final diagnosis: Metastatic adenocarcinoma, consistent with the patient's history of colorectal carcinoma.

The cancer had resurfaced. I was a volcano ready to erupt as the pressure mounted. I would explode if I didn't let out steam, but I couldn't. I couldn't scream or cry. I tried. I couldn't. We rode in silence, and I rested my head against the window. As my despair replaced my anger, I debated whether to fling myself out of the moving car. Michael was never the conversationalist on these drives, and this time, neither was I. There was nothing worth saying. What was there to discuss when you found out you now have stage four colon cancer, with a five-year survival prognosis of just 11%? The most optimistic life expectancy for me was now thirty months. When I later shared the news with my siblings, their tears could have breached a dam. The talk with my dad proved much harder; although he kept trying to convince me I would be fine, the brittleness in his voice spoke volumes. I couldn't imagine what he was going through. A parent should never have to bury their child, no matter how old that child may be. I guess that's what I would have been agonizing over if it were any of my children.

A week or so after the diagnosis, Michael and I had a thorough consultation with the Hopkins thoracic surgeon. He explained that since the lymph node had increased to 1.5 centimeters, he would perform a right lower lobectomy, removing the entire lower lobe of my right lung. He scheduled it for September.

In the meantime, despite the gloomy news, daily life continued in the Feffer household. A crucial argument ensued when Joey decided not to try out for the cross-country team. Nick had recently returned from Spain, anticipating training with his younger brother for the upcoming cross-country season.

"What do you mean you're not doing cross-country?" I heard Nick ask.

"I changed my mind," Joey said.

I stopped my chores to hear the developing dispute clearer.

"But why? We discussed it. This was going to be our year. The Feffer boys, just like in our soccer days."

"That's just it," replied Joey. "I've decided to go for soccer instead."

"But. Why?" asked Nick again, slower this time.

"Because I like soccer better. Cross-country is stupid. It's not challenging; it's just running."

Nick's nostrils flared like a raging bull as he glared at his baby brother, contemplating the best way to harm him physically. I couldn't recall the last time, or ever, I'd seen Nick this visibly upset with Joey. Reaching for his sneakers by the side kitchen door, he gazed in my direction and said, "Mom, I'm going for a run."

I slammed the dishwasher shut as soon as Nick was gone. "Was that necessary, Joey?" I said.

"What?" he asked.

"You know darn well what. Did you have to hurt Nick like that?"

"I don't want to run anymore. What's the big deal?" Joey said.

"It's bad enough you changed your mind when you knew he was looking forward to the two of you running together, but did you also have to insult him? Did you have to say that *his* sport, in which he most excels, is not challenging?"

"He kept pushing me for an answer, and well, it's not."

"Joey," I said, "who do you think you're talking to? You decided against running after your disastrous 4k run on the Fourth of July. You spent most of the summer lying on the couch with your laptop, watching soccer. I told you numerous times to go practice for the

4k, but you never did. I guess you figured if Nick could do it, it couldn't be that difficult. But you were wrong. It was hard, and you were in pain. It was challenging after all, but you would never admit it."

"You're right, Mom. It was after the 4k. I was in pain, and I said to myself, 'Why am I doing this? It isn't even fun.' Soccer is much more fun *and* challenging."

"Joey, I hope you know this is not club soccer or middle school soccer. It's high school soccer, which is very competitive. And *if* you should make the team, you might be a bench warmer."

"Well, Mom, I guess I'll just have to find out."

About a half-hour later, Nick returned and disappeared to his room. I joined him there shortly after.

"How was your run?" I asked.

"Good. It was hot, though. I need to hydrate better," Nick said, removing his sweat-drenched tank top, revealing the well-chiseled chest of a top athlete.

I closed his bedroom door behind me and asked in a hushed voice, "Feeling better about Joey?"

"Not really, but it's okay. I'll get over it."

"I'm kinda surprised by your reaction, though. I didn't think you cared that much about Joey being on the team with you."

"Why?" he said. "We both enjoyed being co-captains of the middle school soccer team. I expected this to continue on the track team. Our cross-country and track teams would have been unstoppable with Joey." He paused for a moment as he leaned against the wall, under a poster of runners captioned: *Winners: While most are dreaming of success, winners wake up and work hard to achieve it.* "I guess this was my chance to truly be his older brother, you know, show him the ropes."

"I see." I paused as the multiplication days cued into my mind. "It'll be okay, Sweetie."

"I guess, Mom."

~

SEPTEMBER CAME AROUND and fall sports at the high school kicked into full gear. Nick and Jackie were on the cross-country team, while Joey was on the soccer team. A week into the month, I was on my way to have my right lower lobe excised. My dad called me that morning, offering me his prayers and support. A tear slid down my cheek as I thanked him. When I arrived at Johns Hopkins with Michael, my mother-in-law, Rony, and Edith greeted me. Seeing them all that early in the morning pleased me. I was most surprised when Danielle and Mikey appeared. They had flown in from Boston the night before to tell me how much they loved me and to keep vigil with their father.

The surgeon removed my lobe uneventfully via the scope. But the recovery was just as painful as I remembered as the chest tube re-inflated my lungs. Michael's family lived in Annapolis and visited me during my week-long hospital stay. Edwidge flew to State College, picked up the children after a cross-country meet, and brought them to see me. Later, Michael visited me and taxied the kids home. Edwidge stayed a couple of nights at the hospital and helped me walk around the halls. When she flew back home, my oldest brother, Evans, flew in. Michael stayed with me for the remaining days while his oldest sister, Susan, cared for my kids. My youngest brother, Roland, a pediatric cardiologist, visited me at home and handed me a tear-jerking poem he wrote for me.

Feeling loved and appreciated by my family and friends gave me the courage to face additional chemo. I couldn't have done it without them. Chemo terrified me. Before, I hadn't known what to expect; I had only heard how terrible it was. This time, I was a veteran. I knew *exactly* what to expect. It shattered any hope of my neuropathy abating; more chemo would only aggravate that situation.

I consulted with my Hopkins oncologist about the need for more chemo. "Couldn't we wait a few months before starting?" I asked. My question drew a vacant stare. I felt nervous but persisted. "I mean… couldn't we wait to see if the surgery cured me? That's not unreasonable, is it? After all, the other lymph nodes in the area were negative, and the margins were clear. Only that one node was cancerous, maybe, well... maybe the cancer didn't have time to spread?"

"No," she said, fixing her gaze on me. "You have stage four colon cancer. Your prognosis is already precarious. If we don't start the chemo by the time your surgery heals, you will die much sooner."

Her bluntness hit me like a dodgeball. I didn't appreciate it. I considered radiation, but the data was scant. Defeated and demoralized, I succumbed to another round of chemo.

Since I had "failed" the previous chemo, I received a new cocktail of drugs to be administered at our local hospital in Pennsylvania. It was another twenty-four-week regimen, with the infusion scheduled for every other week. It would start in November, like last time. I would be sick for the holidays again, but most of all, I would be ill for four out of my five children's birthdays. I felt depressed and angry, emotions I didn't fully express the first time around. My tone set the stage for the household. After school, the kids would run to my room to recount the day's events. They were excited to share their news with me. But over that winter, they became hesitant to enter my room; a depression lingered, a sadness poisoned the air. It affected anyone who entered. The weight of my illness was crushing us all.

The previous course of chemotherapy thinned my hair; this one balded me. I woke up with clumps of hair on my pillow and severe nosebleeds that needed cauterizing by an ENT specialist. But the excruciating headaches were the worst. They made it difficult to fall asleep and greeted me when I awoke. They were the head-holding type of headaches that made me afraid to turn too quickly, lest my head explode.

I relayed my complaints to my local oncologist, who simply said, "Well, we can skip next week if you'd like."

No, I didn't want to skip weeks. I wanted to stop. I wanted the torture to stop. Hopeless, I asked, "What are my chances of being cured?"

"Cured?" he asked, unsure if he heard me correctly. "No, you shouldn't think of your disease as being curable. Instead, you should think of it as a chronic condition… like diabetes… you know, an incurable disease that you'll always need occasional treatments for."

Occasional chemo treatments? No. I couldn't do it anymore. Eventually, I contacted a specialist at UPMC in Pittsburgh for a second opinion about my treatment and inquired about any existing trials I could participate in. Since he was kind enough to answer my questions by email, I set up an office consultation with him.

We met in his office later that month. He was a soft-spoken Asian male who listened as I complained about the side effects I regularly experienced with the drugs and how I thought they would kill me faster than the disease.

"You should stop the chemo," he said. "You've been on some of these drugs for too long. If they were going to work, they would have already. Besides, your tumor may have already mutated, and…"

I didn't hear anything else after "stopping the chemo." I wanted to hug the doctor.

"Stop the chemo for now," he said again, "and we'll see what happens. In the meantime, we'll do some studies on your last tumor tissue, which we'll obtain from Hopkins, and analyze it for better treatment options like immunotherapy if the cancer should return."

I was hysterical with joy. The outcry erupting from within me sounded strange. It had been so long since I'd laughed, I barely recognized it. Like a lost child, it was sorely missed. Michael and I conversed during the entire three-hour drive to State College. Upon arriving home, I immediately called the cancer center to cancel my chemo. I also notified the visiting nurse agency to inform them that I would no longer require their services. I shared the encouraging news with my siblings. Most of them were pleased for me, except for my physician brothers. They thought my decision was reckless and accused me of doctor shopping for the perspective I wanted to hear. They weren't entirely wrong. But I also felt the doctor told me what he did because he knew my 11% survival prognosis was dismal. *Why put her through all this when she's going to die anyway?* He must have thought. *She's probably ready to die.*

Perhaps I was prepared to die. I don't know. All I knew for sure was that I was tired of positive thinking. I had a friend in Altoona who received a diagnosis of pancreatic cancer. She contacted several hospitals for treatment, and they all refused her, claiming her cancer was too advanced. Alternatively, they advised her to prepare her will. She declined, opting instead for self-cure and positive thinking. She retreated to her church and prayed with her priest. She died within a month.

No one ever talks about these people. We only hear about the miracles.

I lay quietly in my bed during one of my headaches, fearing a blood vessel rupturing in my brain. That was not going to happen. I tried persuading myself to *think positive*. But when has that ever worked? Two years ago, I spotted that tinge of blood in my stool. I had hoped it was hemorrhoids. It wasn't; it was a mass in my colon. I tried to think positive again that it was benign. It wasn't; it was an aggressive tumor. After surgery and chemo, the cancer came back— in my lungs this time. All the positive thinking I summoned didn't prevent any of it. Now I was supposed to trust this new chemo cocktail would cure me? Me? A fifty-two-year-old Haitian American woman with metastatic colon cancer and an 11% five-year survival? I couldn't do it anymore. I wanted no part in the theatre of the absurd. I was tired of the isolation, tired of living in fear—or just living. I was ready to become proactive. Maybe I was going to die, but I would do it on my terms. When I conveyed how I felt to my sisters, they sounded disappointed and didn't understand.

"You can't give up," they said. "You have to fight."

Fight what? I never understood what people meant when they said that. I'm not afraid of a fair fight; I've been fighting all my life. But how do I fight this invisible and seemingly invincible enemy? What were the rules of engagement? Even the doctors didn't know. Whenever I'd show up in Pittsburgh for my appointments, the oncologist always appeared stunned to see me. I could practically hear him musing *She's still alive? Wow, who would've thought?*

"Don't misunderstand," I told them. "I'm not giving up. I still plan on doing all my PET scans and my blood work. But I'm through with the chemo. I can't do it anymore. These drugs are killing me faster than the disease. If it comes back, then I'll deal with it. I had an exemplary life." I added softly, "and... and I love you guys, and I love my family, but if it's my time..."

They didn't want to argue any more and finally said, "We love you, too."

As much as I adore my parents and brothers and sisters, the only person who had a right to weigh in on my decision was Michael. Besides being a brilliant physician who understood the circumstances, my husband was the one I had promised to stay with, in sickness and in health. "Am I making the right choice by stopping the chemo?"

He didn't respond for several minutes, then said, "I can't begin to imagine the pain you must be going through, so I can't make that decision for you. I'm here to support your decision, whatever it is."

I felt as if gravity no longer pulled on me. The burden of stopping the chemo, the guilt, the disagreements, all of it flew off my shoulders. "Take care of the kids," I whispered.

He nodded.

"I love you," I said with glistening eyes.

"Ditto," he replied, holding me in his arms. I don't suppose he trusted himself to say anything more.

I left our bedroom and headed straight to my favorite room, my library-office, to contemplate my next move. It occurred to me Joey had written a letter to Natalie Babbitt, author of the novel *Tuck Everlasting*, about death and dying as part of his Letters about Literature when he was eight or nine. At that moment, I felt the need to re-read it. I went to Joey's section of my file cabinet and pulled out the green portfolio labeled 2007–2008. After passing by the French and the geometry pages, I found the literature section.

Joey had written to Ms. Babbitt about Grandpa Feffer's heart attack. At that time, he was afraid his grandfather would die. Grandpa Feffer did pass away several months later due to complications of pneumonia. Eight years before his myocardial infarction, he had been diagnosed with pancreatic cancer. Everyone feared for Grandpa's life back then. But, with surgery and chemo, he recovered. Until Grandpa Feffer, my kids never confronted the death of a close family member. I worried about how they would deal with mine. I also couldn't imagine it being any easier seeing me confined to a bed, bleeding, vomiting, and losing weight. That's not how I think they would want to remember me. That's not how *I* wanted them to remember me. Joey wrote in his letter to Ms. Babbitt: *The spring isn't real, and people can't live forever, but I believe that living a happy and joyous life is equivalent to living forever.*

I stopped my chemo in March 2015, and shortly afterward, the headaches stopped. The fog in my brain melted like ice cream on a summer day. I focused on affairs needing my attention, beginning with paying for our annual Homeschool Hersheypark Day. I was determined to go and have a fun time—since it might be my last. I then prepared Jackie's, Joey's, and Nick's course schedules for the next school year and handed them to the school. I also began studying with them and preparing them for the upcoming AP exams. Next, I turned my attention to our finances. I reviewed my life insurance policy to see if it covered the kids' college expenses. I also refinanced our house. Since I had been grooming Jackie to be our financier, I showed her and Michael where I kept all our bank and investment statements and their corresponding passwords. I also showed them how I paid the bills and organized those documents; Jackie took over paying and filing the reports as I watched.

Unlike some other people in the world, I had a birth certificate, and soon I'd have a death certificate. So, I drove to the local funeral parlor to make my arrangements. I didn't want to leave it to Michael or the kids. I spoke with a young woman who answered all my questions about the services they provided. I decided on cremation. The last thing I needed was for my kids to "talk" to me or carry flowers to my grave perpetually. I envisioned a festive, Mardi Gras type burial ceremony where all my friends and family danced in the street, remembering those "good ol' times" with me. Yes, that's it. I want laughter and dancing when I'm gone because I want the living to go on living. And as I took the scenic route home, I felt a calm sense of control.

In his 2014 ESPY Awards speech, Stuart Scott said, "When you die, it does not mean you lose to cancer. You beat cancer by how you lived, why you live, and in the manner in which you live."

And just like that, as I prepared to die, I lived.

PART V

FLYING

Ends are not bad things; they just mean that something else is about to begin.

And there are many things that don't really end, anyway, they just begin again in a new way. Ends are not bad and many ends aren't really an ending; some things are never-ending.

— C. JOYBELL C.

MATURING

JACKIE: 14–17 (2013–2016)

Six months had elapsed since I quit my chemotherapy, and I felt... healthy. Seeing that death was in no hurry to claim me, I decided to follow Dylan Thomas's advice "and not go gently into that good night." Instead, I focused all my energy on my three youngest children. I hoped I could see them graduate high school before my remission ended. Besides putting them on a firm footing for life, I would conclude this schooling endeavor.

In 2014, Jackie officially entered her freshman year at State High. She continued to excel in all her classes, notably in business and finance. She was also one of the two students chosen to be the Roar Store's accounting managers, a school-based, student-run enterprise that sold State College High School apparel and merchandise. During the summer of 2015, Jackie got a job as a busser at a nearby steakhouse. Owing to her vibrant personality and work ethic, her boss promoted her to hostess in a short few month. As Jackie's sophomore year approached, we found ourselves reclining in lounge chairs on our patio, drinking iced tea, and basking in the few remaining days of summer.

"When are you going to give your two weeks' notice?" I asked.

She rose and took off her sunglasses. "What two weeks' notice?" she said.

"Your job at the restaurant, of course. Do you have others?"

"I'm not quitting my job."

It was now my turn to rise. "Did we not just go over your schedule for this year? You can't take all these courses, *and* run cross-country, *and* work. That's impossible."

"Mom, I can do it. I don't want to quit my job. I won't work after school. I'll only do weekends."

"You're not working, Jackie. You can't," I said, resuming my recumbent position.

"Mom, I'm putting most of my money in my college account. Didn't you say we had to contribute to our college expenses?"

Touché.

"Yes, Jackie," I said. "Scholarships, essay contests, and competitions, that's how I expect you to contribute, not by working."

"Why can't I work during the school year? Dani did."

She knew the last part was a mistake as she watched me spring up from my lounge chair like a Jack-in-the-box. "Don't ever say that to me again," I said, pointing a finger at her. "You know what I always say: Every child is different. I will not feel guilty if I did one thing for one child and something different for another."

"Sorry. All I meant is I can do it."

"Is your memory so short? What happened this past May, during AP season? You couldn't sleep; you were anxious; you couldn't handle the stress. And this time, you want to take three more APs, including the economics one with me, and continue to work? That's too much, sweetheart. You can't perform well with that amount of pressure. So no, it's not happening." I repositioned myself in my lounge chair, turning away from her.

Once Jackie realized I wouldn't compromise, she ran inside. She'd probably seek out her brothers to discuss their common "mom problem." Since becoming teenagers, that's the one area where my three agreed. Jackie would probably run to her twin first, believing she would find an ally in him. She would often be proven wrong. Joey might disagree about how I managed *his* life, but he usually agreed with me regarding Jackie's and Nick's. He once confided in me that Jackie lacked motivation for schoolwork, and Nick was surveying colleges based on their track team's success instead of their academic offerings. It might seem easy to infer that Joey was a tattletale or wanted me to be as angry with the other kids as I often was at him, but the truth is Joey cared about them. When it came to competition and schoolwork, he and I were much alike. At times, I thought we were too much alike, resulting in our frequent arguments. We didn't like people telling us what to do. Some kids, however, needed it.

Moments later, Jackie came back outside. "Okay, fine, Mom, maybe it was too much. I decided to drop AP Art History."

It wasn't the resolution I had hoped for. I would have preferred Jackie quit her job, but it would have to suffice.

"Okay then, and you'll only—"

"Okay," she said and hastened away.

I continued soaking in the sunshine, wishing I could solve all my altercations with my children as quickly as the ones with Jackie.

Just a few weeks later, while the two of us were at the kitchen table, shucking corn, Jackie said, "Mom, I feel lost."

I knew before I took the bait, I would require a refill of my empty wine glass. Reaching for the bottle of pinot noir and trying to delay the inevitable, I teased, "Where did you last see yourself? Get it? Lost?"

"Mom, that wasn't even close to being funny."

"I thought so," I said, taking a sip of wine. "Okay, shoot. Why do you feel lost, Sweetie?"

"I don't know what I want to do with my life. I don't have a passion for anything. I'm average at everything. Sometimes I don't feel like I belong in this family, like... like the rest of them."

"Sweetie, first of all, you're intelligent and above average in everything. And second, stop trying to be like your siblings; just be who you are."

"That's just it, Mom. I don't know who that is."

"Well, how are you going to find out?"

"I should go away."

"Away where? For the summer? Like the scuba diving camp?"

"Well, yeah, sort of. No, not really. Like going away to Spain for the school year, like…"

Like Danielle did in France, is what she intended to say and wisely trailed off. "To Spain? You hope to find yourself there?"

"I don't know. Maybe. Now that everyone knows Joey's skipping his sophomore year and graduating with Nick—"

"Oh, God, don't remind me." Poor Nick. He was not happy about that.

"Well, neither am I because everyone keeps asking me if I'm graduating early, too. If I say no, they'll say, 'you're not as smart as your twin.' But if I go to Spain, I can say, 'no, I'm going to spend a year abroad instead.'"

I put my glass down and said, "Jackie, you're not going. School Year Abroad is expensive. I'm not going to spend that kind of money because you're embarrassed to tell your friends you're not graduating early with Joey. Stop letting people's opinions of you matter. This world will devour you." Her bored facial expression begged me not to deliver one of my familiar "believe in yourself" speeches. So, I changed tack. "Danielle had to convince me why it would be advantageous to study in France for a year. She had a plan. You have none. You sound like one of these rich kids who have to 'find themselves' and end up wasting their parents' money. I don't believe in that kind of stuff."

Jackie blew her nose and held back the tears that moistened her eyes. To my astonishment, she stood firm and debated me.

"I may not have all the details of my plan yet, Mom, but you know I learn best immersed in the world, not a classroom. I chose Spain because I enjoy learning Spanish. I want to be fluent in it." She hesitated briefly, then added, "Just like Dani was in French when she got back from France."

She moved from the table and ran up the stairs to her room. Flustered yet impressed with how Jackie defended herself, I rose from the table to continue my meal prep. Mikey was coming home from his summer internship, and I wanted to grill jerk chicken, boil corn on the cob, and cook rice and beans, one of his favorite meal combos. I placed the cobs in the pot of boiling water and then grabbed the chicken from the refrigerator to begin the seasoning process. I turned to lay the chicken package on the kitchen counter and almost toppled into Jackie.

"Oh, sorry, I didn't know you were behind me."

"Mom, what if I apply for the merit-based scholarship? If I get it, can I go?"

"Jackie, money isn't the only reason I'm against this. Besides learning Spanish, you haven't quite convinced me *why* you should go. What's your main goal? And are you planning this for junior or senior year?"

"I was considering junior year, so I can come back and graduate with my friends as a senior."

"Your junior year is Nick's and Joey's last year here, and when you return, they'll be off to college. Do you want to spend two years without them?"

"I guess. I don't know."

"Well, mull it over some more, and we'll discuss it next week."

"Thanks, Mom," she said and disappeared to her room.

"I'm not promising anything," I shouted after her. That evening, after dinner, I decided to give Danielle a call.

"Hi, Dani. Your sister wants to spend a year abroad studying in Spain."

"Oh, what a terrific idea. I'm certain Jackie'll love it."

I felt betrayed. After an hour on the phone listening to Danielle's many reasons why her sister's escape to Spain would be beneficial, I was more open to the idea than I expected.

I asked, "Okay, if I let her go, when would be a better time, junior or senior year? I'm leaning toward senior year."

"Junior year," Danielle said.

0 for 2.

"I'm surprised," I said. "When you came back for your senior year, most of your friends were gone. You said your senior year would have been a complete waste of time if it wasn't for your research project at Penn State and your record-breaking swim season."

"Yeah, wow, that seems like such a long time ago now," she said. "But Jackie and I are different. She has lots more friends than I did. And I'm also considering college applications. Sure, there were some seniors in France with me trying to complete college applications and procure recommendations, but it's a less arduous process to handle back home. My French teachers got to know me and were able to write detailed letters. They barely knew the seniors when they arrived in September and probably wrote generic recommendations for them due by November."

"Hmm, good point. I leaned more towards the family angle, how she'll be without her brothers for two years. She's close to them, and if she goes her junior year, she'll come home to a house with only her parents."

"Ha, that will probably be the hardest part," Danielle said. "I know I couldn't do it."

I told Jackie the following day to go ahead and apply for the scholarship. The money part was still an issue, so I figured she could go if she got the award. In the meantime, I planned to discuss the subject with her father. After Danielle's successful school year in France, I knew my husband was persuadable.

A few months later, the School Year Abroad accepted Jackie to their program. I talked with Michael in his workshop as he practiced with his latest welding toy.

"You're determined to send all my kids away from me, even my Bubbles?" he asked as he removed his welding mask and laid it on his worktable.

"I couldn't deprive her of this opportunity, especially since I allowed Danielle to go, although I would never admit that to her. She also got the merit scholarship to defray the cost."

"I'm going to miss her," he said and sighed.

"It's only for nine months. Jackie will be back before you know it."

"No, it's not that," Michael said. "Danielle grew up so fast. I blinked, and she was an adult. I want to hold on to my baby Jackie as long as possible. And now, she's going off to Spain."

I walked over to my husband. "You can hold on to me," I said, putting my arms around his perspiring neck.

He hugged me back. "Our kids are growing up too fast, Carline. We should have frozen them as toddlers when we had the chance."

NICK: 15–18 (2013–2016)

"Weren't you ever a teenager?" Michael asked as he pulled the covers down and slid into bed. "Have you never experienced a sense of youthful exuberance?"

We were deep into another argument—this time about dating.

"Yes, and that's exactly my point," I said. "Our "youthful exuberance," as you put it, allowed us to do stupid things at that age; we reasoned with our hormones instead of our brains. That child does not need girlfriends messing with his head. He's in high school. Now, more than ever, he needs to be focused on his studies like—like Joey." I climbed into bed next to Michael.

"He is not Joey; how many times are we going to go through this?"

"I'm not saying he is," I said. "Only that he should focus on his schoolwork *like* Joey. I'm not even upset with him having a girlfriend; I'm more disturbed by his lying."

"Well, do you blame him?" Michael said, facing me. "You go on and on, telling them it's a bad idea to date in high school."

"And I've also told them never to lie to me and—" A knock on our bedroom door interrupted our dispute.

"Who's there?" I asked.

"It's me," Nick said.

I straightened up and crossed my arms when I heard his voice. "Come in," I said.

"Hi, Mom," Nick began. "I'm sorry I lied to you. Well, I didn't *really* lie to you. I just never told you about my girlfriend."

"A lie of omission is still a lie."

"Okay, well, then I'm sorry I omitted telling you the truth. I didn't plan on having a girlfriend; it just happened."

"Well, why didn't it just happen to Dani and Mikey?" I asked.

"I'm not them," he said.

Michael let out a cough and looked away.

"I'm not telling you to be like them," I said, ignoring my husband. "I only want you to do well in your classes without being distracted."

"That's just it, Mom, I am doing well. I got straight As last marking period in all my classes, *and* even in your economics class, my computer graphics teacher loves me; I'm doing well in band and track. What else do you want, Mom?"

Michael coughed again.

I wanted to tell my son, 'Nick, you are a Black child. That's how the world sees you. I don't want them to assume your success in life is due to affirmative action. You're a Black male in America; you need to work twice as hard as your white friends. You need to stay focused. I want you to go out there and compete with the best of them. I want so much for you. But more importantly, I want you to want more for yourself.'

But I didn't say any of that. I was lying next to a white husband who had never lived in my skin and probing the face of my over-privileged biracial child who never lived in the real world. I knew neither of them would understand my fears. Instead, I said, "Okay, Nick, you're right. You've done well in your academics as well as athletics. But this is only the beginning, sweetheart; college will be another battle. You can't afford to get distracted now."

Nick stared down at the hardwood floor.

"However," I said. "I'm willing to meet you halfway. You already have your girlfriend, and well, that's that, but if your grades start to suffer… well, let's just say, I will not be happy."

His face lit up. "Thanks, Mom," he said as he leaned over to kiss me. "Good night, Mom. Night, Dad."

"Good night," we both replied.

"My God, you're tough," Michael said after Nick had left our room. "Glad you weren't my mom."

"One of us has to be the tough parent," I said, and I kissed him good night.

"You're perfect for the role."

Allowing Nick to have a girlfriend worked to my advantage, as he perfected his time management skills. He knew I would criticize him if his grades dropped even slightly. The summer of 2016 found Nick and me alone at home most days. He spent his time between social media and running, which annoyed me.

"Nick, you could accomplish so much more if you weren't lazy," I said. I feared that might provoke him instead of motivating him. It ended up doing neither.

He only simpered at me and said, "According to Bill Gates, 'you should hire a lazy person to do a difficult job because he'll always find an easier way to do it.'" Pleased with his rebuttal, he added, "Do you want to hurt my chances of working for Microsoft, Mom?"

"Seriously, Nick, what's your plan for the summer besides running? You're not working like Jackie, and you're not attending any camps like Joey. Are you going to dilly-dally all summer doing nothing? Just being lazy?"

"Mom, I'm doing the MOSTEC program," he said, referring to the MIT Online Science, Technology, and Engineering Community program.

"I know, but it's only a couple of hours online per day. Have you explored scholarships, essay contests, anything?"

"I will, Mom."

"Yeah, I know. I've heard that before, but when?"

"Fine, Mom. Now. I'm going to search for scholarships and essay contests now. Okay?" With that said, he pushed himself from the kitchen table and stomped away.

About two weeks later, I was in the supermarket when I received a call from Nick telling me to check my email. I wanted to wait until I got home, but I sensed him smiling on the other end. My curiosity got the better of me. I moved to a side of the aisle by the canned vegetables and opened my email to:

JESSE WILLIAMS ESSAY CONTEST WINNERS ANNOUNCED

Black Male Development Symposium[1]

TOP PRIZE: Nick Feffer (State College, PA)

I came racing home to a grinning Nick eating popcorn at the kitchen table. He was waiting for my arrival.

"How do you do it, Nick?" I said, shaking my head. "You must be the luckiest kid alive."

"Luck has nothing to do with it, Mom. It's my lazy man's motto," he said, grinning.

"When did you write the essay?"

"Two weeks ago, after you yelled at me about how unproductive I was. I went online, and that contest by the Black Male Development Symposium just spoke to me. Jesse Williams' fiery BET speech moved me, and well, having attended the Telluride program last year, the essay just kinda flowed out. I wrote it and submitted it that day."

I stood corrected. Nick did understand the plight of Black males in this country. "You're welcome," I said.

Nick also gained a lot of confidence from having a girlfriend. I understand there is a difference when your mom says you're handsome and when your girlfriend does. But there seemed to be more to it than that. I believe his boldness arose because he had something Joey did not—a girlfriend. A week before junior prom, I overheard Nick say to Joey, "Ask her out, Joey. Julie told her friend to tell me to tell you that she likes you. Go ahead. Don't be afraid."

"Teenagers," I muttered as I tiptoed away.

Nick was thrilled when Joey finally declared he was quitting soccer that fall and joining the cross-country and track teams. He envisioned a beautiful picture of the Feffers cross-country and 4x800-meter relay teams, just as he had a year before Joey disappointed him. After Joey departed from the kitchen, I pulled Nick aside. "You know how your brother is, Nick. When he joins the team, he will try to do well *and* try to beat you. We've seen that play before."

"This time, it ends differently," Nick said. "Do you know why? Because I'm ready for Joey to bring it."

With wide eyes and a gaping mouth, I watched my son swagger away. He was no longer the chubby-cheeked child who whimpered in the closet due to his younger brother's teasing. Nick had matured into a confident, capable young man.

THE 2016–2017 SCHOOL YEAR, Nick and Joey's last high school year and last year at home with me, was like herding cats. Or maybe lions. No words could accurately describe what happened. Jackie had followed in her sister's footsteps and studied abroad in Spain for the year, leaving me alone with three men, a position I had never been in. I added a new word to my lexicon between my teenagers' raging testosterone and defiance: fine.

"I don't want to take violin lessons anymore."

"Why, Joey? You're pretty good."

"Pretty good is a stretch, Mom. I could be good, but that would require too much practice time. There are other things I would rather do."

I could have said, 'Like what?' Instead, I said, "Fine."

"What about you, Nick? Do you want to continue with trumpet lessons?"

"Sure, but I'm not going to do jazz band."

"Why not? You love jazz band. *I* love jazz band."

"The afternoon practices are interfering with track."

"Okay, fine."

"Joey, when is the Linguistic Olympiad exam?"

"Next Tuesday."

"Are you both registered for it?"

"Nick's not taking it."

"Hey, thanks, buddy, I like how you just threw me under the bus," said Nick.

"Don't mention it," said Joey.

"Nick, is that true?"

"Well, kind of, I mean, yeah, I don't want to take it, Mom."

"Why not? All of my kids have done well on that exam."

"I don't know if 'well' is the right word," Nick said.

"Speak for yourself," said Joey.

"Mom," Nick said, ignoring Joey. "I do *okay* on that exam, nothing spectacular. It's given during class time, and I'll be missing a whole day of school and have lots of homework to make up. I don't see the point."

"Okay, fine," I said. I was beginning to sound like a parrot until I added, "But you're taking all the other Olympiads: chem, physics, and bio."

"Can we at least discuss those?" Nick asked.

Time to put 'fine' away. "No."

That senior year, I seemed to have argued about everything with my sons, from their messy rooms to college choices and essays. Joey was most often the culprit, but Nick did contribute when he felt excluded from the arguments.

"Did you reply to the Harvard track coach?" I asked Nick.

"No, I'm still waiting to hear from Princeton."

"You can still reply to Harvard."

"I'm not sure I want to go there."

"Why wouldn't you?"

"Well, it's Dani's school and—"

"And let me guess, Joey might end up there?"

Nick remained silent.

"First of all," I continued, "it's not Danielle's school. That's ridiculous. And—"

"Mom, I want to forge my own path."

"It's all about Joey, isn't it?"

"Maybe it is. Is that a bad thing?"

"Yes. Yes, it is. It's more than bad; it's stupid. It's a prodigious school, Nick. It's Harvard. You may not even see each other."

"Well, then what's the point?"

"Because it's a good school, and you can make time to connect when you want. You must admit it was nice having Joey on the track team and in some of your classes. You guys can go to dinner together in Boston like Dani and Mikey."

"No, Mom. You don't understand. I need to go to my *own* school," he said.

"Nick, it would be funny if you both ended up at Princeton. You know Joey is considering Princeton's economics program."

Nick put his head down, staring at the floor as he often did during these discussions. He didn't find my comment amusing.

"Princeton doesn't even have a bioengineering program," I said. "It doesn't have a medical school. Harvard has both. And remember, I'm not paying to send you to college to run, Nick. You're going to college for an education. You're a good runner, but you're not going to the Olympics."

"So you keep telling me, Mom."

"Well, someone has to," I said.

Nick kept gazing down at the floor again, trying not to cry.

"I'm sorry, Sweetie. I'm not trying to hurt you. I just want you to be realistic. I want you to focus on your studies because there's a whole life after college you need to consider. You're so smart, Nick. I'm confident all the top colleges will admit you, and you could study anything you want. I hate when these colleges call you student-athletes, but the emphasis is mostly on the athlete part."

"Mom, you still don't get it," he said, finally making eye contact.

"Running is part of who I am. It doesn't matter where I go; I intend to run. Yeah, maybe I won't make it to the Olympics, but it doesn't matter, Mom. I still want to run."

"Okay, but—"

"You have no idea how running makes me feel. When I run, I feel free, strong, and fast. Running keeps me from eating junk, drinking soda and alcohol, or taking drugs. It keeps me focused and helps me better manage my homework and studying time. And it's something I'm good at, Mom. I can't *not* run."

After a moment, I said, "I guess I can't argue with that."

"No, you can't."

I drove Nick to most of the universities interested in him as a scholar and track recruit. I lodged in various hotels while Nick ran with the teams. We argued a lot during those long-distance drives, which made me wonder if Nick still thought I was the "best mom in the world," as he did many years ago. Nick finally decided on Dartmouth. With its 269-acre main campus situated on the green hills of New England's Upper Valley, it was the perfect choice for my nature-loving son. We celebrated Nick's decision over a Baskin Robbins banana split for him and a sundae for me.

JOEY: 14–17 (2013–2017)

I had hoped the Tunisia altercation with Joey would have been our last major fight; unfortunately, it proved to be the tip of the iceberg. Like the Titanic, Joey and I headed towards an inevitable crash. A simple question about camps one afternoon in Joey's bedroom charted our collision course.

"The RSI application is out," I said, referring to the Research Science Institute. "Are you going to apply?"

"I don't know, Mom. It's extremely competitive," he said.

"Since when has that ever stopped you? Besides, you lose nothing for trying, Joey."

"Just my time, Mom," he said, glancing up from his book. "Like I have nothing else to do."

"Fine, Joey," I said. "Do what you want. Let's hope you do as well this year as you did last year."

"What is that supposed to mean?" he said, rising from his chair and planting himself directly in front of me.

I couldn't believe he was now taller than me. When did that happen? I had to tilt my head upwards to catch his eyes. Nick had once told me that if Joey turned out to be the tallest child in this family, he would definitely know life was unfair. It seemed life was unfair. "It means you did better as an eighth grader on the Olympiad exams than last year as a ninth grader. And now, it seems all you ever want to do is argue with me."

"Well, maybe, if you hadn't embarrassed me by emailing my coach and getting me kicked off the quiz bowl team—"

"Well, maybe, if you kept your room clean, I wouldn't have to threaten to pull you off the team."

"Well maybe, if you kept out of my room, then—"

"Excuse me, do you pay rent here? One more word out of you and your room will be the garage."

He hurried past me, bumping against me as he made his way out of his room.

"Did you just push me?" I yelled after him as he descended the stairs.

"Did you feel me pushing you?" he called back without turning.

"What just happened?" I heard Michael asking Joey from downstairs. "Did you push your mom?"

I ran down the steps.

"I didn't push her. I brushed up against her," Joey said.

"He pushed me," I said, finally reaching the bottom floor.

Seething with anger, Michael asked Joey, "What is wrong with you?"

"Why do you always take her side? She lies, and you always believe her," he said, tears forming in his eyes.

"You're calling me a liar?" I said.

"You're calling your mother a liar?"

The scene, which we afterward referred to as The Push, progressively unraveled. At one point, we were all shouting and crying. Even Jackie and Nick were crying in their upstairs bedrooms. When the situation quieted down, and everyone retreated to their safe zones, I called Rony. "I need a favor," I said and recounted The Push.

"You're not getting rid of my son," Michael said.

"Yes. I am. Temporarily."

"What makes you presume your brother will take him?"

"Because that's what we do for family."

"Carline, you can't do this. You're not thinking rationally."

"I am not going to have a child push me and call me a liar. I don't tolerate rude behavior from anyone, let alone my child. He's going."

"Carline, please don't do this."

"Do you have any better ideas? Well? Do you? I came this close to smacking that boy," I said, drawing my thumb and index finger close together. "And what would he have done? Hit me back? Better yet, called the police and have me arrested for child abuse?"

"What will Jackie and Nick think of you sending their brother away?"

"What will they think of me if I *don't*? We've all been tiptoeing around Joey for months, ever since he ranted about being removed from the quiz bowl team. We would never have tolerated such behavior from the other kids. What message are we sending them?"

Michael knew there would be no reasoning with me when I was this angry, so he disappeared to his workshop-garage. In the meantime, I climbed the stairs to Joey's room to confront him with the news.

"Pack your stuff; you're finishing the rest of your high school years in New York. You'll be living with Uncle Rony. We leave for New York tomorrow at 7 am."

He didn't seem fazed. He must have heard the conversation Michael and I discussed.

Still, he asked, "Why?"

"Why what?"

"Why do I have to go live in New York?"

"Because I don't tolerate rude children in my house. I don't know; call it the Haitian in me. I wasn't raised in a household where kids spoke back to their parents, pushed, or called them liars. Now, pack."

He remained calm. "What school will I be attending? Brooklyn Tech? Stuyvesant?"

Wow, I was shocked, but I shouldn't have been. Joey had already begun analyzing his new life in New York. He contemplated living without us. Without *me*. Could I *actually* send him away? I must admit I formulated the idea while nursing a bruised ego. Eventually, I thought he would apologize, and we would end this. But what if he didn't apologize? Maybe we both needed a separation.

"I don't know, Joey," I finally said. "We'll figure things out as we go along." I glanced at his chaotic mess of crumpled jeans, sweaty t-shirts, dirty shorts, and smelly socks, all dispersed on the floor resembling a Pollock painting displayed on a beige carpeted canvas, and said, "Start packing. Now."

As I made my way out of Joey's room, I saw Jackie and Nick coming out of theirs. They had ruby-red blotches on their faces with bloodshot, puffy eyes. We stared at each other. Without speaking, they left for Joey's room, and I proceeded downstairs to my office. Minutes later, I heard Michael come back into the house and climbed to Joey's room. I left my office door ajar to eavesdrop on the exchanges taking place upstairs. The muffled word "apologize" was the only one I heard multiple times. After a couple of hours, the meeting disbanded, and I saw Joey standing outside my French office doors.

"Could I come in?" he asked.

"Are you packed?" I replied.

"Well, that's what I want to discuss with you."

"There's nothing to discuss, Joey."

"Can I come in?"

"Fine, come in."

"I'm sorry for what transpired earlier between us."

"Yeah, me too," I said, recognizing yet another of Joey's non-apologies.

"I don't want to live in New York."

"I didn't give you a choice."

"Mom, I apologized."

"Did you?"

"Mom, do you love me?" Joey asked, with water blurring his eyes.

"Don't try to guilt-trip me, Joey. It won't work."

"I want to know, Mom, because if you do love me, I don't understand how you could easily throw me away like that... like... like trash." he stammered as a few teardrops escaped.

"Joey, I'm not throwing you away," I said, trying to hold back my tears. "You don't believe this is hard for me? Do you assume this is all about my pride? Well, you're wrong. This is the hardest thing I could do to my child, but I'm doing it *because* I love you." My tears finally burst through despite my effort.

"I don't follow."

"Maybe once you're a parent, you will. Joey, we used to relate well to each other. You used to be my Pumpkin, my genius baby boy. But ever since you started high school, it feels as if you can't stand the sight of me. I know teenagers are a bit rude, and they're trying to test out their new sense of independence on their parents, namely their mom. I get it. Lord knows Danielle did it. But your attitude is beyond rude; it's... it's anger. I'm perplexed as to what I did to provoke such resentment." I stopped as he took a seat on the black leather armchair in my office. I tried to discern some comprehension on his face.

Finding none, I continued, "Sometimes, I wonder if it's because I got cancer again. Maybe you're afraid I will die this time, so you want to detach yourself from me. Sometimes I suspect it's because of the depression I sustained with the second round of chemo, and I guess I was lost back then, angry even, and I shut everyone out. I'm sorry; I thought I was dying. It was never about you guys. It was all the medications; they aggravated my depression." I paused, wiped away tears, and exhaled.

"This is a long shot," I said, "but it could also be... that maybe...

you could be jealous of Nick? You're the one who listened to me and kept your focus on your studies and not on girls. And yet, Nick is in the papers every day for track, and he's popular with the ladies, and... well, maybe you hate how I took 'fun' away from you."

Joey sighed. "Mom, you're wrong on so many levels."

"Okay then, enlighten me."

"You're right; maybe I have been upset these days. I didn't do as well as I wanted on the Olympiad exams and being on the soccer team was not as exciting as I anticipated—don't, Mom, don't give me that look."

"What look?" I asked, feigning innocence.

"That one. The 'I told you so' one. Although you and Nick were right, I had to come to that conclusion on my own. And now, I did. Anyway, I was also mad when you pulled me off the quiz bowl team. You humiliated me, Mom."

"It was only temporary. But I'm sorry about that. Maybe I shouldn't have removed you from the team. I did warn you, though. And you should know by now I follow through with my threats. I don't bluff."

"Does that mean I'm still going to New York in the morning?"

He caught me off guard. Boy, he was good. "I don't know, Joey," I said. "I'm doing something wrong. I hate this hostility between us. Before our relationship disintegrates completely, maybe we should try something different."

"Why New York? Why your brother? Why not Aunt Edwidge in Florida?"

"Well, he raised two wonderful young men."

"So did your sister."

I searched his face and found the tiny toddler who used to hide in my headboard cabinet in my bedroom when we played hide and seek, the same one who outed me as the tooth fairy to his twin sister so many years ago. I confessed. "My brother would be tougher on you than my sister. She would pamper you and act as if you're there for a vacation."

"I knew it," Joey said. "You're sending me to Uncle Rony's as a punishment."

"No, not a punishment, exactly." I continued. "Also, because New York is closer than Florida, and if you were in New York, I would visit you every weekend because I would miss you so much."

"I would miss you, too, Mom."

We rose from our chairs and hugged for a long time. There was no further discussion about going to New York.

My relationship with Joey improved for a couple of months afterward. But, by the following year, his senior year, it chilled again and advanced at warp speed towards the iceberg, beginning with the senior prom incident. Nick and Joey had decided to split up and attend the prom with their respective friends. Nick and his girl-friend planned to go to a friend's house for the pre-prom dinner, and Joey's group would come to ours. I was overjoyed and made sure everything was perfect, from the gold tablecloth and napkins to the home-cooked meal. I thought the evening had been successful, but for some reason, it didn't seem Joey concurred.

"How was the prom?" I asked when Joey came down for break-fast the next day.

"It was okay," he said, reaching for a bowl from the cupboard.

"*Just,* okay?"

"Yeah, okay."

"Did your girlfriend enjoy it?"

He put the jug of milk down on the counter, stared at me, and said, "She's not my girlfriend, Mom. We're just friends. I told you that before."

"She's a girl, and she's your friend, so she's a *girl*-friend, right?"

"Whatever," he said as he poured the milk over his Frosted Flakes.

"What's your problem, Joey?"

"Nothing, Mom. I'm tired, and I don't feel like talking about the prom. I said it was okay."

"Well, at least, you could say thank you. I labored to create a perfect evening for you and your friends."

He said, "Thank you," and resumed eating without glancing up from the cereal box.

The Titanic struck the iceberg when Joey was named a Presidential Scholar for Pennsylvania. The award came as no surprise to any of us. When Joey looked up the remaining four or five finalists, he told me, "I'm pretty sure I've got this, Mom. The other guys are good, but I'm an All-American track runner, *and* I'm smart. I'm well-rounded." I questioned his flawed perfection, but he turned out to be correct.

He received three tickets for the award ceremony. Customarily, the two parents and a teacher would attend. I was ecstatic when he shared the good news with me. I hugged him and didn't want to let go until I heard, "I hope you don't mind, Mom, but I've decided to take Dad and Jackie."

My arms loosened around him. "Excuse me?" I said, pulling out of our hug.

"I've decided to take Dad and Jackie to the Presidential Award ceremony in D.C.," he repeated, but with a much slower cadence. "I'm hoping it motivates Jackie to try to win the award next year."

"What about me?" I said. "I always go to these award ceremonies."

"I know you do," he said, "but this time, I want it to be Dad's turn. You flew to Florida and Tunisia with me, to California with Mikey, to Georgia with Nick, to D.C. with Dani, and many more. It's Dad's turn."

"Joey," I said, rubbing my eyes, "do you ever wonder why your dad's and my relationship works so well? It's because Dad and I care about different, but equally important, things. We don't dictate to each other who should go where. Things usually fall into place. Who was your flag football coach? Who took you guys to hockey practice? Who made it to all your soccer games, particularly your away doubleheaders in Pittsburgh? Who also fell asleep at your music recitals and award ceremonies? Dad does the sports things, and I do the educational stuff. That's why you're so 'well-rounded,' as you put it."

231

"Are you saying Dad wouldn't want to go?"

"No, he would go, but he doesn't live for these moments as I do. I penciled it in my calendar as soon as you told me you might win," I said, pointing to the American Cancer Society calendar on my office wall. "I assumed I was going."

"Well, you shouldn't have," he said. "It's my award, and it's my decision."

His words echoed in my brain. I stared at Joey, waiting for him to say something. He stared back at me.

"Trust me, Joey, I won't make that mistake again," I said as I settled back in my office chair, swiveling literally and figuratively away from him.

It should have been a joyous occasion, mainly since Jackie was back from Spain. But it wasn't. We had a tense celebratory dinner that day. Whenever any of the kids won an award or had a dazzling musical or athletic performance, we usually celebrated by going out to dinner, cooking their favorite meal, or getting their favorite dessert. Mikey's dessert is chocolate cake, Nick's is ice cream cake, and Joey's is cheesecake. There was no cheesecake on the table that evening.

When Joey shared his Presidential Scholar news with the family at the dinner table and who he was taking, his father's first question was, "Why isn't your mother going?"

"I thought it should be your turn this time, Dad," he said.

"But your mom always goes to these things, and she did play a role in your educational success."

"Why am I going, Joey, and Mom isn't?" asked Jackie. "It doesn't make any sense."

Joey started to feel frustrated, and his error began to sink in.

"Guys," I said finally. "It's Joey's award, and he wants the both of you to go, so go. It's that simple."

Everyone looked at Joey, puzzled. I imagined they all thought *This is not how things operate at our house. Mom arranges everything and decides who goes where. Joey should know this by now.* We ate dinner in a rare silence.

To add further insult to injury, a week before the award ceremony in D.C., the teacher told Joey he couldn't make it due to a family emergency.

"Are you coming with us, then?" Michael asked me.

"Nope," I said.

"Why not? Joey said he invited you."

"No, he didn't. He said there's an extra ticket if I want to come. That's not the same as inviting me."

"Come on, Carline, please come. It's on Father's Day and our anniversary. We should be together."

If not for Joey, I should have gone for Michael's sake. It was Tunisia all over again. I didn't like how things ended back then. I was too stubborn. It seemed like I hadn't learned, or I was too old to change. "It's too late, Michael," I heard myself saying. "That kid hurt me. This entire episode has left a bitter taste in my mouth and an emptiness in my heart. He's already writing me off as if I had nothing to do with his educational achievements." With that, I cried. The last time I grieved so profoundly was when I got my cancer diagnosis. This pain felt worse.

"I can't see you like this," Michael said as he put his arms around me. "I shouldn't go either."

"No, you should go. In Joey's juvenile way, he was trying to do something good for you and Jackie. He has never been close to you, and this is how he hoped to improve his relationship with you before leaving for college. I don't believe Joey realized how much it would hurt me. I suspect he also wanted to tell me his success is his own, and he's in charge of making these decisions.

"Anyway, I've already committed to driving Nick and his relay team back from Nationals in North Carolina that weekend. Enough crying," I said, wiping away any remaining wetness off my face. "I'm fine. I also made hotel reservations for you and Jackie in D.C. You guys will have a lovely time. It'll be a nice way to catch up with your Bubbles since she returned from Spain."

That long-anticipated weekend arrived and proceeded as planned. After running the 4x800-meter relay with his team in

North Carolina, Joey left the next day with his father and Jackie for D.C. I stayed with Nick and the rest of the team for their distance medley relay scheduled for the following day. We all had breakfast together as a family. The kids wished their father a happy Father's Day and wished us a happy anniversary. Joey gave me an awkward hug, and I wished him good luck at the ceremony. As if on a movie set, I suppose we both wanted to cut out the preceding months' scenes and run another take with a happier ending. Instead, we said our goodbyes and walked away.

After the relay, I blasted the car radio for a lively trip home, singing with Nick and his teammates, trying to subdue the pain. When the trio returned from D.C. a few days later, no one talked much about it, except to say it was okay and that Betsy DeVos sent a taped video instead of appearing in person as Arne Duncan had at Danielle's Presidential ceremony. Joey didn't show me his Presidential Scholar medallion until many months later.

In the summer of 2017, Jackie, Nick, Michael, and I accompanied Joey to Ireland for the International Linguistic Olympiad, where he earned a silver medal. This award ceremony fared better than the previous one, but the bar was already at its nadir. The CTY's *Imagine* magazine published Joey's "Linguistics Olympiads: Puzzles and So Much More" essay.

Initially, unpleasant memories come to mind when I analyze Nick and Joey's last year at home with me, though in retrospect, there were some wonderful ones as well. Both of my sons received the Biology Olympiad prize at the senior award ceremony, and our local newspaper gave Nick the student-athlete award. Joey was named the salutatorian and received the Principal's Award, and Nick played his trumpet in the symphonic band before taking his seat with Joey and his fellow graduates. We hosted a lovely graduation party for the boys with all our family and friends, where the large banner showed Joey wearing his Harvard sweatshirt and Nick wearing his Dartmouth one.

My favorite memory was when Joey and Nick chose, independently and unknowing of the other's decision, to write about the other for their National Merit Scholarship essays: *Tell us about a person who has influenced you in a significant way.*

To my relief, their sibling rivalry had ended. The brotherly love their essays conveyed made me prouder than any award. Like Nick's *Drachewelt*, the ice dragons and fire dragons, as different as they may be, each with its strengths and weaknesses, learned how to harmonize with the other.

OUR ENDING

JACKIE: 18 *(2018)*

I was already disappointed no one accompanied me to Boston Logan Airport. Then I realized I'd also forgotten the hastily made "Welcome Home Jackie Feffer" sign. Still, I was glad that my baby girl was coming home. At least her welcome home banner had arrived on time, and there would be a good turnout for her surprise party this weekend—the one she would most likely be expecting. Jackie is the kind of person who puts a lot of thought into any gift she gives someone, and she demands the same dedication in return. Once, when she was around nine years old, she got up early to prepare breakfast for her siblings for an entire week. At the end of that week, she asked Joey to make breakfast for her the following day.

"No," he said with no hesitation.

"Why not?" she asked.

"I don't do breakfast," he said while polishing off the pancakes Jackie had just made for him.

"But, I've made breakfast for you this entire week."

"... and I thanked you."

I felt a twinge in my chest as I listened to their conversation while washing my coffee mug at the kitchen sink. I was *not* getting involved.

"... well, no one asked you to," I heard Joey saying. "I prefer spending these extra hours going over my schoolwork, not making breakfast for everyone."

"Mom," she called, dragging me into the argument. "Mom, did you hear what Joey said? It's not fair. It's not right."

"Well, they're not the same thing, fair and right," I corrected. I had their attention now. "It may not be fair that Joey wants to be selfish and can't reciprocate the kindness you showed him by preparing breakfast for him," I said, glowering at Joey, "but he is right, Sweetie, no one asked you to. When you do something nice for someone, you should do it because you want to, and not because you expect anything back."

"But, Mommy," she said and cried.

Arriving at the airport, I ran to the international arrivals area and waited expectantly with the conglomeration of people surveilling the entryway for their loved ones. My heart somersaulted when I finally saw my baby girl. Jackie made it safely home, back on U.S. soil, after being gone for nine months. After hugs and kisses, we made our way toward the exit with her luggage.

Scouting around, she said, "Are any of the other kids here? In the car?"

"No, Sweetie," I said, anticipating the question. "The boys are at a track meet, Mikey has finals, and Danielle's at her boyfriend's graduation. But we will see her tonight after dinner."

"She's not even having dinner with us?"

"No, she's having dinner with her boyfriend and his family. They booked it months ago. Remember how difficult it was getting dinner reservations in Boston during Dani's graduation week last year? That's another reason we're having dinner together at the hotel tonight."

Jackie lowered her chin to her chest.

"By the way," I said, "Danielle made the reservation for us in this beautiful five-star hotel. She said our cheap hotel days are over now that she's working and making *mucho dinero*. She said nothing is too expensive for her baby sister's first day back in the States." And I placed an arm around Jackie's shoulders.

"Except for spending time with me," Jackie mumbled.

"That's not fair, Jackie. You know everyone would have been here if they could. What am I? Chopped liver? I'm enjoying having you all to myself while we catch up on your Spain experience, and I catch you up on the hell your brothers have been putting me through. Wait here with your luggage. I have to go to the bathroom before we hit the road," I said and rushed away before she had a chance to answer.

I entered a bathroom stall, locked the door, and took out my cell phone. I texted the family the picture I took of Jackie as she arrived from the customs area and sent it to them with the caption: "She's back! Call her." I hesitated before adding the "call her" because I believed they would regardless, but I was unwilling to take any chances. Jackie already felt depressed. The phone calls and texts began arriving as soon as we finished loading the car.

"Hi, Bubbles," Michael said, "welcome back to the U.S."

"Hi, Daddy."

"I miss you so much, Bubs. I wish I could stay and talk, but unfortunately, I have a case to start. I just needed to hear your voice. Call you later. Love you."

"Love you too, Dad. Bye."

Joey was next. "Hi, Jackie, welcome back. I had no one to tease when you were gone. We have a lot to talk about."

"I know," she said. "Oh, by the way, congratulations, I heard you're one of the finalists for the Presidential Scholar Award. That's so cool."

"Thanks. Fingers crossed. Later."

The rest of the texts and phone calls from friends and family were similar as they welcomed Jackie back home. They brightened up the mood in the car as I drove to the hotel. After we checked in and ate a light dinner in our room, we heard a knock on our door. I opened it, and Danielle ran into the room and jumped on the bed, hugging her little sister.

"Welcome home, babe!" she shouted.

Jackie hugged her back. "Thanks," she said. And with that, the sadness and accusations vanished into the ether as Jackie met Danielle's grinning face.

We checked out of the hotel the next day and drove home with Danielle and Mikey. Danielle came back with us to celebrate Memorial Day weekend/Jackie's welcome home party, and Mikey ended another grueling MIT semester. The timing worked out perfectly, and so did Jackie's party.

JACKIE SPENT the rest of the summer reconnecting with her friends who graduated while she was in Spain. One day toward the end of the summer, I decided it was time to plan for the upcoming school year one last time. "Jackie, Sweetie, you haven't completed any college applications yet. The Common App has been out for over a month."

"I know, Mom. I'll do it later. Right now, my friends are going to be leaving for college, and I won't see them for a while."

"Jackie, who are you kidding?" I said. "Most of your friends are staying right here and going to Penn State, and besides, going away doesn't mean much these days in this social media age. There's texting, and Snapchat and FaceTime, and God knows what else."

"Well, I can't do lunch with them over Snapchat, so can I go to lunch with Rachel? She leaves for college tomorrow."

"Jackie, your friends are already in college. They know where they're going. You do not. Shouldn't you start concentrating on that? Do you have any ideas about the colleges you'll be applying to? What you're planning to study? By this time, when Dani was applying to colleges, she knew the ones she wanted and had several drafts already written."

"Now I know why you don't like other people comparing us. You do it often enough; you don't need others to do it for you," she snapped.

Did my ears just deceive me? I could not believe Jackie just said that to me. "Careful," I said. "I was anticipating a nice, relaxing year after the hellish one I just had with the boys. It seems I might be wrong. A word of warning, Jackie, don't push me. I don't have any more patience. Now, go pull up the Common App prompts and start formulating ideas and outlines of what to write. After we've reviewed a few of them, you can have lunch with your friend. Then I want to see some drafts by next week."

"Okay," she said, barely audible, as she stomped away.

I didn't see any drafts that week or the following week. This time, Jackie's excuse was that she was going for cross-country captain and needed to socialize with her teammates, primarily the freshmen. We both knew that wasn't the reason. Jackie is bright and witty, but her older siblings have always overshadowed her. She avoided deciding on college choices because she was nervous she might not follow in their Ivy League footsteps. I recalled Danielle's stating years ago that pressure makes diamonds, but I knew that pressure also makes dust. The pressure on my baby girl was tremendous. I didn't want her turning into dust. I knew I would have to tread lightly.

"Jackie, doesn't a cross-country captain have to, you know, *enjoy* running? You hardly did any mileage this summer and declined all the invitations Nick offered you to run with him. What makes you captain material?"

"I didn't believe Nick wanted to run with me, and if he did, his pace would be too fast. And Mom, you don't have to be the fastest on the team to be captain. You have to be a good organizer and someone the girls can relate to; someone *como yo*," she said, pointing to herself. "I plan to lead the stretching tomorrow, and afterward, I will mingle with the freshmen."

It worked. A week later, Jackie's teammates voted her as one of the three cross-country captains. And she excelled at it, as she joked with the girls and gave them pep talks before the meets. She also roped me into hosting a tie-dye event and a sleepover at our house for over fifty high school girls and graciously volunteered her dad to help build her team's float for the homecoming parade.

Meanwhile, Jackie earnestly worked at all her subjects and school activities like FBLA, quiz bowl, and forensics. She also resumed her after-school hostess job. In time, Jackie appeared more relaxed and less pressured, so I decided to resume college talks. This time, she was much more receptive. A couple of weeks later, she acquired all her necessary recommendations and finished her college essays.

"Are you going to retake the SATs?" I asked.

"Nope," Jackie said. "I only missed a couple of questions on the last one. My scores should be good for most schools and maybe even the Presidential Scholar Award."

To our disappointment, her score wasn't good enough for the Presidential Scholar Award. Joey called us from Harvard to inform us that Jackie's name did not make the list for consideration for the award. Jackie tried to hide this unpleasant news and asked instead, "How does Joey find out about these things?"

"He googles it like everyone else, I imagine. Your brother lives for these kinds of things. By the way," I said, twirling my chair away to face her, "shouldn't you be applying to other colleges and writing more essays, you know, just in case?"

"Just in case, what?" she said, entering my office. "You don't think I'm as smart as the others to get into Harvard?"

"No, Sweetheart, I never said that."

"You didn't have to, Mom; you showed it. Everything was always about them—Danielle's IQ, Mikey's music, Nick's running, and of course, your genius, Joey."

Her hidden disappointment about the Presidential Scholar news emerged and was rearing its ugly head at me. "Jackie, I celebrated every one of your sibling's achievements because I wanted to encourage them and let them know their hard work paid off. Just like I did for you. I even acknowledged some of the efforts that fell short and told you how proud I was of you for trying. I know how it must feel competing in such a large family; I've been there. I come from an overachieving family, too, you know. I wasn't the best student or the most outstanding athlete in my family. But I think I was the most courageous. I never give up, not on myself nor my children. Sweetie, I know it must be frustrating that the subjects you find difficult are painless for Joey. But other things like your wit, sense of humor, and personality that don't often make the headline news aren't as easy for them. And, in the long run, yours may be more important." I paused, pursing my lips for a moment and deciphering my daughter. "This isn't about me, and you know it. *You're* the one that's afraid you may not be accepted into Harvard, and you're just projecting that onto me." I rose from my chair and hugged her. "I think you're smart and beautiful and funny, and if Harvard doesn't accept you, then it's their loss."

She hugged me back and said softly, "I'm sorry, Mom. Thanks."

"Seriously, though," I said, "shouldn't you consider other schools to see what they have to offer? For all the grief you guys give me about Joey, I believe you only chose Harvard because of him."

"That's not true," she said, flopping herself in the adjacent armchair. "Besides, would it be a bad thing? I thought you liked Harvard."

How on earth was I having this conversation again? One kid *didn't* want to go to Harvard because of his brother; this one *did* want to go because of that same brother. "Yes, Jackie, I do like Harvard—*for Joey*. Maybe there's another school better suited *for you*."

"Well," she said, rising from the chair, "early action decision should be coming out soon. If I'm wait-listed or rejected, I'll consider other schools. But for now, I don't want to talk about it anymore. I gotta meet a few friends to finish our accounting project. Bye, Mom."

"Enjoy," I said as she left my office.

Later that week, Joey called to tell us that Harvard's acceptance email was expected out around 5 pm.

"How does he *do* that, Mom?" Jackie asked again.

The accepted students received their emails around 5 pm, and this time the list included Jackie. Harvard accepted her. So, in the end, Jackie did not have to worry about not living up to the high bar set by her siblings. Like me, Harvard had recognized her unique quality. The rest of her applications and brochures found their way to the trash as she accepted Harvard's offer. The twins would be together again. Joey would protect her, just like in their Montessori days. Her siblings called to congratulate her, and Michael and I took her out to dinner. We celebrated Jackie's accomplishment and that our last child was going off to college.

NEW BEGINNINGS (2018)

In family life, love is the oil that eases friction, the cement that binds closer together, and the music that brings harmony.

— FRIEDRICH NIETZSCHE

On Christmas of Jackie's senior year in high school, we gathered around the Christmas tree, opening presents, and sharing details of our respective lives. Joey seemed different—at ease—happy—*really* happy. I guess these few months at Harvard and away from me gave him the independence he had always yearned. A little over a month prior, when we visited Joey in Boston and met up with the rest of the family for dinner to celebrate the twins' eighteenth birthdays, he asked me not to be offended by his messy dorm room.

"As long as it's not in my house, Joey, I don't care."

"My dorm room is spotless," Nick said after being seated at the restaurant. "I can't stand a cluttered room. I don't know how I tolerated it before."

Wonders never cease.

Watching my family together, all home for Christmas, brought a sense of fulfillment and joy, although it would be short-lived.

"I love these shirts, Mom," Joey said.

"I'm glad, Sweetie, but a tad surprised. Nick was the one who loved clothes, not you. Are you trying to impress Malia Obama?"

He glanced over at Jackie, and they had one of their silent telepathic twin conversations. "She's not my type, Mom."

"What was that with Jackie? Are you seeing someone? What *is* your type? Is she Black? Asian? Latina? White?"

"No, Mom," he said in a grave tone. "It's not a she. It's a he."

Everyone stopped opening presents.

"Ha-ha, funny, Joey. You almost had me there for a minute," I said.

"I'm not joking. Mom, Dad, I'm gay."

It was a pin-drop moment as the room silenced itself. I gauged the other's reactions, but no one seemed as shocked as Michael and I were. "Did everyone know?" I finally asked.

"I told Jackie shortly before she left for Spain. I told Nick around senior prom, and I told Mikey and Dani a few weeks ago, around Thanksgiving, when they visited me in Boston."

"Why didn't you tell us, Joey? Why didn't you tell *me*?"

"Come on, guys," ordered Danielle to the other kids as she rose to her feet. "Let's go. Joey needs to talk to Mom and Dad."

The other kids got up with some of their presents to regroup downstairs. Jackie lightly kneaded Joey's right shoulder as she passed him, then turned to me and said, "It's not that serious, Mom."

"It is to me," I said and directed Joey toward our bedroom. The three of us marched to the bedroom and closed the door.

"This was not the way I rehearsed telling both of you, but now that I have, well...?"

"Well, what? You needed to rehearse before talking to us? Did you not have enough faith in us to know we would always love you?" I asked.

"I knew intuitively you would still love me," Joey said, "but I didn't know what your initial reaction might be."

"Love you, *intuitively*? What does that even mean?"

"Mom, I think sometimes you love the person who you want us to be. Not who we are. You spent your entire life planning our lives, shaping and molding us. Did you ever question who we were or wanted to become?"

I felt attacked, but I've grown used to it, dealing with my children over twenty-odd years. "Joey, I wasn't molding you. I was preparing you for the world. I was laying the foundation for building your strength, perseverance, and confidence, enabling you to succeed in whatever you choose to do. I was helping you grow into the person you were meant to be. Sweetheart, what you decide to major in college and who you love is totally your choice. Like our school objectives, I just provided the guidelines. The paths are yours."

After what seemed like a long moment of silence, Michael asked a series of questions: "Are you sure, Joey? How do you know? When did you know?"

"Yes, I'm sure, Dad," he said. "I suspected as much around middle school, but I knew by the time I officially started high school."

"How could you not share this with us, Joey?" I asked. "How could you shut me out of this part of you? I'm your mother. I'm supposed to know these things,"

"I wanted to, Mom, but... but you had cancer," he said. "You had cancer, Mom."

Suddenly, the ground seemed unlevelled, as if I wore mismatched shoes. "It doesn't matter, Joey," I said, "you should have told me... told us. You shouldn't have to... to pretend around us. We're your parents. That's why we're here—for our children. Oh my God," I said as I plunked down on my bed and sobbed. "Those last years were so... so bad. You were angry. I was angry. You should have told us, Joey."

When is the best time for a mom to get cancer? I remembered asking myself. When your kids are teenagers, I had answered—wrongly. Now I know the correct answer—never. There was never a good time for a mom to be ill. Your kids always need you. The umbilical cord is never truly cut.

"I wanted to, Mom, but you and Dad were dealing with a lot. I didn't want to add my confusion to it. By the time I reached high school and realized I was gay, I figured I could pretend for another three years until I fled to college." He paused. "It's why I was so annoyed after prom when you wouldn't stop asking if my date was my girlfriend."

"Did your date find out? Is that why you were bitter?"

"No, we didn't like each other like that. I made sure not to go out with any girl I knew romantically liked me. I would never want to lead anyone on. I was irritated because I was tired of pretending. I saw other gay couples at the prom, and I felt like a phony."

Mom, how can I kill myself? I remembered how Joey had inno-cently asked that question years ago. Did he revisit the thought when he realized he was gay? As a parent, I had often wished I believed in something or someone. A higher power of some sort who could wave a magic wand and make me feel confident my daughters would be safe while studying abroad. A higher power to help me believe my sons wouldn't be shot by the police or anyone else because they wore a hoodie. A higher power who would simply take away my cancer. But I couldn't. I didn't believe in that. This was one instance where I was happy we didn't belong to any reli-gious group. I wouldn't want my son's soul to be damned. I wouldn't want him to be among the statistics of gay and trans-gender youths who commit suicide every year. What a waste that would be—the future of humanity, deprived of Joey's genius. Of his humor. Of his love.

At Nick's soccer field all those years ago, what about the woman who assumed we were all Christian? I now felt guilty for judging her because I had done the same thing, believing all my kids were straight. What about when Joey wrote to Robert Frost about bully-ing? I remembered a line in Joey's essay that said something like... *thank you for writing this radical poem that tells individuals like me that being different is fine and that you do not have to change yourself to please others.* Was that an unintentional cry for help?

While Joey and Michael spoke, I began reliving all the conversations I'd ever had with my son. I grasped at any clue that might have alerted me to Joey's sexual orientation, trying to pinpoint the exact moment. There must have been signs. I knew I had high expectations for my kids, but I had even higher ones for myself. And I failed. I failed at the most fundamental part of being a mom—I didn't know my child. If nothing else, I thought being a stay-at-home mom had provided me with the benefit of knowing one's child for as often as I was with them. I became stuck in a guilt loop until I heard:

"... and I failed you, Mom," Joey said.

"What? What are you talking about?" I asked.

"I thought I failed you, Mom. I was no longer your perfect genius boy, and I was upset. I didn't want to be gay. I didn't choose to be gay."

"Oh honey," I said as I rose and hugged him. "You'll always be my perfect, genius baby boy, and nothing will ever change that. Society tries to make us hate ourselves, don't let them do that. You have to love who you are. I love you so much."

Michael joined our group hug as he also told his son how much he loved him.

I mastered the art of pretending as I interjected "oh's" and "ah's" during our lively conversation around our Christmas meal. But the discussion couldn't humor me, and the food tasted like cardboard as the feeling of despair overwhelmed me. I impersonated a cheerful mom because I didn't want Joey to assume my sadness meant I was disappointed in him. Quite the contrary, I was disappointed in myself.

I still found myself fraught with guilt months later and kept re-examining different scenes in my head, wondering how I could have responded differently—better, somehow—to Joey's past behavior. Nick finally took me aside after one of his races at Dartmouth.

"Stop beating yourself up about it, Mom. Stop trying to relitigate the past and just push on forward."

"Easier said than done, Nick. I don't know if I can. I'm his mother. I should have known."

"I'm his brother, and I didn't know. I used to talk to Joey about girls all the time in our rooms, on runs, and he pretended to agree. He was good at that. He was so, so good at pretending. I was mad at him when he told me because I felt stupid. And you know what he said? He said I was so happy trying to teach him and feel like an older brother that he was happy for me. *For me?* Can you believe that? I hugged him afterward, and I told him I was happy for him also. Happy he didn't have to hide anymore; he could come out and be himself. I sometimes go to Harvard and spend a weekend with him and his friends, and sometimes he comes to Dartmouth and watches me run. We've gotten closer, Mom. I'm happy about that, too."

EPILOGUE (2018)

Other things may change us, but we start and end with the family.

— ANTHONY BRANDT

I sit here at the kitchen table, the same one Michael built so many years ago. I run my hands over its smooth surface. It is as strong as its construction day and has witnessed many of our family's joys, sadness, and fears.

"A family that eats together stays together," I had often said.

Today it stands holding all my children's portfolios, essays, and awards, as I peruse them, putting the final touches on my memoir. I finally understand why the timeline of history was difficult for all my kids to comprehend. I too, failed to grasp this elusive thing we call "time." It seems like only yesterday I prepared to die, and four years later, I'm still very much alive. It seems like only yesterday I played hide and seek with my toddlers. Now I fear they may wander too far away for me to find them.

Danielle joined the crew team at Harvard and served as president of the Haitian club. She graduated with honors with a bachelor's degree in developmental biology and a minor in anthropology. She resides in New Jersey and travels widely for her job in healthcare management consulting. Danielle took the MCAT and may apply to medical school next year if she wants a change because, well, that's how my multi-talented child rolls.

Mikey competed with the MIT Quiz Bowl team and served as president of the triathlon club and Alpha Phi Omega service fraternity. He was also inducted into Phi Beta Kappa. In four years, he graduated with a Bachelor of Science *and* a Master of Engineering with a major in computer science and a minor in music. He will work for a computer software company in D.C. in the fall of 2018. He still composes all sorts of music and hopes to put his scores on the internet for movies or computer games because he's still my musician.

Nick finished his first year at Dartmouth. He intends to major in bioengineering with a minor in computer science. He runs for Dartmouth's varsity track and field team. Nick also has a part-time job working in a video game design lab and plays the keyboard and trumpet in a rock band because he's still my creative child.

Joey finished his first year at Harvard, where he intends to major in economics or applied math. He is also part of the tutoring staff for HOPE (Harvard Organization for Prison Education and Reform), traveling to a juvenile detention center once a week to help inmates with coursework to complete their GED. Joey called me a few months ago to tell me how much he loves me. He also apologized—a genuine apology—for the pain he caused me by not taking me to his Presidential Scholars ceremony. Joey moved me to tears. I played it off. "You're just saying that because you want to look good in my memoir."

"I always have a plan," he said.

Of course, he does. He's still my calculating child.

My baby Jackie is still at home with me, but not for much longer. I am reminded every day that she's no longer a baby. Today when we shopped for prom dresses and accessories, her red sequined gown shimmered upon her radiant nutmeg skin, perfectly capturing the elegance of my grown-up baby girl. The shopping made me reminisce about our dress-up days. Jackie has many friends and plans to major in psychology and perform stand-up comedy at Harvard because she's my social child.

I glide my hands across my kids' portfolio photos with their smiling faces staring at me. I close my eyes and see them as babies, as toddlers, as teenagers, reminiscing and missing our beautifully chaotic life.

In front from left to right: Danielle and Jackie.
In back from left to right: Mikey, Joey, and Nick.

POSTSCRIPT:
DINING ROOM RECOLLECTIONS

BY JOEY FEFFER

I had not sat in my chair for a while before now. Well, I guess it is not really my chair; it was Dani's, but when she moved away, I inherited it. The seat was mine for two years, but after Mikey left, no one had fixed seats anymore. Everyone sat wherever they chose —there were more than enough seats to choose from, after all— until we started eating at the countertop. There were too many empty chairs at the kitchen table, and who would want to make the long trek to the dining room anyway?

Our dining room is a small rectangular enclave near the entrance to our house. It has bright yellow walls and tall windows that admit sunlight, making the room feel peaceful and safe as if neither stress from work nor pain from swim practice could hurt anyone in there. In the center of this fortress, surrounded by eight wooden chairs, is my father's crowning achievement: our kitchen table. My dad built the table from scratch, but you would never be able to tell. The light oak wood is sanded so perfectly you could never feel the cuts made by an amateur carpenter. And the green Formica inlay appears so natural it seems it should have always been next to the wood as if trees were meant to grow in the middle of quarries. My dad decided to make the table soon after my mom discovered she was pregnant with twins. My parents had shopped around for a table bigger than the one that seated them and their three children, but after having no luck at the store, my dad announced he would make one himself.

"A big family needs a big dinner table," he insisted.

My mom agreed: "A family that eats together stays together."

And we did.

On Sunday mornings, my four siblings and I woke to the tempting sizzle of fresh bacon. We sprinted out of bed and raced down the stairs to the dining room—pushing any sluggish kid out of the way—to ensure we could get some food before the others greedily scarfed it down. On some weeknights, Mikey and Nick argued about who was the best GameCube player, but their disputes were put on hold when they saw my mom's signature Haitian spaghetti on the table. The cheesy goodness of the dish made them forget there had ever been any conflict at all. Most nights in between, we quickly and silently wolfed down pasta topped with my dad's divine tomato sauce. But then I would mention how Jackie's face resembled a squash, or Nick would spill his juice on his clothes, and the non-stop sound of five young children laughing would reverberate throughout the house.

During the day, we appropriated the dining room for several other uses. Sometimes after lunch, we filmed our imaginary Food Network show, "Little Cooks," which consisted of us microwaving frozen foods while explaining the most critical steps to our nonexistent audience. Other times, we laughed our heads off, watching our dad play the air guitar and dance around crazily as he shook our ice-cold chocolate milk for us.

Occasionally, to escape the barren confines of our basement, we did schoolwork in the dining room. Once, our mom had us draw periodic tables on large tee-shirts as a science project. She wanted to teach us the elements' positions by having us create pajamas that showed the full table in all its glory. With colored markers in hand, we started on our canvases. But after my mom left us unsupervised —she had to go pay bills or something—we inevitably used the markers, not on the shirts, but on each other. I can still see Nick and Jackie howling and screaming as reds and blues and greens ran across their skin until our mom came and told us to get back to work.

Almost ten years have passed since then. Jackie will be gone in a few months, and a year after that, Nick and I will leave too, flying from the nest as our siblings before us have. But my mom and dad will stay here. And this dining room and all the memories we had in it will be with them. And though we will live far apart, do different things, and lead separate lives, on Thanksgiving and Christmas and any other day we feel like it, we will come back here. We will all help prepare the turkey and stuffing, and then we will sit in our old seats around the table and relive the memories of our time together. And maybe make a few more.

ACKNOWLEDGMENTS

One of the unexpected joys in writing this book was deepening my relationships with old friends. Dr. Grace Hampton was my first non-relative reader. I want to thank her for providing an outside lens and helpful critiques about my book. I'd also like to thank Nathalie Augustin, one of my oldest elementary and high school friends, for her critical edits and advice. I have to thank Marie B. Leon, who is more like a sister than a friend, who supported me throughout this process.

I'm appreciative of the new friends I've made in the process of writing this book, like Rev. John Harwood, who never knew my kids or me before this, and whose insights and comments helped tremendously. I also want to thank my friend (an author himself), Terry Walters. He patiently answered all my questions and helped me navigate the publishing world. I want to thank my friend, coffee buddy, and fellow cross-country mom, Astrid Degleris, for being my sounding board as I considered many different directions to take with my book.

Most importantly, I want to thank my family. I couldn't even begin to undertake the task of writing this book without their support. I want to thank my "cousin" Claudette Crow for listening and encouraging me to find my voice. My nieces and nephews (you know who you are!) helped motivate me when I needed it. Thank you to my dad, Roland Crevecoeur, and my siblings—Edith, Evans, Rony, Edwidge, and Roland—for encouraging me to write this book years ago and reading my drafts, and enhancing my drafts with their recollections. And thank you to my mom, Mercia Crevecoeur, for being a wonderful role model and giving me the courage to deal with life's hardships.

I want to thank my children—Danielle, Michael, Nicholas, Joseph, and Jacqueline—for being the inspiration for my book and reading and editing my drafts.

I want to thank my husband, Michael, for the patience and love he provided when I set out to write this book and for always being the wind beneath my wings.

Finally, to the teachers, coaches, instructors, host families, and friends—anyone who played a role in shaping my children's lives and helped to make them the beautiful adults they are today—know that I am truly grateful.

ABOUT THE AUTHOR

Dr. Carline Crevecoeur is a wife, mother, doctor, and teacher. She is also a SCASD School Board Director. Carline resides in Centre County with her husband, Dr. Michael Feffer.

NOTES

2. OUR BEGINNING (2000)

1. Books like Usborne's *Railways and Trains* worked well because each page had four or five different pictures.

4. THE LEAP (2001–2004)

1. Utilizing David Macaulay's book *Castle*.
2. In 2014, the double review of the portfolio in Pennsylvania ended, and the educator's assessment was the sole requirement to be submitted to the school district
3. I also consulted books such as *Genius Denied* by Davidson, *The Well Trained Mind*, by Wise, and a *Mind at a Time*, by Mel Levine, MD. Later, I would add *Academic Competitions for Gifted Students*, by Tallent-Runnels, and Candler-Lotven.
4. Intermediate units in Pennsylvania are regional offices that provide services to public schools, charter schools, and homeschoolers.
5. These books ranged from classics like *Bobby Fischer Teaches Chess* by Bruce Pandolfini to *Sharpen Your Tactics* by Lein and Archangelsky. My favorite chess book was a yellow paperback titled *The Chess Tactics Workbook*, by Al Woolum. We also used Polgar's *Chess: 5334 Problems, Combinations, and Games*
6. Written by Sallie J. Miller and Susan F. Stallings, *Administrator*, September 2003
7. Such as *Jane and Johnny Love Math*, by Lupkowski and Assouline.

6. SUBJECTS

1. We used *Handwriting Without Tears*.
2. We practiced typing with software such as *Typing for Kids* and *Type to Learn 3*.
3. *Weekly Reader* and *Time for Kids*
4. My dad came initially to the US on a scholarship to study math.
5. I used books such as Scholastic's *Favorite Poetry Lessons*, by Paul B. Janeczko, along with Scholastic's series of *Poetry for Young People*. K12 Literature also had wonderful poetry lessons for the young child.
6. Usher's *Annals of the World*, *The Jerusalem Bible*, and *The Heart of Islam*, along with books by Richard Dawkins, Christopher Hitchens, and Philip Yancey. We also used books such as *The Religious Experience of Mankind*, by Ninian Smart, *When God Was a Woman*, by Merlin Stone, and *World Religions at Your Fingertips* by McDowell and Brown.

7. One of my favorites was *Teacher Created Resources: World Religions* by Arquilevich, written for sixth- to eighth graders and containing quizzes and exercises.
8. From Edith Hamilton's *Mythology*, and *The Meridian Handbook of Classical Mythology* to Ovid's *Metamorphoses* by Ambrose.
   D'Aulaires' Book of Greek Myths and the *Book of Norse Myths. Epic of Gilgamesh, Tales from Africa* retold by Kathleen Arnott, *American Indian Myths and Legend* selected and edited by Erdoes and Ortiz.
9. Concept cited from Russell Roth's "On the Instrumental Origins of Jazz" in American Quarterly Journal, Vol 4 (4)
10. We used The *Come Look with Me Series* about "American Indian Art" by Stephanie Salomon.
11. I later enrolled Danielle and Mikey (and later the younger ones) in Creative Oasis, where they learned proper pottery techniques.
12. We again used the *Come Look with Me Series* about "Art in Early America."
13. Using *Short Lessons in Art History: Artist and Their Work* by Phyllis, Clausen, and Barker. I also used the Art Activity packs by Mila Boutan.

9. GROWING PAINS (2004–2009)

1. Term coined by James R. Flynn, and used By M. Gladwell.
2. K12 curriculum and the *History of Us* books.
3. From Montessori Resources and Curriculum Program Catalog.
4. For the slavery and the Civil War units, I purchased several DVDs such as *Glory: The 54th Massachusetts Regiment*, PBS' *Reconstruction: The Second Civil War*, Burn's: *The Civil War*, Simon's BBC video: *Schama's Rough Crossing*, and Haley's *Roots*.

11. BREAKING AWAY

1. This app may seem similar to the more well-known program MapMyRun. However, Mikey created this app before MapMyRun had a mobile version; at that time, it was only a website. Mikey wrote all of the code using Apple's X-code software and the Google Maps API.
2. *The New Jim Crow* by Michelle Alexander; *Slavery by Another Name* by Douglas A. Blackmon; *The Immortal Life of Henrietta Lacks* by Rebecca Skloot; and one of my favorite but hardest to read without crying: *At the Hands of Persons Unknown: The Lynching of Black America* by Phillip Dray.
3. I had ordered it from webelements.com after I saw a similar poster hanging in one of Danielle's summer classes at the University of Pittsburgh at Johnstown's LEARN Program
4. I ordered them from Carolina Biological supplies.

12. SUMMER FUN

1. LEARN camp at the University of Pittsburgh at Johnstown or the youth triathlon at Garver Memorial Park.

17. MATURING

1. The Black Male Development Symposium was initiated by the leadership of Chicago's Third World Press, one of the oldest African American publishing houses in the United States. The venue was established as a national tour that promoted community discussions on the plight of African American Males.